THE JERSEY SHORE:
ATLANTIC CITY TO CAPE MAY

INCLUDES THE WILDWOODS

Nun's Beach Community Day and Surf Invitational, Stone Harbor Barry D. Mastrangelo

THE JERSEY SHORE: ATLANTIC CITY TO CAPE MAY

INCLUDES THE WILDWOODS

Jen A.
Miller

The Countryman Press
Woodstock, Vermont

This project is dedicated to my grandfather, Anthony Verzella. He passed away while I was writing this book, and every time I was down the Shore, I couldn't help but think of him, whether it was memories of taking boats out to the bays for crabbing, or sitting around the campfire in Avalon Campground. Without you, I never would have come to love the Shore. Without you, I never would have been propelled to always do my best.

We welcome your comments and suggestions. Please contact Great Destinations Guide Editor, The Countryman Press, P.O. Box 748, Woodstock, VT 05091, or e-mail countrymanpress@wwnorton.com.

ISBN 978-1-58157-089-2

Cover photo © Steve Greer Photography
Interior photos by the author unless otherwise specified
Book design by Bodenweber Design
Composition by Melinda Belter
Maps by James Miller, © The Countryman Press

Published by The Countryman Press, P.O. Box 748, Woodstock, Vermont 05091

Distributed by W. W. Norton & Company, Inc., 500 Fifth Avenue, New York, NY 10110

Manufactured in the United States of America

10 9 8 7 6 5 4 3 2 1

GREAT DESTINATIONS TRAVEL GUIDEBOOK SERIES

Recommended by *National Geographic Traveler* and *Travel + Leisure* magazines.

[A] CRISP AND CRITICAL APPROACH, FOR TRAVELERS WHO WANT TO LIVE LIKE LOCALS.
— *USA Today*

Great Destinations™ guidebooks are known for their comprehensive, critical coverage of regions of extraordinary cultural interest and natural beauty. The authors in this series are professional travel writers who have lived for many years in the regions they describe. Each title in this series is continuously updated with each printing to insure accurate and timely information. All the books contain more than one hundred photographs and maps.

Current titles available:

THE ADIRONDACK BOOK

ATLANTA

AUSTIN, SAN ANTONIO
 & THE TEXAS HILL COUNTRY

THE BERKSHIRE BOOK

BERMUDA

BIG SUR, MONTEREY BAY
 & GOLD COAST WINE COUNTRY

CAPE CANAVERAL, COCOA BEACH
 & FLORIDA'S SPACE COAST

THE CHARLESTON, SAVANNAH
 & COASTAL ISLANDS BOOK

THE CHESAPEAKE BAY BOOK

THE COAST OF MAINE BOOK

COLORADO'S CLASSIC MOUNTAIN TOWNS:
 GREAT DESTINATIONS

THE FINGER LAKES BOOK

THE FOUR CORNERS REGION

GALVESTON, SOUTH PADRE ISLAND
 & THE TEXAS GULF COAST

THE HAMPTONS BOOK

HONOLULU & OAHU:
 GREAT DESTINATIONS HAWAII

THE HUDSON VALLEY BOOK

THE JERSEY SHORE: ATLANTIC CITY TO
 CAPE MAY (INCLUDES THE WILDWOODS)

LAS VEGAS

LOS CABOS & BAJA CALIFORNIA SUR:
 GREAT DESTINATIONS MEXICO

MICHIGAN'S UPPER PENINSULA

MONTREAL & QUEBEC CITY:
 GREAT DESTINATIONS CANADA

THE NANTUCKET BOOK

THE NAPA & SONOMA BOOK

NORTH CAROLINA'S OUTER BANKS
 & THE CRYSTAL COAST

PALM BEACH, MIAMI & THE FLORIDA KEYS

PHOENIX, SCOTTSDALE, SEDONA
 & CENTRAL ARIZONA

PLAYA DEL CARMEN, TULUM & THE RIVIERA
 MAYA: GREAT DESTINATIONS MEXICO

SALT LAKE CITY, PARK CITY, PROVO
 & UTAH'S HIGH COUNTRY RESORTS

SAN DIEGO & TIJUANA

SAN JUAN, VIEQUES & CULEBRA:
 GREAT DESTINATIONS PUERTO RICO

THE SANTA FE & TAOS BOOK

THE SARASOTA, SANIBEL ISLAND
 & NAPLES BOOK

THE SEATTLE & VANCOUVER BOOK: INCLUDES
 THE OLYMPIC PENINSULA, VICTORIA & MORE

THE SHENANDOAH VALLEY BOOK

TOURING EAST COAST WINE COUNTRY

WASHINGTON, D.C., AND NORTHERN VIRGINIA

YELLOWSTONE & GRAND TETON NATIONAL PARKS
 AND JACKSON HOLE

YOSEMITE & THE SOUTHERN SIERRA NEVADA

If you are traveling to, moving to, residing in, or just interested in any (or all!) of these enchanting regions, a Great Destinations guidebook is a superior companion. Honest and painstakingly critical, full of information only a local can provide, Great Destinations guidebooks give you all the practical knowledge you need to enjoy the best of each region. Why not own them all?

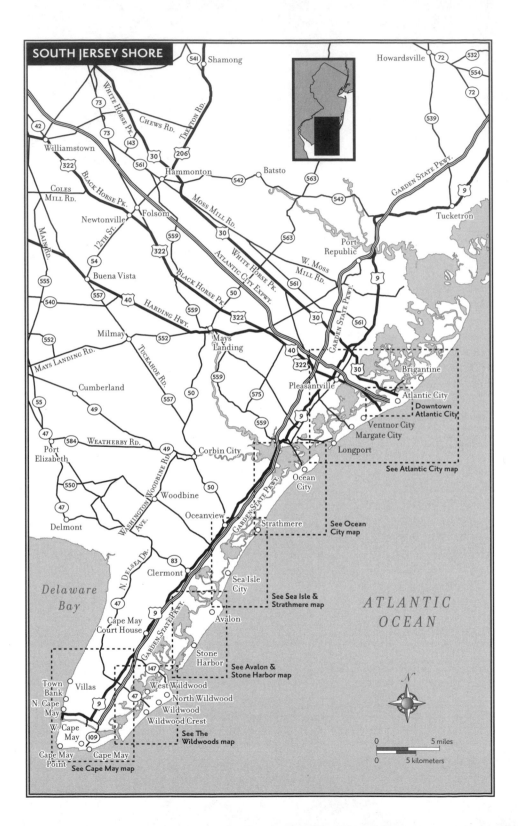

Contents

Acknowledgments

Thank you, family—parents Bob and Mary, siblings Jim, Tracy, and Mike Miller—for putting up with me while I worked on this book, and for always being the rock on which I lean. Our summers at the Shore formed the idea and the framework of this book—thanks for being there at the true beginning, and at the end, of this project. Special thanks to Jim, my older brother, who did the wonderful maps you'll see herein. We both have a book, so we're even. For now.

Thanks to everyone who pointed me in the right directions. I never would have found those little nooks and crannies without your suggestions: Chuck Darrow, Jay and Mary Ann Gorrick, Ruth Hershey Lincoln, Melissa Jacobs, Evan McIntyre, Lauren McCutcheon, Chuck Schumann, Bob and Linda Steenrod, and Marlene Testa, to name a few. Thank you, too, to the crew at 551 W. 22nd Street for letting me make the dining room table my temporary office.

I tried to work as anonymously as possible to ensure that my opinions and judgment wouldn't be clouded, but I couldn't have written this book without the help of public relations and marketing people from around the Jersey Shore. My heartfelt thanks to Michael Bruckler, Elaine Zamansky, Brian Cahill, and Courtney Birmingham in Atlantic City; Michele Gillian and Kathryn A. Caraballo in Ocean City; Ben Rose and the Doo Wop Preservation League in the Wildwoods; Carolyn Connors, and, once again, the Steenrods, in Cape May; and Michelle Goldstein, who represented the entire area.

Special thanks to the team at The Countryman Press who made this book possible: Kim Grant for believing that a book about the Jersey Shore was an excellent idea, and for guiding me along the way; Jennifer Thompson and Kermit Hummel for their advice and direction; and Bill Bowers for his incredible editing prowess.

To my fact checkers, Lindsay Hicks and my sister Tracy—a thousand thank-yous. You made this process much easier for me, and any errors are mine. Thanks to Mickey Verzella, Anthony Bucci, Aimee Topping, Conor Urian, Tracy (again), and my mom for shouldering dog walking and watching duties while I was out researching this book.

Finally, heaping thank-yous to my two writing mentors, Andy Solomon and Maury Z. Levy—without you guys, this book, and my writing career, never would have happened.

INTRODUCTION

So you've decided to go down the Shore. It's not to the beach or even to the shore—when you travel to the southern coast of New Jersey, you're going down the Shore where, within 45 miles, you can find everything from the flash of casinos to gourmet dining to relaxed seaside communities to pristine beaches. Your Jersey Shore vacation is what you make of it, and I'm here to show you how.

History

The Shore as we know it today wouldn't have existed without Philadelphia, or its steamy summers. In 1790, Philadelphia was America's largest city (with 42,000 people), and living conditions weren't ideal, especially in the summer, when temperatures could reach past 100 degrees Fahrenheit with high humidity.

The Shore area was first inhabited by Native Americans, then by farmers who let their animals graze on the land. Fishermen soon followed and set up small towns along the water.

In the 1850s, railroads started bringing people to the coast, and by 1880, a new rail line opened between Philadelphia and Atlantic City. Vacationers soon followed, and spread south. Congress Hall opened in 1816 in Cape May. Few in town believed it would succeed—why would that many people ever want to stay in their corner of the world? Townspeople even nicknamed the building "Tommy's Folly" after Thomas Hughes, who built the hotel that still stands today and forms the cornerstone of a thriving, bustling Shore town.

By the 1950s, going down the Shore was a tradition for families from the Philadelphia area, and the subtle difference between the towns still holds today. Ocean City was the family-friendly spot (no alcohol allowed, even as BYOB); Sea Isle City, Avalon, and Stone Harbor were the quieter towns with a preppy appeal and bar scenes; Wildwood was where the action was without the gambling. It was even known as Little Las Vegas because Vegas performers, including the Rat Pack, flocked to the Wildwoods when the heat turned up too high in the desert.

Many Victorian buildings in Cape May were destined for demolition then, but a push by local citizens in the 1960s and 1970s saved her gems, and started a redevelopment phase that eventually swung up to the Wildwoods, though they work to save their Doo Wop motels, as opposed to gingerbread cottages.

What you'll find today is a Shore in its prime. People have realized the value of shore homes, and real estate prices have gone through the roof. Where you could maybe buy a lot or two for $20,000 in the 1960s (as my grandfather had the opportunity to do), you'd be hard pressed to find one under $500,000 now—they're selling for over a million in some locations.

This hasn't stopped vacationers from coming down to enjoy the sights, the sounds, and the water. If you're reading this book, you're probably one of them. Whether you found the Shore by accident, or have been coming here since you were a baby, there are plenty of new things (or new-to-you things) to see and do down the Shore.

Transportation

If you're coming from the Philadelphia area, you're probably driving down the Atlantic City Expressway, accessible via I-76 in Philadelphia, then NJ 42 in New Jersey, which feeds into the Atlantic City Expressway. If you're headed to points south of Atlantic City, you can hop onto the Garden State Parkway (exit 7S), which ends in Cape May.

If you're coming from New York, make your way to the Garden State Parkway and ride it south through the state (jumping onto the Atlantic City Expressway if that's your final destination).

These highways can be extremely crowded and congested in season, especially on Friday evenings and Sunday evenings and nights. Many people have found backroads around the mess, usually via Route 55. But there are more backroads routes than grains of sand on the beaches, and too many to reprint here. They're a combination of small town and country roads, and can make for excellent sightseeing. Stop at a roadside stand if you see one. They give new meaning to "Jersey fresh."

Atlantic City has an international airport, but it's small. Most travelers reach the Jersey Shore via the Philadelphia International Airport, the region's main hub. Many of the Atlantic City casinos run bus transportation from Philadelphia, or you can take the New Jersey Transit train into Atlantic City.

New Jersey Transit runs bus service through the Jersey Shore, but it's not always dependable, or efficient. You'll have better luck with in-town transit systems, such as the Atlantic City Jitney and Cape May Trolleys.

HOW TO USE THIS BOOK

If I were to write about every place to eat, stay, and play down the Shore, you'd be reading an encyclopedia. So instead I've written a selective guide and recommended what I believe are a range of choices, from budget-friendly to beyond luxurious, from romantic to family-friendly. It's a guide to help make your experience a fantastic one.

Organization

This book is organized geographically along the southern part of New Jersey's coast, north to south starting in Atlantic City and ending in Cape May. I've separated each chapter by island—Atlantic City includes Ventnor City, Margate, and Longport, and Avalon and Stone Harbor are grouped together, for example. I've also included highlights of nearby inland towns. The chapters are then organized by what you'll be looking for—lodging, dining, recreation, culture, and shopping. You will find everything in that category, no matter where on the island it may be, in that chapter. For example, in the Wildwoods chapter, all lodging facilities in North Wildwood, Wildwood, and Wildwood Crest are in one section, organized by town and then alphabetically within that town. The end of each chapter also includes events (weekly where there are enough to include) and information you might need, such as emergency numbers and contact information for realtors in towns where most lodging is available by renting private residences.

Prices

Prices of everything at the Shore change all the time, so I've created price ranges for lodging, dining, recreation, and cultural attractions. These prices reflect the ranges that you will find during the height of tourist season—in many locations, the prices for lodging are much lower in the shoulder and off seasons. Weekends and holidays usually carry extra fees in season, too. Sales tax in New Jersey is 7 percent.

Price Codes

Code	Lodging	Restaurants (per entrée) and attractions (per adult)
$	up to $75	up to $10
$$	$76–150	$11–$25
$$$	$151–$250	$26–40
$$$$	more than $250	more than $40

Seasons

For the purpose of this book, "in season" means May through September. Off season means everything else. These dates reflect the unofficial beginning of the summer—the dates surrounding Memorial Day weekend—and the end—Labor Day weekend. But every spot has a different idea of what "in season" means, so these are approximations only. I've tried to mark when hours shift in the off season, but those can change from year to year, or even week to week. You're best served by calling ahead of time if you're visiting outside of those holiday weekends. Most smaller places in Ocean City, Sea Isle City, Avalon, Stone Harbor, and the Wildwoods are closed in the fall, winter and spring, but Atlantic City and Cape May maintain almost full operations year-round.

1

ATLANTIC CITY

The Original Seaside Resort

INCLUDING VENTNOR CITY, MARGATE, LONGPORT, BRIGANTINE, AND GALLOWAY TOWNSHIP

You might already know Atlantic City as a gambling town, and you wouldn't be wrong—gambling has been legal here since 1976, and Atlantic City is home to 11 casino hotels and a popular destination for those looking to play poker, roulette, blackjack, baccarat, or the slots. But this playground by the sea has a much longer history than gambling, and Atlantic City and its neighboring towns on Absecon Island offer everything from the busy, big, and bright casino scene to peaceful beaches, gourmet dining, and wildlife refuges.

In the 1850s, railroads started bringing people to the what is now Atlantic City, and by 1880, a new rail line between Philadelphia and Atlantic City opened, carrying vacationers from Philadelphia who were looking for a little fun while escaping broiling city summer temperatures. Hotels, housing, restaurants, concert halls, and amusements soon followed. By the turn of the 20th century, Atlantic City was the place to go for your family vacation.

But it hasn't always been a boomtown. Atlantic City started to slide in the 1950s, when the benefits that drew most people to the Shore, like cooler temperatures and a place to swim, weren't so unique as more Americans put air conditioning and pools in their homes and backyards. Air travel was not just for the rich and famous anymore, which made cross-country—or even cross-continent—trips possible for more people. Atlantic City was no longer the only option.

In 1976, New Jersey legalized gambling in Atlantic City, in the hope that the increased revenue would pull the city out of its economic slump. In 1978, Resorts Atlantic City, which had previously been two Quaker-owned hotels, became the first casino in town. Others quickly followed, including Donald Trump, whose name is plastered on three Atlantic City casino hotels. Gambling has given the town a boost, but it has also brought its own demons, like crime, gambling addiction, and poverty, which is why, even today, some parts of Atlantic City are not safe at night.

Atlantic City has long played second fiddle to Las Vegas, and not without reason. It's much smaller, with limited room for expansion. It didn't help the town's reputation that many visitors were senior citizens brought in on bus tours. That image started shifting in 2003 when Stephen Wynn, who is credited with starting the luxury casino trend in Las Vegas, opened The Borgata in Atlantic City. This 43-story casino hotel set out to woo the

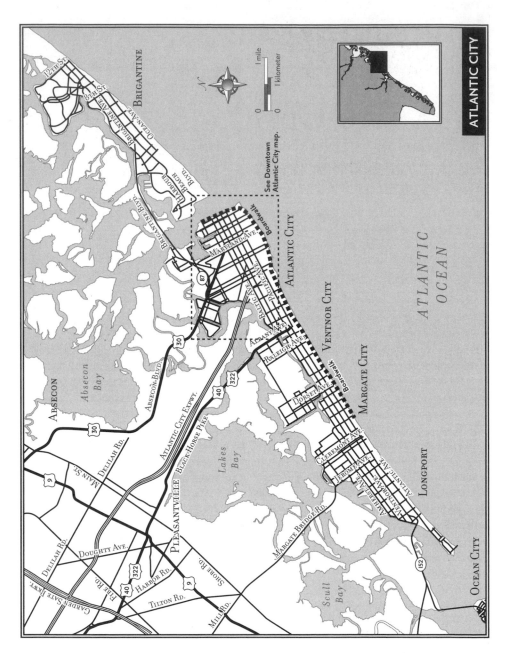

young, hip, and rich crowd back to Atlantic City. It's been a hit—the second Borgata tower is scheduled to open in 2008, and it prompted other casinos in Atlantic City to renovate and improve their aging properties, which brought new nightlife, restaurants, shopping, and spas to America's playground. Pinnacle Gaming is planning to open a $1.5 billion casino resort at the location of the old Sands Hotel and Casino in 2011. In late 2007, MGM Mirage unveiled plans for MGM Grand Atlantic City, a 60-acre, $5.5 billion project with three towers.

Atlantic City Hilton Casino Resort Atlantic City Hilton Casino Resort

Today you'll find that the two sides of Atlantic City—the historic seaside town and gambling mecca—coexist without stepping on each other's toes. Most of the flash and glitz is contained in the Boardwalk and marina areas. Restaurants range from pizzerias and ice cream stands to luxury dining. And of course there is the beach, which is one of the few beaches in southern New Jersey that doesn't require a beach tag.

Atlantic City is surrounded by Brigantine to the north and Ventnor City, Margate, and Longport to the south. These towns are more typical of the sleepier, family-friendly shore spots you'll read about later in the book. The lodging is more B&Bs and hotels, or you can rent a home for a week. Combined, Atlantic City and her neighbors make for an interesting visit. Within a 10-mile span, you can fly high on parasail, nosh on gourmet fare, go all in at the poker table, gawk at Tiffany's diamonds, lie on the beach, or tour a 65-foot wooden elephant. An elephant? Read on.

LODGING

ATLANTIC CITY

Atlantic City Hilton Casino Resort
609-347-7111
www.hiltonac.com
3400 Pacific Ave., Atlantic City 08401

This AAA four-diamond-rated hotel is at the southern end of the Boardwalk, so it's a bit removed from the heart of the action. But Hilton regulars cherish that breath of fresh air—sans noise—while still being close enough to walk down the boards. The Hilton is the most traditional of the Atlantic City casinos—the acts are considered "classics." $$$–$$$$.

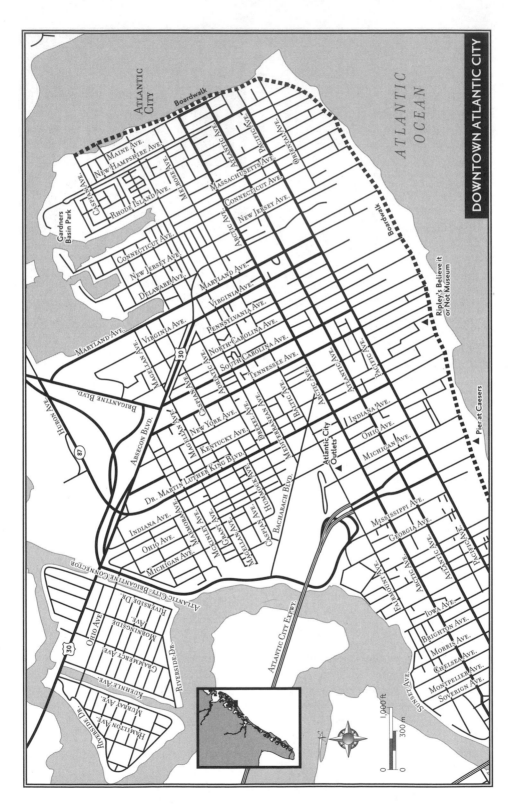

Classic Room at the Borgata. Borgata Hotel Casino & Spa

Bally's Atlantic City

609-340-2000
www.harrahs.com
1900 Boardwalk, Atlantic City 08401

Kick back in style at this casino hotel, whose rooms provide plenty of space to relax and unwind. They're contemporary in more than one way. The hotel is ecofriendly through Bally's Green Earth program. $$–$$$$.

Shave and a Haircut

Gentlemen, you have the room. Or, at least you have these rooms at The Barber Shop at the Borgata, which is a guys-only spa and salon. The highlight is the straight razor shave, which includes a pre-shave oil, then hot towel and after-shave treatment. The Barber Shop also offers haircuts plus guy-friendly manicures and pedicures. No one said looking good had to make you girly, especially if you stop here for your treatments.

Borgata Resort & Spa Hotel Casino

1-866-692-6742
www.theborgata.com
1 Borgata Way, Atlantic City 08401

This is the newest casino hotel in Atlantic City and caters to the affluent crowd looking for a city-like experience at the Shore. The rooms are sleek and modern with clean lines throughout. Every room includes marble bathrooms and showers, customized lighting, and floor-to-ceiling windows. $$$–$$$$.

Caesars Atlantic City Hotel Casino

1-800-443-0104
www.caesars.com/atlantic_city
2100 Pacific Ave., Atlantic City 08401

Hail Caesar! This Ancient Rome–themed casino is located at the center of the Atlantic City Boardwalk. It has four towers of rooms—Ocean Tower was just renovated and redecorated into suites. Luckily for you, the rooms are more Tuscan villa than ancient Italian conqueror—the colors are cool neutral tones with an accent or two

The Boardwalk

Atlantic City is a spot of many firsts—first picture postcard, first beach patrol, first use of the word "airport"—but its best known export is the Boardwalk.

The Boardwalk (always a capital B in Atlantic City) wasn't built as a way for tourists to walk along the beach, or as a pathway to 47 blocks of casinos, restaurants, and shops. It was born out of frustration. Alexander Boardman (get it? Board walk), a conductor of the Camden & Atlantic Railroad, was fed up with tourists bringing the beach with them into his railcars. So, using wooden planks, he made a collapsible footpath prototype. His idea was such a hit with hotel owners—they didn't like sand in their lobbies, either—that in 1870 the city built a 10-foot-wide boardwalk 1.5 feet off the sand. It wasn't a continuous, permanent fixture as it is today. Instead, the Boardwalk was made of 12-foot-long sections that could be picked up and moved in the event of high tide and storms, and in winter.

The Boardwalk was so successful that it became a tourist attraction itself, and it still is today, year-round. The Boardwalk was 7 miles long before a giant hurricane in 1944. Today, it's more than 4 miles long and the hub of activity in Atlantic City. It's the easiest way to get to and from most of Atlantic City's casinos, with lots of restaurants and opportunities along the way.

At the South Jersey Shore, you'll find boardwalks in Ocean City, Sea Isle City, Avalon, Wildwood, and Cape May, though those in Sea Isle City and Cape May are made of concrete. The concept caught on, with boardwalks now all over the country, from California to Hershey Park. But Atlantic City's Boardwalk is still the only one to carry the capital B.

---

that remind you you're supposed to be having a Roman holiday. $$$–$$$$.

Harrah's Atlantic City

1-800-2-HARRAH
www.harrahs.com
777 Harrah's Blvd., Atlantic City 08401

Harrah's is one of the three casinos not on the Boardwalk strip. Instead, it's tucked along the bay with the Borgata and Trump Marina. The newest addition is the Bayview Tower, which—you guessed it—offers views of Absecon Bay. The latest and greatest thing to do at Harrah's is to visit the Pool which is 86,000 gallons of relaxation and is the site of poolside events, including luaus and live music. $$–$$$$.

Irish Pub Inn

609-344-9063
www.theirishpub.com
164 St. James Place at the Boardwalk, Atlantic City 08401

The Inn is a cozy, comfy, and budget-friendly Victorian spot in Atlantic City. It's more like some European accommodations, in that guests share a shower, which keeps the cost down. For those who are a little more reserved, the Inn has rooms with private showers, too. They also offer single-occupancy rooms if you're flying solo—a rarity in the area. $–$$.

Resorts Atlantic City

1-800-336-6378
www.resortsac.com
1133 Boardwalk, Atlantic City 08401

Resorts was the first casino in Atlantic City but has been catering to vacationers since 1929, when it was known as the Chalfonte-Haddon Hall Hotel. Today, the Ocean Tower, which was part of that original structure, keeps a vintage feel by paying homage to Atlantic City's rich history with nautically decorated rooms and pictures from Atlantic City's past. Resorts added the

Resorts Atlantic City Resorts Atlantic City

Rendezvous Tower in 2004. These rooms are more bold and bright than what you'll find in the Ocean Tower. $$–$$$.

Sheraton Atlantic City

609-344-3535
www.starwoodhotels.com
2 Miss America Way, Atlantic City 08401

The Sheraton is primarily a business hotel—it's attached to the Atlantic City Convention Center. It's an ideal place to stay if you want to be a bit removed from Atlantic City's gambling scene, since there is no casino in the Sheraton, but it's close enough to the action that you can walk there. As of press time, the Sheraton is also home to the Miss America memorabilia—dresses and shoes from pageant contestants are on display on both floors of the grand foyer. But Miss America recently moved her offices out of the Sheraton, so call ahead to make sure the glitter's still there if you plan to visit. $$–$$$.

Showboat Casino Hotel

1-800-621-0200
www.harrahs.com
801 Boardwalk, Atlantic City 08401

The theme here is Mardi Gras with a heavy dose of music—the House of Blues is located inside the casino hotel. If you're bringing a lot of people, or just want a lot of space, rent out one of the 22 House of Blues studios, which include a spacious living room plus a multi-jet-spray enclosed glass shower—in the bathroom, of course. $$–$$$$.

Tropicana Casino & Hotel

1-800-843-8767
www.tropicana.net
2801 Pacific Ave., Atlantic City 08401

"The Trop" has the most hotel rooms of any spot in Atlantic City. They're spread through four towers, so make sure you memorize which tower your room is in before you hit the casino floor. If you'll be spending most of your time gambling, try the North Tower—it's the most recently renovated and has the best rooms. If you're coming to the Trop to enjoy the nightlife and shopping of The Quarter, which is a Cuban-themed area with shops, restaurants, and bars, stay in the Havana Tower. It's closest to the nongambling action. As of press time, the Tropicana's gaming license was in flux. For the latest, go to www. atlanticcitynj.com. $$–$$$.

Trump Marina Casino Hotel

1-800-777-1177
www.trumpmarina.com
Huron & Brigantine Blvd., Atlantic City 08401

Smoking

As of press time, smoking was still allowed in Atlantic City casinos. It's banned in bars and restaurants throughout New Jersey, but the casino lobby is a powerful one. Even so, legislators, backed by health officials, casino employees, and the blatant fact that smoking kills, keep chipping away at the smoking-permitted ruling and are still at work.

There's now a partial smoking ban in the casinos, and many proudly display their nonsmoking sections and advertise their nonsmoking towers of rooms. As of press time, seven of Atlantic City's casino hotels said they would ban smoking in their gaming areas—all their gaming areas—by the spring of 2008.

More than a few casino officials told me that they expect the casinos to be entirely smoke-free by the time this book comes out. To find out the latest scoop, call the casino where you'd like to play, or visit www.atlanticcitynj.com.

This is one of the few casino hotels that isn't on the main Boardwalk strip. Trump Marina includes rooms and suites, plus Crimzen, a spa and health complex that includes a spa, a 3.17-acre recreation deck, jogging track, and tennis and basketball courts. Like Trump's two other hotels in Atlantic City, the Marina is a five-star, diamond-award-winning hotel, as rated by the American Academy of Hospitality Services. $$–$$$.

Trump Plaza Hotel & Casino

1-800-677-7378
www.trumpplaza.com
Mississippi Avenue at the Boardwalk, Atlantic City 08401

You can't miss Trump Plaza if you're coming into town via the Atlantic City Expressway. It's smack at the end of the ramp. The 39-story hotel also offers lots of luxury and is a five-star, diamond-award-winning hotel, as rated by the American Academy of Hospitality Services (as are Trump's other two hotels in town). It's close to the center of the Boardwalk action and just a short walk to the Pier at Caesars. $$–$$$$.

Trump's Taj Mahal Casino Resort

1-800-825-8888
www.trumptaj.com
1000 Boardwalk at Virginia Ave., Atlantic City 08401

India meets Atlantic City at this prong of Trump's Atlantic City empire. It's a big one, too—the building has 4.5 times more steel than the Eiffel Tower. If you've got money to burn, check out the Alexander the Great Suite. It's 4,500 square feet, including a sauna, weight room, bar, lounge, and pantry that'll set you back about $10,000—per night. For the rest of us, the rooms at the Taj are recently renovated to be more sleek luxury done in warm tones rather than over-the-top flash and bling. Like Trump's other two hotels in Atlantic City,

Atlantic City Pet Hotel & Grooming

609-348-8660
www.atlanticcitypethotelandgrooming.com
547 N. Trenton Ave., Atlantic City 08401

Atlantic City isn't the most pet-friendly place in New Jersey (pets aren't allowed on the beaches, on the Boardwalk, or in most hotels), but you can still bring your cat, dog, or even parrot along for the ride. While you're playing, they can stay at Atlantic City Pet Hotel and Grooming, which was started by Jackie and Scott Winston after they were thrown out of their room because of Jackie's service dog. Unlike a kennel, none of the animals are caged, and the dogs are walked—individually, not in groups—several times a day. Shuttle service for the pets is provided to and from Atlantic City hotels, and you can pick up or drop off your animals 24 hours a day. It is a 24-hour town, after all.

the Taj is a five-star, diamond-award-winning hotel, as rated by the American Academy of Hospitality Services. $$–$$$$.

BRIGANTINE

Speidel House

1-866-266-3705
www.speidelhouse.com
3001 Bayshore St., Brigantine 08203

The Speidel house was built in 1927 but wasn't quite complete—the Depression put a stop to that. In 1937, Charles Speidel bought it, hence the name. The bed & breakfast is now owned by Rose and Glenn Kaiser and features five guest rooms, each decorated according to the tastes of either a member of the Speidel family, or friends and family of the Kaisers. If you're a history buff, take the Amber Room, which features war memorabilia. Romancing? Go for the Florence Room, which has an in-room

Jacuzzi. No matter which room you pick, make sure to sit on the back deck of the Speidel House to watch the sunset over the water. $$–$$$.

VENTNOR CITY

Come Wright Inn

609-822-1927
www.comewrightinn.com
5003 Ventnor Ave., Ventnor City 08406

Stephen and Dianne Wright make their house your home—literally. The couple lived in this Victorian home for over a decade before converting it into a six-bedroom B&B. All proceeds go to the church across the street, the Way of Life Assembly of God (the Wrights are missionaries). This doesn't mean that the hotel is lacking in any of the conveniences you'd expect from a B&B. It's been meticulously renovated and maintained to reflect its turn-of-the-20th-century heritage. If you're looking for space, the two-bedroom Rossing Suite is your best bet—it has excellent views of the ocean and a private sitting room and is the largest accommodations in the inn. If you're traveling by yourself, the Huntsford Room is one of the few single-occupancy places in the area. $$–$$$.

GALLOWAY TOWNSHIP

The Colonial Inn

609-748-8999
www.colonialinnsmithville.com
615 E. Moss Mill Rd., Smithville 08205

This eight-room B&B located in Historic Smithville is designed to evoke America during the Revolutionary War with its simple décor and a heavy emphasis of finely crafted wood pieces, from the beds to the dressers and even the walls. Five of The Colonial Inn's rooms have views of Lake Meone, and select rooms have tubs, fireplaces, and cathedral ceilings. $$–$$$.

Seaview Resort & Spa

609-652-1800
www.seaviewmarriott.com
401 South New York Rd., Galloway 08205

This Marriott property was recognized as one of the world's best golf resorts by *Travel & Leisure Golf* magazine. The resort (and the golf courses, of course) are set back into New Jersey's pinelands. Marriott bought the property in 1984 and has been expanding and renovating it ever since, keeping that turn-of-the-20th-century charm in its 297 rooms while creating a resort that pleases today's travelers. (Destination weddings are popular at Seaview as well). $$$–$$$$.

DINING

ATLANTIC CITY

Adam Good Deli

609-344-6699
The Tropicana
2801 Pacific Ave., Atlantic City 08401

Quick service, hearty servings, and low prices make Adam Good Deli a damn good bet. It's close to the Boardwalk entrance to the Tropicana, too, if you want to stop in for a midday meal. Breakfast, lunch, dinner. $.

Angelo's Fairmount Tavern

609-344-2439
www.angelosfairmounttavern.com
2300 Fairmount Ave., Atlantic City 08401

There's no fuss or muss at this corner tavern, but the food is good and served in larger-than-life portions. The menu is, of course, Italian (there's a reason it's known as "Little Italy by the Sea"), but also leans toward seafood, pasta, and fried items. For the full experience, ask to taste their homemade wine. Lunch, dinner. $$.

Atlantic City Bar & Grill

609-348-8080

Bobby Flay Steak Borgata Hotel Casino & Spa

www.acbarandgrill.com
1219 Pacific Ave., Atlantic City 08401

This favorite-with-the-locals hangout has become less of an unknown gem, but who can blame visitors for wanting to chow down on the rib or crab platters? Expect a party atmosphere in the later hours. Lunch, dinner, late night. $–$$.

Back Bay Ale House
609-449-0006
backbayalehouse.com
800 N. New Hampshire Ave., Atlantic City 08203

What better way to celebrate a good day than with a sunset toast? The folks at the Back Bay Ale House do just that every day that the sun is shining (and setting). If you're in the mood for fries, go for the Old Bay variety. The spice (traditionally used for crab dishes) makes all the difference. Breakfast, lunch, dinner in season. No breakfast September, October, and mid-March through May. Closed late October through mid-March. $$.

Beach Bar at Trump Plaza
1-800-677-7378
www.trumpplaza.com
Trump Plaza Hotel & Casino
Mississippi Ave. at the Boardwalk, Atlantic City 08401

You might expect just appetizers at this bar on the beach, but they also dish up salads and pizza, and they have a raw bar. Still, the main attraction is the drink menu, which is loaded with what you'd need a blender to make: margaritas, daiquiris, coladas, plus island-themed drinks like Myers's Rum Runner and the Mango Mojito. Lunch, dinner in season. $–$$.

Bobby Flay Steak
1-866-692-6742
www.bobbyflaysteak.com
Borgata Resort & Spa Hotel Casino
1 Borgata Way, Atlantic City 08401

World-renowned celebrity chef Bobby Flay put his first steakhouse at the Borgata. Architect David Rockwell, who's designed Broadway sets and a Cirque du Soleil theater, and renovated FAO Schwartz in New York, engineered the dining space, which is light and airy given the heavy presence of wood and glass. Steak takes the spotlight here, but don't skimp on dessert. The banana split is divine. Dinner. $$$$.

Buddakan
609-674-0100
www.buddakanac.com
Pier at Caesars
1 Atlantic Ocean, Atlantic City 08401

This is the third Buddakan restaurant from restaurateur Stephen Starr (the original is in Philadelphia, the other is in New York City). A trip to Buddakan is much more than just a sumptuous, modern Asian meal. It's a dining experience, set in the dim, cool dining room where you eat under the gaze of a big Buddha. Lunch, dinner. $$$.

Café 2825
609-344-6913
2825 Atlantic Ave., Atlantic City 08401

This nook of a restaurant seats only 48, which keeps it an intimate fine dining experience, especially given that owner Joe Lautato, or a member of his family, greets guests every night of the week. Reservations recommended. Dinner. Closed Sunday and Monday. $$$.

Capriccio
1-800-336-6378
www.resortsac.com
Resorts Atlantic City
1133 Boardwalk, Atlantic City, NJ 08401

Capriccio has one of the best views of any restaurant in Atlantic City—its terrace offers both Boardwalk and ocean views for ample people and beach watching. That's not to detract from the food, which is gourmet Northern and Southern Italian dishes. Try Chef Steve Klawitter's signature dish, osso bucco. The Sunday brunch is a treat

Sunday brunch at Capriccio Resorts Atlantic City

and, at a fixed price, a smart splurge. Reservations recommended. Closed Monday and Tuesday. Dinner. Brunch Sunday. $$–$$$$.

Caruso's

609-340-7585
www.hiltonac.com
Atlantic City Hilton Casino Resort
3400 Pacific Ave., Atlantic City 08401

You'll find traditional and contemporary Italian cuisine at this casino restaurant. Sunday brunches here are popular, too—the made-to-order omelets are a must-do. Dinner Monday, Tuesday, Friday, and Saturday. Brunch Sunday. $$$.

Chef Vola's

609-345-2022
111 S. Albion Pl., Atlantic City 08401

This restaurant, which has been dishing up Italian cuisine in Atlantic City for almost 90 years, is a local favorite, and a Zagat favorite, too—they rated it one of the best restaurants at the Jersey Shore. No credit cards. Reservations required. BYOB. Dinner. Closed Monday. $$.

Cuba Libre Restaurant & Rum Bar

609-348-6700
www.cubalibrerestaurant.com
Quarter at the Tropicana
2801 Pacific Ave., Atlantic City 08401

Step back into 1950s Havana at Cuba Libre, which is both restaurant and bar. The food is, of course, Cuban, which carries influences of Spanish, African, Creole, and Asian cuisines. In keeping with Cuban tradition, the bar leans toward rum-infused drinks, and Cuba Libre even has its own brand of rums. In the summer, don't be surprised to find Latin dancing and DJs at night, and Latin floor shows. Lunch, dinner. Late night Friday and Saturday. $$–$$$.

Restaurant Hours

If you're looking at some of these restaurants and wondering why they're only open a few nights a week, check where they're located. Many casino restaurants will close for a night or two during the week because the casino offers so many other restaurant options. For example, Atlantic City Hilton Casino Resort, home to Caruso's, also has Peregrines' and the Oaks Steakhouse, which are open on some nights when Caruso's is not. Resorts, home to Capriccio, also has Gallagher's Steak House to offer fine dining on nights Capriccio is closed.

Dock's Oyster House

609-345-0092
www.docksoysterhouse.com
2405 Atlantic Ave., Atlantic City 08401

Dock's Oyster House has been a local favorite since long before the town was a vacation spot, let alone a gambling destination. Harry "Dock" Dougherty opened the oyster house in 1897. It's still family owned and operated, now by Frank Dougherty, who also runs the Knife & Fork Inn. As you can imagine, there's a lot of fresh seafood at Dock's, and their wine list has been recognized with an award of excellence by *Wine Spectator*. For a bit of history, choose from "Dock's Classics," which are recipes and dishes, such as crabmeat au gratin, lobster tail, and fried oysters, that have been on the menu since 1897. Dinner. $$$.

EVO

609-441-0400
www.evorestaurantlounge.com
Trump Plaza
2225 Boardwalk, Atlantic City, NJ 08401

You can't get much closer to the Boardwalk than at EVO—you eat right on it. Well, at your table, which is on the Boardwalk, with big umbrellas at every table for shade. Like a good chunk of Atlantic City restaurants, EVO's menu carries an Italian influence in items like personal pizzas and seafood linguine. The raw bar is a highlight, with fresh selections like oysters and littleneck clams. Indoor seating available. Lunch, dinner. Late night Friday and Saturday. $$–$$$.

Flying Cloud Café
609-345-8222
www.atlanticcityflyingcloud.com
800 New Hampshire Ave., Atlantic City 08401

This casual restaurant has a simple menu that leans heavily on the seafood, which makes sense for where it is: it's literally on a dock and, weather permitting, you can eat dockside at their outdoor bar and grill. Even if you're inside, the view is superb. In addition to being surrounded by ocean, owners Ross and Mary Anne Constantino decorate the interior ceilings with baseball caps from around the world. Lunch, dinner in season. Closed in January. Call for off-season hours. $$.

Harrah's Waterfront Buffet
609-441-5000
www.harrahs.com
Harrah's Atlantic City
777 Harrah's Blvd., Atlantic City 08401

The all-you-can-eat buffet is a casino tradition. Harrah's has the newest kid on the block with an impressive setup. Their Waterfront Buffet has 620 seats and offers nine different food stations to dish up anything you're craving on your first, second, or third trip back to fill your plate. Lunch Tuesday, Wednesday, Saturday, Sunday. Dinner Monday, Thursday, Friday, Saturday, Sunday. Brunch Saturday, Sunday. $$.

Irish Pub
609-344-9063
www.theirishpub.com
164 Saint James Pl., Atlantic City 08401

I hit the Irish Pub on a weeknight in the summer, noshed on some pub grub, and chatted with a father-and-son pair who'd lost a bundle that day at the poker table. It's that kind of congenial place where you can talk to strangers over food and a pint, and one of the homier places in Atlantic City. If

Rolling Carts

If that walk to the next casino seems like too long a trip, hop in a rolling cart. Don't worry—it's not considered uncouth. Rolling carts have been around almost as long as the Boardwalk. The drivers wait all over the Boardwalk and at every casino exit onto the Boardwalk. Plenty cluster around the Pier at Caesars, too, if you need a ride after shopping and/or dining.

Here's how much it'll cost you. Count the blocks to prevent being overcharged, and it's customary to tip your driver:

1–5 blocks: $5 for one or two people, third person is an extra $3

6–12 blocks: $10 for one or two people, $3 third person

13–21 blocks: $15 for one or two people, $5 third person

22–32 blocks: $20 for one or two people, $5 third person

1/2 hour tour round trip: $25 for one or two people, $5 third person

1-hour tour round trip: $40 for one or two people, $5 third person

Bar at the Irish Pub

you're looking for a full meal, the Irish Pub is more than willing to accommodate, though the bar is a major draw, as are the hours. Food is served until 5 AM. $.

Knife & Fork Inn

609-344-1133
www.knifeandforkinn.com
Atlantic and Pacific Ave., Atlantic City 08401

The Knife & Fork has a history as colorful as Atlantic City itself. Opened in 1912, it's survived two family feuds, two shutdowns, and two renovations to remain as a classy restaurant right off the Boardwalk strip. In its latest incarnation under Frank Dougherty, who also owns Dock's Oyster House, the Knife & Fork offers an extensive surf and turf menu that uses local ingredi-

ents, from the seafood in your entrée to the tomatoes in your salad. The Knife & Fork also offers more than 1,000 wines and a full bar. If you're not in the mood for a big, sit-down meal, you can eat on the "porch," which is an enclosed lounge with two plasma screen TVs. Dinner. Lunch Friday. $$$.

Los Amigos

609-344-2293
www.losamigosrest.com
1926 Atlantic Ave., Atlantic City 08104

Los Amigos couldn't look more out of place. Nestled against the bargains and bargain hunters who flock to The Walk, this 100-year-old, bright pink, green, and yellow Mexican restaurant is the one who looks like the tourist. The cuisine is Mexican and

Club Life

If you're looking to party it up in Atlantic City, the town that's "always turned on" has plenty of night-club options. The music is loud and pumping, and most of the clubs have dancers shaking it on the floor or on the bar. What's hot and what's not changes quickly in Atlantic City. For the latest, click through www.ac2night.com.

32 Degrees
609-572-0032
32lounge.com
Quarter at the Tropicana
2801 Pacific Ave., Atlantic City 08401

Casbah
609-449-1000
www.casbahclub.com
Trump Taj Mahal
1000 Boardwalk at Virginia Ave., Atlantic City 08401

Club Worship
609-236-2583
www.hob.com

House of Blues
www.hob.com
801 Boardwalk, Atlantic City 08401

40/40 Club
609-449-4040
www.the4040club.com
2120 Atlantic Ave., Atlantic City 08401

Mixx
609-317-1000
www.theborgata.com
Borgata Resort & Spa Hotel Casino
1 Borgata Way, Atlantic City 08401

mur.mur
609-317-1000
www.theborgata.com
Borgata Resort & Spa Hotel Casino
1 Borgata Way, Atlantic City 08401

Providence
609-345-7800
www.providenceclubac.com
The Quarter at the Tropicana
2801 Pacific Ave., Atlantic City 08401

The Wave
609-441-2000
www.trumpmarina.com
Trump Marina
Huron & Brigantine Blvd. Atlantic City 08401

Tex-Mex, and all spicy. But the main event here is the margaritas, which are big, strong, and enough to make you drop if the shopping didn't get to you first. Lunch, dinner. Late night Monday through Saturday. $$.

Mia
609-441-2345
www.miaac.com
Caesars Atlantic City Hotel Casino
2100 Pacific Ave., Atlantic City 08401

Famed restaurateur Georges Perrier brings the ridiculous success of his fine dining eateries like Philadelphia's Le Bec-Fin and Brassier Perrier to Atlantic City through Mia. This über-luxe Mediterranean Italian restaurant is set inside soaring towers at Caesars, which gives your fine dining a light, airy effect. Dinner. Closed Sunday and Monday. $$$.

Noodle Village
609-340-2000
www.harrahs.com
Bally's Atlantic City
1900 Boardwalk, Atlantic City 08401

Get your comfort foods quick at this new noodle bar. The speedy service doesn't compromise the quality, though—Chinese and Vietnamese selections, like dumplings and congee, are authentic, and the drink menu matches. It's conveniently located next to Bally's Asian table games and exposed to the action through its low walls. Night owls will appreciate the hours—it's 24 hours on Saturdays and open noon to 6 AM the rest of the week. $–$$.

Old Homestead

1-866-692-6742
www.theborgata.com
Borgata Resort & Spa Hotel Casino
1 Borgata Way, Atlantic City 08401

The Atlantic City outpost of this venerable New York City steakhouse fits right in with the luxury and style that the Borgata is known for. You can't go wrong with the 36-ounce Gotham Rib Steak. For a gourmet twist on an old favorite, the 20-ounce Kobe beef burger, which is served with Tater Tots, is a treat and a challenge. I made it through about 16 of those ounces before I cried uncle. Dinner. $$$$.

OPA Bar & Grille

609-344-0094
www.opa1.com
1700 Boardwalk, Atlantic City 08401

The atmosphere is always exciting at OPA, whether you're eating inside or out. Outside, you can watch the buzz of the Boardwalk; inside, the open kitchen. The food is American with a dash of Mediterranean, especially Greek. The bars on both levels are popular, as is the martini menu. $$–$$$.

Phillips Seafood

609-348-2273
www.phillipsseafood.com
Pier at Caesars
1 Atlantic Ocean, Atlantic City 08401

The Atlantic City location of this Maryland seafood giant is all about, of course, seafood. Check out the rolling oyster cart, which will come to your table to shuck your oysters. Another popular event at Phillips is the Sunset Happy Hour, where you watch the sun go down from your perch on the third floor of the Pier at Caesars while enjoying drink specials. Phillips also has a takeout window on the Boardwalk, also at the Pier at Caesars. Lunch, dinner. $$.

Sonsie

609-345-6300
www.sonsieac.com
Pier Shops at Caesars
1 Atlantic Ocean, Atlantic City 08401

Chef Martin Doyle has created a mixed menu of local favorites, like brick oven pizzas and simple spaghetti, with gourmet fare, like seared rib eye, roasted monkfish, and squid ink linguine at Sonsie. The wine list offers more than 300 selections, stored in a walk-in wine cellar. They have a pastry chef on site, too, so don't skip dessert—or, come back for breakfast. Breakfast, lunch, dinner. $$$.

The Trinity

609-345-6900
www.trinitypubac.com
Pier Shops at Caesars
1 Atlantic Ocean, Atlantic City 08401

Firewaters

Like beer? Then Firewaters at the Tropicana is a must visit while you're in Atlantic City. They have 50 beers on tap, and 101 different brews in bottles.

If you can't decide, tell the bartender what beers are your favorites, and he or she will make a recommendation. Or peruse the "menu," which is a thick book describing their beers. If you're a sports fan, the TVs are usually tuned into the game of the day, or ESPN.

Lunch rush at the White House Sub Shop

The bar at this Irish pub was imported from Ireland, so Trinity is the real deal. It's a surprisingly cozy and intimate spot at the Pier, which is more known for its flashy and pricy restaurants. The smoked salmon with toast points appetizer was affordable for this traveler, but tasted like it should have cost much more. The Trinity shifts over to a bar scene late at night. Call ahead for the live music schedule. Lunch, dinner, late night. $$–$$$.

White House Sub Shop
609-345-1564
2301 Arctic Ave., Atlantic City 08401

It's all about the food at this sub shop, which has been in business since 1946. Frank Sinatra was a fan, and I can see why. The sandwiches are huge and stuffed with meat, cheese, and whatever else you like. The White House Sub Special is always a hit. Even though I ordered a half size, I was full past dinnertime. No credit cards. Lunch. $.

BRIGANTINE

Laguna Grill & Martini Bar
609-266-7731
www.lagunagrill.com
1400 Ocean Ave., Brigantine Beach 08201

This beachside eatery is almost two different restaurants in one. The deck is ultra-casual—feel free to have a drink while still in your bathing suit. Dinner is a different story. You won't need a jacket, but flip-flops and tank tops are out. Their specialties are the filet and crab cake surf and turf. Don't miss out on the "martini" part of the name. The menu includes 25 varieties. For a sweet treat, try the Creamsickle martini. It's a grown-up version of a childhood classic (Popsicle stick not included). Breakfast, lunch, dinner. Deck: $$. Dining room: $$$.

VENTNOR CITY

Annette's Restaurant
609-822-8366
104 N. Dorset Ave., Ventnor City 08406

This little brick-front restaurant looks like your mom's kitchen on its inside, and the food is good and filling like a home-cooked meal. Eat at one of the benches or in the middle of the room at what looks like—you guessed it—mom's kitchen table. It's loud like a family reunion, too, so be prepared to have your conversation overlap with someone else's. If it's too noisy, try to grab one of the outdoor tables. Breakfast, lunch. $.

Custard's Last Stand
609-823-4033
107 N. Dorset Ave., Ventnor City 08406

For a sweet treat post-meal, or something to cool you off in the middle of the day, Custard's dishes up, of course, custard, but also milkshakes, smoothies, and sundaes. Eat inside in the cool air or outdoors at one of the many shaded octagon tables. Open noon–midnight Sunday through Friday and noon–1 AM Saturday in season. $.

Manna
609-822-7722
www.mannaventnor.com
7309 Ventnor Ave., Ventnor City 08406

It's New American at this exclusive 20-seat restaurant. The items on the menu change with the season, as chef/owner John Merlino likes to use whatever's fresh at the time. The wild mushroom bruschetta is highly recommended, as is the linguine and clams. Reservations are recommended, even for lunch, and an absolute must for dinner. BYOB. Lunch, dinner. Closed Monday and Tuesday. $$$.

Johnny's Café and Bakery
609-822-1789

www.johnnyscafeventnor.com
7303 Ventnor Ave., Ventnor City 08406

All the cooking and baking are done on site at this Italian restaurant, which carries a casual and laid-back vibe. Don't overlook the bakery part at Johnny's. Owner John Liccio owned a bakery before turning this Ventnor City spot into a restaurant. BYOB. Breakfast, lunch, dinner. $$.

Osaka Sushi & Japanese Steak House

609-823-8616
www.osakasushinj.com
5200 Ventnor Ave., Ventnor City 08406

It's sushi and Japanese cuisine served with flair at this Ventnor City spot. They have just about every type of sushi and hand roll you could imagine, plus an excellent selection of hibachi dinners. BYOB. Lunch, dinner. $$.

Sage

609-823-2110
5206 Atlantic Ave., Ventnor City 08406

This 75-seat restaurant is the latest creation from Lisa Savage, who had been in Ventnor City for 13 years before trying her luck on the mainland. She brought the best from that venture to Sage, putting items like fried artichoke hearts and seared scallops on the menu. No credit cards. BYOB. Dinner. $$.

MARGATE

Bobby Chez

609-487-1922
8007 Ventnor Ave., Margate 08402
www.bobbychezcrabcakes.com

No need to go out on a boat for fresh seafood. Bobby Chez offers gourmet seafood dishes, including jumbo lump crab cakes, broiled crab cakes, lobster mashed potatoes, and coconut shrimp as carry-out

entrées. Just reheat at home. Expect long lines at the holidays. Open 11 AM–7 PM. $$.

Casel's Supermarket

609-823-2741
www.casels.com
8008 Ventnor Ave., Margate 08402

While most big grocery stores down the Shore are inland, Casel's is just blocks from the beach, and has free parking for customers. Expect all the brands you know and love, plus a deli, bakery, and assortment of beach items like pails, wiffleball bats, and boogie boards. Open 8 AM–6:45 PM Monday through Wednesday, 8 AM–7:45 PM Thursday and Friday, 7 AM–7:45 PM Saturday, 7 AM–7 PM Sunday in season. Call for off-season hours. $–$$.

Dune

609-487-7450
www.dunerestaurant.com
9510 Ventnor Ave., Margate 08402

The Philadelphia Inquirer praised Dune as serving "easily some of the most sophisticated food down the shore." The setting is vintage beach with old woodwork and black-and-white photographs decorating the walls. The menu has twists on restaurant staples, with items like grilled bluefin tuna steak, mussels steamed in pancetta, Champagne, and chervil broth, cracked wheat salad, and Hawaiian walu on the bill. Menu changes daily. BYOB. Dinner. Closed Tuesday. Closed late December to April. $$$.

Luciano Lamberti's Sunset Marina

609-487-6001
www.sunsetonthebay.com
9707 Amherst Ave., Margate 08402

Luciano Lamberti's started as a simple pasta house, but has become more of a destination for unique Italian dishes since the restaurant on the bay opened in 2000.

Many of the traditional recipes have been passed down through the Lamberti family. Go with selections from the pizza menu, or indulge in one of the many pasta dishes, which, according to Italian tradition, are big, big, big. Lunch, dinner. $$.

Stewart's of Margate

609-823-6700

www.drinkstewarts.com

7801 Ventnor Ave., Margate 08402

The first Stewart's root beer stand opened in 1924, and while this Margate outpost serves its share of flavored colas, it's also a great spot for burgers, fries, and hot dogs. Eat in or take out. Just don't forget to grab a Stewart's root beer in a glass bottle. Lunch, dinner in season. $.

Tomatoe's Restaurant

609-822-7535

www.tomatoesmargate.com

9300 Amherst Ave., Margate 08402

The sushi is the main attraction at this recently renovated Margate restaurant. Don't let the size fool you—even though Tomatoe's seats 250 people, you'll still need a reservation, especially in season. The décor is a mashed-up mix, from kitschy wall murals to Oriental accents. Extensive wine list as well. It's very much a see-and-be-seen place. Dinner. $$$.

LONGPORT

Ozzie's Luncheonette

609-487-0575

2401 Atlantic Ave., Longport 08403

Talk about retro charm: this eatery, which has been serving up breakfast and lunch in Longport for more than 50 years, is decked out in mid-20th-century style with black-and-white checked floors, red leather seating and stools, and pictures of Longport from years past on the walls. For breakfast,

order anything you think you could imagine in omelet form, and lunch sandwiches are enough to hold you over until dinner—and then some. I liked the "I Heart Longport" mugs that wait at the counter for your morning cup of coffee. Those seats are prized spots in the restaurant, so get there early to grab one, or be prepared to wait. Breakfast, lunch, dinner. $.

GALLOWAY TOWNSHIP

Athenian Garden

609-748-1818

619 S. New York Rd., Galloway Township 08205

This Zagat-rated restaurant is a hidden treasure tucked away in Galloway Township. But those in the know are familiar with its authentic Greek fare. You can even see how fresh your seafood is on the open fish display. BYOB. Lunch, dinner. Breakfast Saturday and Sunday. $$.

Goodies Pushcart Style Franks

609-652-0544

615 E. Mossmill Rd., Shop 16, Smithville 08205

Goodies isn't actually a pushcart, but it does sport those Sabrett umbrellas you see all over the streets of New York City. Aside from hot dogs, Goodies sells ice cream, sodas, lemonade, nachos, hot cider, and cocoa. If you're a true hot dog fan, try "the works," which comes with sauerkraut, onions, cheese, chili, mustard, ketchup, and relish—and a knife and fork so you get it all. Lunch, dinner. $.

Ram's Head Inn

609-652-1700

www.ramsheadinn.com

9 West White Horse Pike, Galloway 08205

You don't get much more classic than Ram's Head. The men still wear jackets, and

Caesar salads are still prepared at your table. The food is traditional American, too, like filet mignon and beef Wellington. Zagat named it one of the best restaurants at the Shore. Lunch, dinner. Closed Monday. $$$.

Smithville Bakery
609-652-6471
615 E. Mossmill Rd., Shop 20, Smithville 08205

Check out this an old-fashioned bakery parlor, which opens bright and early at 7 AM. You can eat breakfast in or take your pastries, rolls, or cookies outside to eat by Lake Meone. They also make cakes and pies for takeout. Breakfast, lunch. $.

Smithville Inn
609-652-7777
www.smithvilleinn.com
1 N. New York Rd., Smithville 08205

This popular wedding spot is also a cozy and intimate restaurant with lake views. The menu goes beyond surf and turf—poultry dishes are also a Smithville Inn specialty. Sunday brunch is a popular option, so don't doze too long over your morning paper. Breakfast, lunch, dinner. $$.

Spa Life

Looking to relax? Atlantic City has plenty of spa options. Here are a few highlights:

Bluemercury
609-347-7778
www.bluemercury.com
Quarter at the Tropicana
2801 Pacific Ave., Atlantic City 08401

Crimzen
1-800-777-8477
www.trumpmarina.com
Trump Marina Casino Hotel
Huron & Brigantine Blvd., Atlantic City 08401

Elizabeth Arden Red Door Spa
609-441-5333
www.reddoorspas.com
Harrah's Atlantic City
777 Harrah's Blvd., Atlantic City 08401

Elizabeth Arden Red Door Spa
609-404-4100
www.reddoorspas.com
Seaview Marriott Resort
400 East Fairway Lane, Galloway 08205

Larimar
609-441-1600
www.larimarsalonspa.com
Pier at Caesars
1 Atlantic Ocean, Atlantic City 08401

Spa at Bally's
609-340-2000
Bally's Atlantic City
www.harrahs.com
1900 Boardwalk, Atlantic City 08401

Spa at Trump Plaza
1-800-677-7378
www.trumpplaza.com
Trump Plaza Hotel & Casino
Mississippi Ave. at the Boardwalk, Atlantic City 08401

Spa Toccare
609-317-7555
www.theborgata.com
Borgata Resort & Spa Hotel Casino
1 Borgata Way, Atlantic City 08401

ARTS & CULTURE

Atlantic City Art Center

609-347-5837
www.acartcenter.org
New Jersey Ave. and the Boardwalk, Atlantic City 08401

This three-gallery art center features work by local and national artists. Exhibits change monthly and bimonthly. The Art Center also sponsors gallery talks, concerts, readings, and art demonstrations. Open 10 AM–7 PM. Free.

Atlantic City Historical Museum

609-347-5839
www.acmuseum.org
701 Boardwalk, Atlantic City 08401

Atlantic City's museum features a rotating plus a permanent exhibit. The permanent one, called Atlantic City, Playground of the Nation, is chock full of artifacts from Atlantic City's rich history, including postcards, song sheets, photographs, and Mr. Peanut. Make sure to pick up your complimentary Heinz pickle pin. Open 10 AM–4 PM. Free.

Civil Rights Garden

609-347-0500
www.njcrda.com/civilrightsgarden.html
1014 Atlantic Ave., Atlantic City 08401

This public sculpture garden, which pays homage to the leaders of the Civil Rights Movement, features 11 granite columns set among richly landscaped winding pathways and gardens. A bell is rung several times a day, driving home Martin Luther King, Jr.'s "Let Freedom Ring" speech, which is, in part, inscribed in a reflecting pool. It's attached to the Carnegie Library, a 1904 Beaux Arts–style building that was recently renovated into part of the Richard Stockton College's Atlantic City campus. Open 9 AM–5 PM. Free.

Dante Hall Theater of the Arts

609-344-8877
www.dantehall.org
14 North Mississippi Ave., Atlantic City 08401

Yes, the casinos are chock full of entertainment stages, but Dante Hall is the only fine performing arts space in Atlantic City. It was built in 1926, originally as the social hall for St. Michael's Roman Catholic Church, which explains the cathedral elements in the architecture. In 2003, after an extensive renovation project, the building was reopened as Dante Hall and is home to performances in classical and world music, opera, children's theater, entertainers, and regional production companies. Prices vary per performance.

Magic Masters

609-449-1800
www.tropicana.net

Quarter at the Tropicana
2801 Pacific Ave., Atlantic City 08401

Can you figure out how he did it? Take a look at Magic Masters, a live magic show that is held in the very vintage-looking Dickens Parlour Theatre. If you can't catch the show, or want to try tricks on your own, Magic Masters also sells magician's tools, including cards, coins, and books. $$.

MARGATE

Margate Players
609-487-7783
www.margateplayers.org
7804 Amherst Ave., Margate 08402

You'll find all your old favorites, like *Little Shop of Horrors, Annie,* and *Joseph and the Amazing Technicolor Dreamcoat* at the Margate Players, who take the stage at the Margate Performing Arts Center. They also run one show a year cast exclusively with young actors. $$.

Miss America

I stopped at the Sheraton Atlantic City to tour the convention hotel for this book. I told myself to be all business, but I couldn't help but let out a decidedly girlish coo when I stepped into the grand foyer, which showcased Miss America gowns from the first pageant to the latest winner.

No bones about it, Miss America started as a beauty contest. Talent wasn't added until 1935. In 1945, Miss America became a scholarship-granting organization, something the group still pushes (and pushes, and pushes) today. The contest first hit the small screen in 1954 and became one of the longest-running live events in television history.

Even if I thought the competition was just silly, I still watched every September. I made fun of the girls and their unnaturally bright white smiles and the silliness of a beauty pageant still having so much draw. But apparently I wasn't the only one who thought Miss America was falling behind the times. In 2006, after being dropped from her longtime broadcast home of ABC, Miss America moved to Las Vegas and was televised on Country Music Television in January, not on the traditional September date. CMT dropped the pageant after one year, and it was picked up by The Learning Channel for 2007, adding in a reality television element and another January show date.

Also in 2007, the Miss America organization moved out of Atlantic City. When I visited the Sheraton, the Miss America's offices had been located in the building. But soon after that visit, they announced that they'd be moving their offices to nearby Linwood. And even though the press release announcing that movement was filled with zip and vigor, anyone could see that moving out of your 85-year home in Atlantic City to an office inland was a far fall.

You can still find pieces of Miss America lore in Atlantic City—Miss America Way is still a street in town, and she's too much a part of the city to go away completely. As of press time, those dresses from previous winners are still on display at the Sheraton, as is a video montage of greatest hits from the annual show. I've included that information in the lodging section of this book because, even though I think it's an outdated competition, it's still a part of the town's history, and I can't help but think that the gowns are gorgeous and worth stopping in for a peek.

GALLOWAY TOWNSHIP

Noyes Museum of Art
609-652-8848
www.noyesmuseum.org
733 Lily Lake Rd., Oceanville 08231

This art museum grew out of Fred W. Noyes, Jr.'s and Ethel Noyes's love of art. The couple, who also developed Historic Smithville, were art and antiques collectors and wanted to create a greater public awareness of New Jersey artists. Today, the museum has many items from the Noyes' collection and focuses on artwork that is local and/or artwork that exhibits the art and cultural heritage of southern New Jersey. If you hunt, check out the collection of vintage bird decoys. Open 10 AM–4:30 PM Tuesday to Saturday and noon–5 PM Sunday. $.

ATTRACTIONS, PARKS & RECREATION

ATLANTIC CITY

Absecon Lighthouse
609-449-1360
www.abseconlighthouse.org
31 S. Rhode Island Ave., Atlantic City 08401

If you're looking for a workout with your view, climb the 228 steps to the top of New Jersey's tallest lighthouse (and the third tallest in the U.S.). It was built by General George Mead in 1857 and looks over both Atlantic City and nearby Brigantine. Open 10 AM–5 PM July and August, 11 AM–4 PM Thursday through Monday September through June. $.

Atlantic City Aquarium
609-348-2880
www.acaquarium.com
New Hampshire Ave. and the Bay, Atlantic City 08203

The Atlantic City Aquarium is the best spot to take a look at what lives in New Jersey waters—or even touch a few critters at the touch tank—without getting too dirty. In this three-story aquarium's 11 tanks, you'll see native inhabitants, including sea bass, sand tiger sharks, stingrays, and horseshoe crabs. You can also learn about what makes boats go—whether of the sailing or the motor variety—in permanent exhibits like The Art of Sailing and A Ship's Bridge. Don't miss the third-story observatory—it offers fantastic views of where the ocean meets the bay. Open 10 AM–5 PM. $.

Atlantic City Cruises
609-347-7600
www.atlanticcitycruises.com
800 North New Hampshire Ave., Atlantic City 08401

For a high-flying thrill, try parasailing. For a closer-to-the-water experience, consider a whale watching trip. Both are offered through Atlantic City Cruises. Parasailing is not as

Absecon Lighthouse Absecon Lighthouse

Skee-Ball

Skee-Ball is a simple game. Put your coin in the slot for eight chances to roll a ball up a ramp to rack up points. The games come in all shapes and variations now, and with most machines, you score points for tickets that you can turn in for a bouncy ball, a radio, or a stuffed animal. But at the heart of this classic game is the same goal: Skee-Ball is all about the 50-point high score.

Skee-Ball was born in 1909, when it was invented and patented by J.D. Estes of Philadelphia. It wasn't exactly what you find on the boardwalks today—it was an outdoor game with 36-foot alleys. In 1928, the alleys were cut to 14 feet, which made it a game that could be played by more people of almost any athletic ability (today's ramps are between 10 and 13 feet). The size and shape change, plus the price, also helped the game spread in popularity, especially at the Jersey Shore.

"One of the reasons Skee-Ball is so popular is that it's akin to bowling, which is already a popular sport," says Angus Kress Gillespie, professor of American studies at Rutgers University and coauthor of *Looking for America on the New Jersey Turnpike*. "Skee-Ball is a feasible alternative to a full-length bowling alley. The real estate on a beachfront boardwalk is so expensive in terms of rent that no business could afford a full-scale bowling alley. What you have in effect is miniature bowling, same as miniature golf."

In 1932, Atlantic City was host to the first national Skee-Ball tournament, and since then, it's spread to other Shore towns, and across the country. Skee-Ball's even taken center stage in Hollywood, making cameos in the movies *Chasing Amy* and *Dogma*, and appearing in episodes of *The Simpsons*, *Rugrats*, and *SpongeBob SquarePants*. It's stayed a staple of Boardwalk amusements for many of the same reasons it was so popular to start—it's affordable, easy to maintain, and because it's fun.

"Another part of the appeal of Skee-Ball is that there is some skill involved and therefore it lends itself to competition," says Gillespie. "The fact that it's competitive works to the proprietors' advantage because people try to outdo one another."

Probably that more so than the tickets and the prizes you can earn.

"roller coasterish" as you might think—it's a floating feeling without the stomach turmoil of a roller coaster plunge, which is why kids and adults can go high flying (Ricky Hopkins, teenage son of Atlantic City Cruises owner Jeff George, likes it, in part, because "there's no butterflies.") If you're more comfortable at sea level, Atlantic City Cruises offers a variety of choices, from dolphin and whale watching trips to moonlight dance parties to the Morning Skyline Cruise, which takes you through the back bays to view the Atlantic City skyline. Sightseeing cruises in season only.

Atlantic City Surf Professional Baseball
609-344-8873
www.acsurf.com
545 North Albany Ave., Atlantic City 08401

Root, root, root for Atlantic City's home team May through August. It's a minor league ball club, so while you might see a few more errors on the field, you'll pay a lot less for a baseball experience than you would at a Major League Baseball stadium. $.

Boardwalk Hall

609-348-7000

www.boardwalkhall.com

2301 Boardwalk, Atlantic City 08401

Boardwalk Hall might look like just another big convention hall if you're visiting to see one of the knockout acts that regularly perform there, like Bruce Springsteen, Jimmy Buffett, or Bon Jovi. But when what was then called Convention Hall opened in 1929, it was a marvel of modern architecture. Situated on 7 acres of concrete and coming in at a then unheard-of $15 million price tag, Convention Hall was the largest auditorium in the world to be built without posts or pillars. The 137-foot arched roof with 10 steel trusses was designed to hold itself in place, which allowed unparalleled and unobstructed views of whatever was happening onstage under that proscenium arch.

Convention Hall was also home to the world's largest pipe organ, a Midmer-Losh Company instrument that had more than 33,000 pipes. The building's ballroom had another, though smaller, organ built by the W.W. Kimball Company.

In its time, Boardwalk Hall has seen musicals, boxing, the Harlem Globetrotters, ice hockey, indoor football, polo, bowling, Ice Capades, bike races, Judy Garland, horse shows, and, of course Miss America, which first sent its most beautiful woman in the country—at least for that year—down the runway in 1933 and again in 1940. It wasn't until 1946 that the organization attached itself to the building as its home until she left for Las Vegas in 2006. It's also the only place in Atlantic City the Beatles ever played. (The boys from Liverpool were taken out of the building by laundry truck to avoid 19,000 screaming fans.)

In 1998, Boardwalk Hall started a five-phase, $90 million renovation project to bring her up to modern concert venue standards while also taking asbestos out of the ceiling. The project was finished in 2001 (though construction was halted so that the 1999 Miss American Pageant could be held there).

Boardwalk Hall, in a lot of ways, is used today as it was when it first opened. The events held on her show floor and stage are the same hodgepodge of shows, festivals, sports events, and competitions, though it was home to more conventions before (which are now held at the Atlantic City Convention Center). But one major tenant has left the building: the last Miss America to cry and wave down the long runway was Jennifer Barry, Miss Oklahoma and then Miss America 2006, when the pageant left for Las Vegas. Boardwalk Hall still thrives, though, and rocks, too. I took in a Jimmy Buffett concert in the summer of 2007. Even though the stage was more Caribbean cool and margaritas, and the sight of thousands of people moving in unison to "Fins," was startling, Boardwalk Hall still managed to exude her sense of history—no posts or pillars necessary.

Atlantic Surf Sessions

609-517-5069

www.atlanticsurfsessions.com

Mississippi Ave. and the Boardwalk, Atlantic City 08401

If you've ever wanted to learn how to hang ten, you can take a one-day lesson with Atlantic City Surf Sessions. They're based in Atlantic City but also teach you how to achieve the feeling of "stoke" in Ventnor and Margate. No need to be of the typical surfing type. Co-owner Don Milora says a lot of their students are young girls and parents with kids. $.

Flyers Skate Zone

609-441-1780

atlanticcity.flyersskatezone.com

501 North Albany Ave., Atlantic City 08401

It's all ice, all the time, at this outpost of the Philadelphia Flyers training facilities. The Flyers don't actually train here—that's at the Skate Zone in Voorhees, New Jersey—but the Atlantic City franchise offers much of the same services to the general public: ice time seven days a week, skating lessons, and hockey camps and clinics (some as short as four days if you're vacationing with the kids). Public skate 1 PM–3 PM Monday through Saturday and 8 PM–10 PM Fridays. $.

Ripley's Believe It or Not

1-877-713-4231

www.ripleys.com

1441 Boardwalk, Atlantic City 08401

Check out the unusual, fascinating, and just plain odd at this branch of Ripley's, which has 400 exhibits, including a lock of George Washington's hair and a 27-room, mini castle carved in wood. Open 10 AM–11 PM Sunday through Friday and 10 AM–midnight Saturday in season. Call for off-season hours. $$.

Shore Bet Deep Sea Fishing

609-345-4077

www.shorebetfishing.com

13 N. New Hampshire Ave., Atlantic City 08203

In season, this fishing outfit runs two trips a day, seven days a week. Bring your own gear, or rent rods on the boat—bait and tackle are included in your fee. If you're a serious fisherman (or hope to become one), book one of Shore Bet's six-and-a-half-hour, all-day trips. For a less intense (or rocking) experience, check out their "no seasickness" trips, which stick to the calm inland waters of the nearby inlets. $$–$$$$.

The Spa at Bally's

609-340-2000

www.harrahs.com

Bally's Atlantic City

1900 Boardwalk, Atlantic City 08401

Don't be fooled by the pastel décor. The Spa at Bally's is a great place to work out, especially if you still like to smash a racquetball. Where in a lot of places racquetball has gone the way of Aquanet and acid-washed jeans, Bally's decided to keep the courts. Call ahead to make sure they're open—Bally's has a lot of regular players. Open 7 AM–7 PM Monday to Saturday and 7 AM–7 PM Sunday. $.

Steel Pier

1-866-386-6659

www.steelpier.com.

1000 Boardwalk, Atlantic City 08104

Live from Atlantic City

You won't be at a loss for stage shows in Atlantic City. Every casino provides entertainment. You can enjoy everything from live music at a casino bar to blockbuster acts at Boardwalk Hall. Here's a quick summary of what you'll find where.

Atlantic City Hilton Casino Resort

The Hilton has a 1,420-seat theater that houses both music and live comedy. The term "legend" tends to apply to the acts that grace the Hilton stage, like Frankie Valli, Blondie, Cyndi Lauper, Kool & the Gang, the Doobie Brothers, Peter Frampton, and KC and the Sunshine Band. The comedy goes big, too, with names like Whoopi Goldberg and Jerry Seinfeld. For tickets: www.hiltonac.com.

Bally's Atlantic City

Bally's cozy 550-seat Palace Theater is the spot for concerts and shows, like *Dancing Queen* and *Ain't Nothing Like the Real Thing*, and audience-participation game shows like the stage version of *The Price is Right*. For tickets: www.harrahs.com.

Borgata Concerts

Most of the Borgata shows are held at two theaters within its walls (though they do run larger shows at Boardwalk Hall). The Event Center is where you'll see most big-name acts, like John Mayer and the Moody Blues since, with 3,700 seats, it accommodates more fans than the Borgata's second venue, The Music Box, which tops out at 1,000 seats. It's a more intimate setting and more often a stage for comedians such as Lewis Black and Lisa Lampanelli than you'd find at the Event Center. For tickets: www.theborgata.com.

Caesars Atlantic City

The Circus Maximus Theater just got a $10 million facelift that has turned this 1,500-seat, stadium-style seated theater into a headlining stage of choice for artists like Tony Bennett, the Steve Miller Band, Sheryl Crow, and Jon Stewart. For tickets: www.harrahs.com.

Harrah's

When Broadway makes its way to Atlantic City, it usually stops at Harrah's—the Concert Venue has hosted hits like *Hairspray*, *Movin' Out*, and *The Producers*. Harrah's also provides live music for their pool guests at the Pool at Harrah's. For tickets: www.harrahs.com.

Resorts Atlantic City

The 1,350-seat, 17,500-square-foot theater at Resorts has hosted a wide range of performers, from Snoop Dogg to Jerry Seinfeld to Tom Jones to Don Rickles. For tickets: www.resortsac.com.

Showboat: The House of Blues

Along with The Borgata and Boardwalk Hall, The House of Blues has brought in A-list acts such as Bonnie Raitt and Brian Setzer, plus comedians and tribute bands. Tickets are general admission, and you can either stand to watch the show or sit on the second level in tiered seating. The House of Blues also holds a Sunday Gospel Brunch, which includes a Southern-style brunch buffet and top Gospel acts from around the country. It takes place, of course, every Sunday at 11 AM. For tickets: www.hob.com/venues/clubvenues/atlanticcity.

Tropicana Casino and Resort

The Showroom at the Tropicana is another multipurpose stage, hosting big shows by top-40 artists and comedians as well as magic shows, boxing, and tribute bands. You'll also find live music in the Quarter, including Latin dancing at Cuba Libre. For tickets: www.tropicana.net.

More Live from Atlantic City

Trump Marina Hotel & Casino

For bigger shows, head to the Grand Cayman Ballroom. If you'd like a revue, then the Shell Showroom is for you. Trump Marina's live shows on "The Deck" are popular in the summer, with events such as Jimmy Buffett tribute bands, and the Jerry Blavat Dance Party. For tickets: www.trumpmarina.com.

Trump Plaza

Trump Plaza plays host to music acts, stage shows, and sports at the Trump Plaza Theater. For tickets: www.trumpplaza.com.

Trump's Taj Mahal Atlantic City

Trump's Taj Mahal brings in the big names to the Mark G. Etess Arena, acts like Beyonce, Liza Minnelli, and the Police. The Taj also has Xanadu, a smaller, more intimate setting that still pulls in big names, like George Carlin and Earth, Wind & Fire. For tickets: www.trumptaj.com.

This Boardwalk attraction, built in 1898, had a date with a wrecking ball (new condos were the reason), but when construction plans hit a snag, the pier that was once home to world-class entertainment and high-diving horses was allowed to stay. As of press time, the folks at the Steel Pier were planning for another season. The rides range from the kid-friendly, double-decker carousel to the shocking thrill of the Slingshot, which does exactly what its name implies—slingshots you over the ocean (while appropriately tied and harnessed, of course). Open 3PM—midnight Monday through Friday and noon—1 AM Saturday and Sunday in season. $.

Web Feet Watersports
609-572-1004
www.webfeetwatersports.com
800 N. New Hampshire Ave., Atlantic City, 08401

If you're looking to explore the back bays of Atlantic City in style, rent or buy a kayak from Web Feet Watersports. Or, if you need a different kind of water thrill, Web Feet also rents surfing kayaks, plus bikes and fishing gear. Owner Dotty Web is a sailing expert if you want to talk shop—or ship. Open 7:30 AM—6 PM Sunday through Thursday and 7:30 AM—9:30 PM Friday and Saturday in season.

BRIGANTINE

Brigantine Golf Links
1-800-698-1388
www.brigantinegolf.com
1075 North Shore Drive, Brigantine 08203

This is the closest golf course you'll find to Atlantic City, and over the last 10 years, Brigantine Golf Links has gotten a $4.5 million facelift. Originally built in 1927 according to classic Scottish links design, Brigantine Golf Links is an 18-hole, par 72 course that comes in at 6,570 yards from the back tees. Since it's built by the water, the course includes marsh, berm, and tidal water hazards. $$.

Marine Mammal Stranding Center
609-266-0538
www.marinemammalstrandingcenter.org
3625 Brigantine Boulevard, Brigantine 08203

Injured whales, dolphins, seals, and sea turtles found in local waters are all brought here for rehab. The public viewing hours are limited for the safety of the animals, but you can also check out the attached shop and exhibits on sea life and how the stranding center works. As of press time, the center was in a state of limbo. Brigantine wants to use the land for further development, and the center doesn't know where it would be moving, if it stays in operation at all. Open 10 AM–4 PM Tuesday through Sunday in season. Free, though donations are appreciated.

MARGATE

Lucy the Elephant
609-823-6473
www.lucytheelephant.org
9200 Atlantic Ave., Margate 08402

In 1881, real estate prospector James Vincent de Paul Lafferty, Jr. built a 65-foot-high wooden elephant in Margate, in the hopes that it would attract visitors and potential real estate buyers. He was right then, and still is today. Lucy's been a tourist attraction, a restaurant, even a home, and is now back to an attraction again. She welcomes visitors to take a walk up into her insides. Make sure you head into the top—her howdah—to get a 360-degree view of Margate. Guided tours available. Open 10 AM–8 PM Monday through Saturdays and 10 AM–5 PM in season. Call for off-season hours. $.

GALLOWAY TOWNSHIP

Antiques Arcade
609-748-6160
615 E. Mossmill Rd., Shop 65, Smithville 08205

Are you "uncontrollable" or a "cold fish"? Find out at the Love Tester, which strikes fear in the hearts of all lovers at the Antiques Arcade in Historic Smithville. You can also test your gunslinger skills at the New Frontier shoot-em-up game, or have your fortune told by Merlin. Open 10 AM–6 PM Monday through Friday, 10 AM–7 PM Saturday, and 10 AM–5 PM Sunday. $

The Bay Course
609-652-1800
www.seaviewmarriott.com
Seaview Resort & Spa
401 South New York Rd., Galloway 08205

Historic Smithville

In the 1700s, Smithville was a stop for stagecoaches traveling between Leeds Point and Camden. When railroads replaced stagecoaches as the preferred method of travel, travel routes—and people— migrated to nearby Brigantine. By the 20th century, Smithville had all but ceased to serve travelers, and many of the buildings were falling apart.

In 1951, Fred and Ethel Noyes, antique dealers from Absecon, and the couple behind the Noyes Museum of Art, bought a dilapidated inn for $3,500 and turned it into a restaurant and inn, reopening in 1952 as the Colonial Inn at Historic Smithville. They started buying historic 18th- and 19th-century homes from all over the South Jersey area and moving them to the site that would become Historic Smithville. Today these homes are filled with shops and restaurants.

In 1975, the Noyes sold Smithville to ABC—yes, as in the television network. Smithville didn't turn out to be the tourist gold mine they thought, so Smithville was sold again, and has changed hands many times since. Today, it's owned by two groups, who work together to make sure Smithville stays on the map this time. It features clusters of shops, restaurants, and plenty of places to stroll, plus a train and paddle boats. Watch out for the tour buses, and the roosters, the latter of which roam the property.

The shops come in all stripes, from kitchen to fashion to toy stores. And even if Smithville was created around the idea of America's past, they embrace cultures from all over through festivals and shops in town. In October, Smithville is host to both an Oktoberfest and Irish Festival. It also counts two Irish import shops—Out of Ireland and Ireland and Old Lace—among its ranks. Don't worry if you don't have the luck of the Irish: Smithville also has The British Connection and Journey through Italy among its many shops.

Historic Smithville

One of two golf courses on the Seaview property, the Bay Course is home of the ShopRite LPGA Classic. It first came to be in 1914 because Clarence Geist, a Philadelphia utilities magnate, couldn't get a tee time at his hometown course. It's a par 71, 6,247-yard, links-style course. $$$$.

Edwin B. Forsythe National Wildlife Refuge
609-652-1665
www.fws.gov/northeast/forsythe
Great Creek Rd., Oceanville 08231

Two wildlife refuges, which were established in 1939 and 1967, came together in the 1980s to form the 43,000 acres of preserved land that is today the Edwin B. Forsythe National Wildlife Refuge. It's located in one of the Atlantic Flyway's most active flight paths, so it attracts birds (and birders) from around the world. You can drive, walk, hike, or run an 8-mile continuous loop through the refuge, or hike one of the shorter trails. Open sunrise to sunset. $.

The Pines Course
609-652-1800
www.seaviewmarriott.com
Seaview Resort & Spa
401 S. New York Rd., Galloway 08205

The Pines Course, much like its fellow Seaview course the Bay Course, was a result of Clarence Geist. The Bay Course was so successful that he created the Pines Course in 1929. It's a par 71, 6,731-yard, Parkland-style course carved into the woodlands, and runs 6,800 yards. $$$$.

Edwin B. Forsythe National Wildlife Refuge Arthur Webster, USFWS

IT'SUGAR

Shopping

Bernie Robbins

609-441-0090 and 609-449-0600

www.bernierobbins.com

Trump Marina and Trump Taj Mahal

Huron & Brigantine Boulevard, Atlantic City 08053 and 1000 Boardwalk, Atlantic City 08401

Dazzle her with what glitters from famous jewelry names like David Yurman, Vera Wang, Judith Ripka, Kwiat, Michael B, and Simon G. Bernie Robbins also stocks luxe watches from Chanel, Fendi, and Tag Heuer. Marina: Open 11 AM–8 PM Monday to Thursday, 10 AM–midnight Friday and Saturday, and 10 AM–10 PM Sunday. Taj Mahal: Open 10 AM–10 PM Sunday to Thursday and 10 AM–midnight Friday and Saturday.

Bijoux Terner

609-345-4088

Pier at Caesars

1 Atlantic Ocean, Atlantic City 08401

Shop 'Til You Drop

If you're looking to get the most punch out of your shopping time in Atlantic City, you'll want to head to one of three (or all three) shopping centers in town. Some of the stores in these complexes are covered in the shopping section of this chapter, but there's no way to include them all—there'd be no room left to write about where to stay, eat, and play in Atlantic City. So here's where to go:

Atlantic City Outlets: the Walk

609-872-7002

www.acoutlets.com

1931 Atlantic Ave., Atlantic City 08401

You can scour for bargains at this expanding outlet mall, which includes discount goods from Adidas, Converse, Coach, the Gap, and Kenneth Cole, to name a few. If you feel yourself about to start wilting from shopping, the Starbucks located at the western end of the shops can give you a pick-me-up. Open 10 AM–9 PM Monday through Saturday and 10 AM–6 PM Sunday in season. Open 10 AM–9 PM Monday through Saturday and 10 AM–5 PM Sunday in the off season.

Pier at Caesars

609-345-3100

www.thepiershopsatcaesars.com

1 Atlantic Ocean, Atlantic City 08401

If the Walk is your bargain spot, the Pier is where you can blow your winnings at luxury retailers like Tiffany's, Burberry, Louis Vuitton, and Baccarat. It's also home to an Apple store if you have a must-need for an iPod (or want to give your e-mail a quick check for free). Don't be intimidated by the big names—the Pier also has mall staples like Ann Taylor and Banana Republic. The Pier is also home to restaurants on its third floor, and The Show, which is a water show with lights and music, held at the western end of the building. Open 11 AM–11 PM Sunday through Thursday and 11 AM–midnight Friday and Saturday. Hours vary for restaurants.

Quarter at the Tropicana

1-800-843-8767

www.tropicana.net

2801 Pacific Ave., Atlantic City 08401

You'll find everything from spy gear to spa products at this indoor shopping area, which is connected to the restaurant complex that has made the Quarter a popular nighttime spot, and a top choice by *CasinoPlayer* magazine. The Quarter has a few national stores, like White House Black Market, Chico's, and Cache, but also shops that are as individual as the shoppers, such as Salsa Shoes, Jake's Dog House, and Magic Master. The Quarter is also home to an IMAX theater, which shows educational and Hollywood movies, some with 3D elements. Open 10 AM–11 PM Sunday through Thursday and 10 AM–midnight Friday and Saturday.

You'll find baubles, bangles, and beads—and then some—at this shop. The accessories, like sunglasses, purses, and jewelry, are very "now," but at a price point that won't make you cringe if it goes out of style next season: everything's $10. Try finding that kind of deal at the Tiffany's location one floor up! Open 11 AM–11 PM Sunday through Thursday and 11 AM–midnight Friday and Saturday.

IT'SUGAR

609-289-4200

www.itsugar.com

Pier at Caesars

1 Atlantic Ocean, Atlantic City 08401

Diets be damned at this all-candy, all the time, two-story Boardwalk shop. Pick from candy-themed clothing and accessories, or make your own candy bar (pick the type of chocolate and goodies dumped inside). Don't skip the re-creation of Lucy the Elephant, made out of jelly beans. Open 11 AM–midnight.

Jake's Dog House

609-344-0060

www.jakesdoghouse.com

Quarter at the Tropicana

2801 Pacific Ave., Atlantic City 08401

This is the place to pamper your pet. Jake's sells everything from dog sweaters to team-themed collars and leashes to gourmet treats. Most of what's sold at Jake's is for dogs, though they do stock cat items, too. Open 10 AM–11 PM Sunday through Thursday and 10 AM–midnight Friday and Saturday.

Lush Cosmetics

609-345-5733

lush.com

Pier at Caesars

1 Atlantic Ocean, Atlantic City 08401

Everything at Lush, which is a British-based company, is handmade and fresh—so fresh that the facial masks come with an expiration date. You can also pick up soaps, lotions, fragrances, and stuff that'll make your bathtime more fun. Open 11 AM–11 PM Sunday through Thursday and 11 AM–midnight Friday and Saturday.

Princeton Antiques and Books

609-344-1943

www.princetonantiques.com

2917 Atlantic Ave., Atlantic City 08401

Salt Water Taffy

Salt water? In your food? Not quite.

There is no salt water in salt water taffy. Heck, there isn't even much water in it. Then how'd this sweet sticky substance get the name? Legend has it that the name stuck because of a man named David Bradley, who sold taffy on the Atlantic City Boardwalk. As sometimes happens to shoreside real estate, the ocean acted up one night and flooded his stand. The next morning, a girl asked for some taffy, and, in an obviously bad mood, Bradley spat back that it wasn't taffy but "salt water taffy." The name stuck.

Get your slice—or stick—of this tasty treat at James' Salt Water Taffy (1519 Boardwalk, Atlantic City 08401, www.jamescandy.com), which has been making salt water taffy since around the time the treat got its official name.

James' Salt Water Taffy

Monopoly

If you've ever passed Go to collect $200 or built the ever-elusive hotels on Boardwalk and Park Place, you know your Monopoly. But did you know where the names of the streets came from? After spots in Atlantic City!

Philadelphian Charles B. Darrow was an unemployed salesman during the Depression and traveled to Atlantic City's Steel Pier, which was then an area where men went to try to find work. When he returned back home—still unemployed—he created the game that is now Monopoly, using Atlantic City's geography to make the real estate buying and selling game.

The game was, at first, rejected by Parker Brothers for "52 design errors." So Darrow and a friend made 5,000 sets and sold them to a Philadelphia department store. They sold out, and Parker Brothers took another look.

Since 1935, the first year of the Parker Brothers edition, 200 million games have been sold. Even if you can now buy Monopolies themed to your alma matter, town, or favorite movie, the original Atlantic City version is still the classic.

If you're hunting for a rare title, they'll search their 250,000-book library and go beyond the shelves if it's not in stock. Open 8 AM–5 PM Monday through Friday and 8:30 AM–1 PM Saturdays.

Spy Shop
609-348-1500
Quarter at the Tropicana
2801 Pacific Ave., Atlantic City 08401

Whether you're a James Bond fan, a spy in training, or just want to keep tabs on the nanny, the Spy Shop will have the gear you need to sneak around. Some of the stuff's pretty high-tech, too. And, no, they won't tell you who buys the pricier items. Open 10 AM–11 PM Sunday through Thursday and 10 AM–midnight Friday and Saturday.

Toon In
609-340-0010
www.toonin.net
1729 Boardwalk, Atlantic City 08401

If you're a fan of movies, cartoons, TV shows, Disney, and/or Betty Boop, Toon In is a must-see. This Boardwalk shop stocks T-shirts, posters, figurines, and more of your favorite characters. Open 11 AM–8 PM.

World Series of Poker Store
609-340-2000
Bally's Casino Resort
900 Boardwalk, Atlantic City 08401

Poker player, or watcher? You'll want to stop at this store, which stocks official merchandise, like shirts, chips, and cards. Open 11 AM–7 PM Sunday through Thursday and 11 AM–10 PM Saturday.

Zephyr Gallery

609-340-0170
www.zephyrgallery.com
Quarter at the Tropicana
2801 Pacific Ave., Atlantic City 08401

The Quitel family has done an excellent job in keeping Zephyr full of unique arts and crafts. It's hard to describe just what they sell because the stock changes according to what they find on buying trips, but it ranges from home décor to jewelry to wine accessories. Whatever it is they have at the moment, it's eye-catching. When Zephyr was located in Marlton, New Jersey—its home before moving to Atlantic City—it was my go-to place to shop for those people who already have everything. Open 10 AM—11 PM Sunday to Thursday and 10 AM—midnight Friday and Saturday.

MARGATE

Paperchase

609-822-4583
8000 Ventnor Ave., Margate 08402

This gift shop might seem a bit jumbled, but that's because they carry whatever fits their fancy, like cards (of course), jewelry, staplers that look like dogs, metal wine holders, and books about the area. Open 10 AM—5:30 PM Monday through Saturday and 10 AM—3 PM Sunday.

Sassy Shoes III

609-823-4969
8003 Ventnor Ave., Margate 08402

This slip of a store carries an impressive stock of designer women's footwear. Check out the name-brand accessories, too, like sunglasses from Prada, D&G, and Cole Haan. Open 10 AM—6 PM Monday through Saturday and 10 AM—5 PM Sunday.

GALLOWAY TOWNSHIP

The Birder's Company Store

609-652-5122
615 E. Mossmill Rd., Shop 9, Smithville 08205

If you're coming to the Jersey Shore to take in the birding sights (or even if you're not), stop in this airy store for an assortment of birdhouses, feeders, and even Birdopoly. Don't miss the outdoor displays, either. You might catch a bird or two enjoying the samples. Open 10 AM—6 PM.

Cook's Corner

609-748-9030
www.cookscorner.net
615 E. Mossmill Rd., Shop 12, Smithville 08205

Find that cookie jar you never knew you wanted, or get gourmet coffees, teas, spices, and oils for your kitchen at Cook's Corner, an all-in-one cooking and kitchen store. You can even watch the coffee beans being roasted in-store and get a quick pick-me-up from the coffee shop. Make sure you look up, too, to see their expansive cookie jar collection that's literally in the rafters (and, no, they're not for sale). Open 10 AM–6 PM.

Prairie Fire

609-748-1555
615 E. Mossmill Rd., Shop 14, Smithville 08205

Get girly at this sunny shop. If you're into Vera Bradley, Prairie Fire has a sizable stock of her bags and purses, plus soaps, personalizable gifts, and silver jewelry that looks more expensive than it actually is (on one trip, I picked up stackable bracelets for $6.99 each). Open 10 AM–8 PM Monday through Saturday and 11 AM–6 PM Sunday.

Smithville Zoo

609-748-1116
615 E. Mossmill Rd., Shop 5B, Smithville 08205

No, this isn't an actual zoo, but you might think so at this shop, which is part toy store and part animal kitsch. Make sure to check out their stuffed animal display, which includes plush animals big and small. Open 10 AM–8 PM Monday through Saturday and 10 AM–6 PM Sunday in season. Call for off-season hours.

Tomasello Winery

609-652-2320 and 609-748-8717
615 E. Mossmill Rd., Shop 11 and Shops 75–76, Smithville 08205

Yes, the tastings at these Tomasello Winery locations, which are within walking distance of each other, really are free. The store in Shop 75 leans toward wine accoutrements, and the location in Shop 11 showcases this New Jersey winery's wares. Make sure to taste Tomasello's fruit wines. The cranberry goes well with turkey dinners and is popular around

---

Jackpot

I'll be the first to admit that I'm not a gambling man—or woman, as the case may be. Even as I toured the 11 Atlantic City casinos conducting research for this book, I avoided the slot machines, tables, and games of chance. I'm more a "sit on the beach and read" than "test Lady Luck" kind of gal.

But on one tour through the Tropicana, a friend coaxed me into sitting down at a $1 slot machine and he put in $5 for me so I wouldn't feel guilty about giving away my money. First spin, nothing. Second spin, the same. Third spin, bingo! I promptly cashed out and traded in my winning voucher for $200. Not bad for a $5 investment. Of course, I had to buy celebratory drinks and then picked up something at one of the shops in the Quarter, but I still made out ahead—at least that night.

I've dabbled in the slots since and haven't won more than a few dollars. I'm still not a gambling woman, and I don't think I'll ever graduate up to the poker or craps table. But drop a quarter or two on my way from the Boardwalk to the restaurant? I'm game.

The only part about the experience I regret is that the casinos don't pay out in quarters anymore—it's all tickets and paper, so if you hit big, you won't be faced with a deluge of quarters. You'll probably win out that way. When crews removed slot machines from the now-closed Sands Casino Hotel, they found more than $17,000 in change on the floor and behind the slot machines.

the holidays. The Cape May white is a popular choice for summer meals. Open 10 AM—8 PM in season, 10 AM—6 PM off season.

ANNUAL EVENTS

February

Atlantic City Classic Car Show
Atlantic City Convention Center
856-768-6900
www.acclassiccars.com
Atlantic City Convention Center

From Model Ts to the hot rod you wish you never sold, the Atlantic City Classic Car Show features models of days gone by—some of which are for sale, too. If a new car isn't in your budget, the show also features car parts and antiques vendors. $$.

Atlantic City International Power Boat Show
212-984-7000
www.acboatshow.com

More than 700 power boats, cruisers, and yachts are on display at this five-day boat show, which draws more than 40,000 people every year. The show also includes free fishing and boating seminars with the price of admission. $$.

Atlantique City Spring Antiques and Collectibles Show
1-800-526-2724
Atlantic City Convention Center

This is the big one—the largest indoor art, antiques, and collectibles show in the world. Twice a year, exhibitors come from as far away as Asia to partake in the buying and selling items from the 18th, 19th, and 20th centuries. $$.

March

St. Patrick's Day Parade
1-888-AC-VISIT
www.saintpatricksdayparade.com/AtlanticCity/index.htm
Atlantic City Boardwalk

Everyone's Irish on St. Patrick's Day. Show your pride at this annual event, which starts at 1 PM on the Boardwalk at New Jersey Avenue and ends at Albany Avenue. Free.

April

Atlantic City Easter Parade
Atlantic City Boardwalk
609-347-5300

Get decked out in your Easter finest—or watch the "best dressed" contestants stroll down the Boardwalk at this annual tradition. The parade starts at 2 PM at Indiana Avenue. Free.

June

Atlantic City Seafood Festival
609-FISH-FUN
www.acseafoodfest.com
Bernie Robbins Stadium

Sample the best of local eateries and restaurants at this annual Atlantic City tradition. The new location at the home of the Atlantic City Surf means that a day of feasting and live entertainment can be followed by a night of baseball. $.

July

Chicken Bone Beach Jazz Series
609-441-9064
www.chickenbonebeach.org
Kennedy Plaza at Missouri Avenue and the Boardwalk, Atlantic City 08401

Until the early 1950s, African Americans were not allowed on all sections of the beach in Atlantic City, so they stayed on the Missouri Avenue area of the beach. It became known as Chicken Beach, a name that sticks today, and Chicken Beach was recognized as a historic land site by the city in 1997. It's the center of weekly jazz concerts on Thursday nights—on the Boardwalk. Free.

August

Atlantic City Air Show
609-345-4524
www.atlanticcityairshow.com
Atlantic City Boardwalk

The United States Air Force Thunderbirds and United States Navy Blue Angels soar and zip over the Atlantic City Boardwalk and coast at this spectacular event. Air show fans will know that having both the Thunderbirds and the Angels at one show is a rarity—because of this, it is the largest military flying event in New Jersey. If you can't make it on the exact day of the show, you can still watch—and hear—the planes practicing the day before. Free.

Puerto Rican Parade and Latin Music Festival
609-347-0770
www.atlanticcityparade.com
Atlantic City Boardwalk

Puerto Rican and Latin heritage are celebrated at this two-pronged event. The day starts with a parade on the Boardwalk that starts at noon, followed by the Latin Music Festival. Free.

October

Atlantic City Marathon

609-601-1RUN

www.atlanticcitymarathon.org

Think you got what it takes to run 26.1 miles in one shot? Give it a try at this annual marathon, which starts on the Boardwalk. The course changes, so check out their Web site to find out where you'll start—and where you'll go.

Atlantique City Fall Antiques and Collectibles Show

1-800-526-2724

Atlantic City Convention Center

This is the big one—the largest indoor art, antiques, and collectibles show in the world. Twice a year, exhibitors come from as far away as Asia to partake in the buying and selling items from the 18th, 19th, and 20th centuries. $$.

Oktoberfest

Historic Towne of Smithville

609-748-6160

615 E. Moss Mill Road, Smithville 08205

Taste the best of German food and drink in a family-friendly setting at this festival, which also draws about 100 arts and crafts vendors to Smithville.

The Jitney

What are all those little blue busses zipping around Atlantic City? No, they're not senior services vehicles or errand trucks. They're a cheap, easy, and efficient way to get around town.

The Atlantic City Jitney Association started in 1915, and it's the longest-running non-subsidized transit company in the country—there's even a Jitney in the Smithsonian Institute.

Today, the fleet is made up of 13 state-of-the-art, air conditioned, 13-passenger vehicles painted in a pretty sky blue. They run 24 hours a day, 365 days a year, and stop all over Atlantic City, including all the casinos. And, yes, they are handicapped accessible. The Jitney costs $2 a ride. That's far from a nickel, which is what the word "jitney" means in Old English, but it's a cheap and easy way to get around town.

EMERGENCY NUMBERS

In an emergency, dial 911.

Poison information: 1-800-222-1222

Non-emergency police: 609-347-5780

HOSPITALS

AtlantiCare Regional Medical Center–City Campus

609-345-4000

www.atlanticare.org

1925 Pacific Ave., Atlantic City 08401

AtlantiCare Regional Medical Center–Mainland Campus
609-652-1000
www.atlanticare.org
Jimmie Leeds Rd., Pomona 08240

NEWSPAPERS

Atlantic City Weekly
609-646-4848
www.acweekly.com

Press of Atlantic City
609-272-7000
www.pressofatlanticcity.com

TRANSPORTATION

Atlantic City Airport Taxi & Car Service
877-568-8294
www.actaxi.com

Atlantic City International Airport
609-645-7895
www.acairport.com

Atlantic City Jitney
609-344-8642
www.jitneys.net

Atlantic City Rent-A-Car
609-344-3001

Avis
609-383-9356
www.avis.com

Budget
609-383-0682
budget.com

Enterprise Rent-A-Car
609-348-2902
www.enterprise.com

Hertz
609-646-7733
www.hertz.com

New Jersey Transit Rail
1-800-772-2222
www.njtransit.com

New Jersey Transit Bus
1-800-772-2222
www.njtransit.com

Philadelphia International Airport
215-937-6937
www.phl.org

Tropiano Transportation Airport Shuttle
1-800-559-2040
www.tropianotransportation.com

New Rail Line?

As of press time, a new rail line is being planned that will be a direct train from New York City to Atlantic City—no stops. For updated information, go to www.atlantic citynj.com

TOURISM CONTACTS

Atlantic City Convention and Visitors Authority
1-888-228-4748
www.atlanticcitynj.com

Atlantic City Regional Mainland Chamber of Commerce
609-345-4524
www.atlanticcitychamber.com

Brigantine Beach Tourism Commission
1-800-847-5198
www.brigantinebeachnj.com

New Jersey Travel and Tourism
www.state.nj.us/travel
1-800-VISITNJ

Ocean City beach

2

Ocean City

Family Fun

Including Somers Point and Egg Harbor Township

Ocean City was founded as a Christian retreat and, in many ways, the laws set by the town's four Methodist founders have kept it a family-oriented town. Its 2.5-mile boardwalk is largely devoid of any of the icky T-shirt shops and tattoo parlors that are popular in some Jersey Shore towns, and the boardwalk has consistently been ranked one of the best in the country. In fact, the entire town was voted Best Family Beach by the Travel Channel.

Like many Shore towns, Ocean City is a barrier island, surrounded by the Atlantic Ocean on its east side and Great Egg Harbor Bay on its west. This provides ample opportunities to enjoy water sports like wave running, boating, fishing, surfing, and swimming. The same is true for Somers Point, which is the town across Great Egg Harbor Bay from Ocean City.

The 7.5-mile-long island was first known as Peck's Beach, after whaler John Peck, who staged his whaling operations here. Since being incorporated in 1897, Ocean City has been and will most likely always be a dry town. This doesn't just mean that you won't find bars or liquor stores on the island. You are not allowed to bring alcohol into restaurants and certainly not to the beach. Even if one entry into the annual Night in Venice boat parade cheekily declared that Ocean City was the wettest dry town at the shore, this no-liquor rule has helped keep Ocean City a family-friendly town.

The main attraction, aside from the beach, is that boardwalk. In season, it's a beautiful jumble of shops, restaurants, amusements, and people—lots of people. On summer morn-

Ocean City Music Pier

The Ocean City Music Pier is a one-stop spot in Ocean City. The building, which is located at 9th Street on the boardwalk, provides shady space and benches for weary travelers, or those just looking to take in the view. It also has public bathrooms, a show space that features concerts, fairs, and festivals, and an information center that is chock full of information for your Ocean City vacation. I recommend picking up one of the coupon books at the information center. You'll find everything from a free ride on Wonderland's giant Ferris wheel to restaurant discounts.

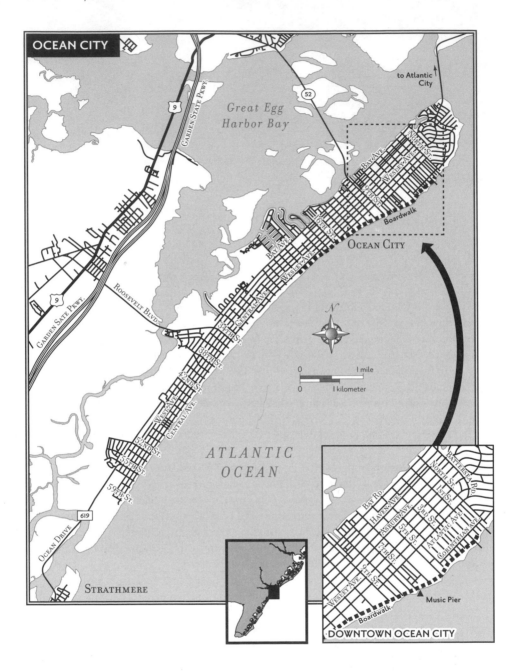

ings, bikes and surreys zip up and down the boards. At night, the boardwalk is packed with people getting from one spot to another, or just taking in the sights.

You'll be hard pressed to find über-fine dining in Ocean City—the liquor situation probably has something to do with that, though the town is chock full of casual, hearty restaurants, and almost all are kid-friendly. Plus, Ocean City is 10 miles from Atlantic City and 30 from Cape May, or you can explore one of the eateries (with liquor licenses) in Somers Point, just on the other side of the bay.

LODGING

OCEAN CITY

Atlantis Inn Luxury Bed & Breakfast
609-399-9871
www.atlantisinn.com
601 Atlantic Ave., Ocean City 08226

Luxury, luxury, luxury at this expansive (and expensive) inn, which was named best B&B at the shore by the *Atlantic City Press* three years running. But the price tag is worth it if it's elegance you're after. You might not even want to leave your room since those at Atlantis include Jacuzzi whirlpool tubs for two, fireplaces, and a grand poster or sleigh bed draped in luxury sheets imported from Milan. Atlantis also has an in-house spa, and on busy weekends, if you're not staying as a guest, you can't even get into the common areas. Yes, it's that exclusive. $$$$.

Bayberry Inn
609-391-1183
www.bayberryinnoc.com
811 Wesley Ave., Ocean City 08226

This inn offers two kinds of rooms—classic nautical and romantic Victorian. The Bayberry, which was built in the early 1900s, is also ideal for a quick trip to Ocean City—where most other accommodations require a two-night stay, you can just drop in for one here, as long as it's a weekday trip. Open in season. $$–$$$.

Beach Club Hotel
609-399-8555
www.beachclubhotel.com
1280 Boardwalk, Ocean City 08226

This hotel is literally on the beach, or as close as you can get to it—the boardwalk is your closest neighbor. The rooms are clean and smoke-free—nothing too fancy, but with the beach outside, are you really going to spend much time in your room? They also have grown-up and kiddie pools, both with ocean views. Open in season. $$–$$$$.

Beach Club Suites
609-399-4500
www.beachclubsuites.com
1217 Ocean Ave., Ocean City 08226

Consider these an upgraded version of the rooms at the Beach Club Hotel (they're owned by the same company). The accommodations are one-room apartments with kitchens, living rooms (with pull-out sofa beds), and separate bedrooms. You can get connecting apartments, too, if your group is large. Like those at the Beach Club Hotel, the suites have ocean views, and there is a pool. Open in season. $$–$$$$.

Biscayne Suites
1-800-452-1003
www.biscaynesuites.com
820 Ocean Ave., Ocean City 08226

You'll have space—lots of space—in any of the rooms at Biscayne. Even the deluxe

---

Causeway Construction

As of press time, NJ 52, the causeway connecting Somers Point with Ocean City, is being replaced, and officials estimate construction and removal of the current causeway will be complete in 2012. In the meantime, driving along NJ 52 between Somers Point and Ocean City can be tricky, and the ride is sometimes rough. But watching the huge blocks of concrete being lifted off the water and set into place is as good as any people-watching. The best view is probably from The Inlet in Somers Point.

When driving along NJ 52, be careful of work trucks and narrow lanes. Or come into town over the 34th Street bridge, which is one exit south on the Garden State Parkway.

suites, which are the smallest, still have living rooms and kitchenettes inside. Don't miss the heated rooftop pool (in season), and views of the beach from the rooftop sundeck. $$$$.

The Bluewater Inn
1-800-367-3042
www.bluewaterinnoc.com
617 East 8th St., Ocean City 08226

This turn-of-the-20th-century hotel recently renovated itself to bring it into the 21st century. This is a drop-your-stuff-and-go kind of place—nothing too showy, but clean and well maintained. Choose from rooms and suites that sleep two to eight people. Open in season. $$.

Brown's Nostalgia
609-398-6364
www.brownsnostalgia.com
1001 Wesley Ave., Ocean City 08226

The building is authentic early 1900s, but the eight rooms inside are a mix of styles (all updated with modern conveniences). One room features a gorgeous Victorian stained glass window; another has seashore décor and stunning Amish quilts on the bed. Brown's also has a two-bedroom apartment with living room and kitchen available. The front veranda is well shaded and a great spot to relax. $$–$$$.

Butterfly Breeze Bed & Breakfast
609-391-9366
www.butterflybreeze.net
637 Wesley Ave., Ocean City 08226

Butterflies are the theme at this bed & breakfast. Each of the seven rooms is named after a different kind of butterfly, and even though you won't be entering into a bug chamber, the rooms are decorated so sweetly that you wouldn't be surprised if a butterfly wandered in. Butterfly Breeze also lets you play detective through its murder mystery packages on weekends in the off season. This is DIY (which is all of the fun), meaning that you'll pick your script and act out the mystery for eight to a dozen of your closest friends, with prizes for the winner. They run couples weekends, too, if you can't corral a big group together but still want to sleuth it out. Open every day in season, weekends only in the off season. $$–$$$$.

Ebb Tide Suites
609-391-9614
www.ebbtidesuites.com
1001 Little Atlantic Ave., Ocean City 08226

If you're not into old-time charm, check out the Ebb Tide Suites. They're newly constructed one- and two-bedroom apartments. All suites have private balconies, and some of the rooms are ADA compliant, built to the design standards of the American Disability Association. There's no pool at Ebb Tide, but guests can use the pool at the nearby Impala Island Inn at no extra charge. $$$–$$$$.

Flanders Hotel
609-399-1000
www.theflandershotel.com
719 East 11th St., Ocean City 08226

This hotel, which opened in 1923, has survived fire, the stock market crash, and a partial conversion into condominiums to remain one of the more luxurious places to stay in Ocean City. It still retains the opulence and glamour befitting movie stars Grace Kelly and Jimmy Stewart, who both stayed at the Flanders. One of the more popular year-round hotels. $$$$.

Homestead Hotel
609-391-0200
www.homesteadhotel.info
805 East Eighth St., Ocean City 08226

In 1927, a fire ripped through Ocean City and destroyed 12 city blocks. The

Homestead Hotel was one of the buildings built in the fire's wake, and the seven-story brick building is still standing. Even if the building has history, the rooms inside are modern, with furniture you'd more expect to find at a new home than a historic hotel. Choose from one-room efficiencies, one-bedroom suites, or go top of the line with a penthouse apartment. $$–$$$.

Inn at Laurel Bay

609-814-1886
www.laurelbayoc.com
400 Atlantic Ave., Ocean City 08226

The rooms at this bed & breakfast are works of art—literally. Murals or mosaics decorate many of the walls, especially in the Roman suite, which features a few lovely ladies painted on the wall—and in the bathroom—in ancient Roman style. The Inn at Laurel Bay also includes The Cottage, a single-family home that sleeps six to eight people. $$–$$$.

Inn the Gardens Bed and Breakfast

609-399-0800
www.innthegardens.com
48 Wesley Rd., Ocean City 08226

Inn the Gardens was built as a private summer home in the early 1900s, and has served as both house and hotel since the middle of the 20th century. Today, the Inn has seven rooms and one apartment, all painted bright white and simply decorated to give them a lively, summer feel. $$–$$$.

Northwood Inn

609-399-6071
www.northwoodinn.com
401 Wesley Ave., Ocean City 08226

The Northwood Inn is a Queen Anne–style Victorian building that was one of the first 200 houses to be built in Ocean City. When innkeepers Marj and John Loeper bought it in 1989, it was nothing but a gutted shell

The Lady in White

Is the Flanders Hotel haunted? Depends on whom you ask.

If you direct your questions to the staff, the answer is a resounding "Yes." But that's not something said in fear. They call Emily, or "the lady in white," their "happy ghost." She's been known to go in and out of walls, unscrew light bulbs, and sing. She's never really caused any trouble, though she did appear, allegedly, in a picture taken at a wedding in one of the Flanders banquet halls.

To get a look at her, visit the second floor of the Flanders to see a portrait painted by Tony Troy. Or hang around the hotel, which is the best way to encounter the young lady with long brown hair who wears a white dress and no shoes.

with potential. John used his skills, gleaned from his years as a boat- and custom home builder, to bring this building back to its original glory, and his craftsmanship is hard to miss, especially on the flooring and staircase. The Northwood has seven rooms and suites, some with in-room Jacuzzis. Don't miss out on the rooftop whirlpool. The sights are as glorious as the building itself. $$$–$$$$.

Ocean City Mansion

609-399-8383
www.ocmansion.com
416 Central Ave., Ocean City 08226

Every room at the Ocean City Mansion is themed, from the Little Cabin Room (fireplace, wood-ringed Jacuzzi, rough wood bedposts) to the Chocolate Room (painted rich brown with the luxuriously draped bed in its own alcove) to the Honeymoon suite (king-size bed with gorgeous cherry headboard, deep plum walls, and 15-foot-high ceilings, including a 300-crystal chande-

Cape May County Dog Park
609-399-6112
www.oceancitydogpark.org
45th Street and Haven Ave., Ocean City
08226

Even though dogs aren't allowed on most beaches at the South Jersey Shore, Ocean City does have a spot for your four-legged friends to play. At the Cape May County Dog Park, you can let your dog off leash to run, sniff, play, and do tricks (or at least try) on ramps and hurdles. The park has three areas of play: large dog area, small dog area, and dog run area for all dogs.

To gain access to the park, you must apply for a "Paw Pass" at City Hall (861 Asbury Avenue, Ocean City 08226, 609-399-6112). You must bring a municipal dog license (which can be from your own municipality) and proof of up-to-date immunizations.

lier). Two of the mansion's rooms, the Collier's Cottage and Arthur's Bungalow, are dog-friendly, too. $$$–$$$$.

Oceanic Motel
609-399-6101
www.oceanicmotelnj.com
1110 Wesley Ave., Ocean City 08226

You can relax at this recently renovated motel. The rooms certainly inspire relaxation—they're all decorated with a very beachy feel, from the flip-flop borders to the nautical striped bedspreads. Even if things sometime lean more toward the tropical than Jersey beaches, the calm is universal. $$$.

Osborne's Inn
609-398-4319
www.osbornesinn.com
601 East 15th St., Ocean City 08226

If you've got kids, check out Osborne's Inn. One of their apartments is stocked with

cribs, high chairs, and toys. The Osbornes, who have been running the inn for more than 30 years, keep this apartment that way for when their kids and grandkids come to visit. When they're not in town, the room is available for you to rent. As for the other rooms, the inn has both rooms and apartments for however many guests—of whatever age—you're bringing with you. Open in season. $$.

Plymouth Inn
609-398-8615
www.plymouthinn.com
710 Atlantic Ave., Ocean City 08226

Step back to the turn of the 20th century at this bed & breakfast. The common areas and rooms have been renovated back to the way the Inn looked in 1898. The rooms meticulously match the time period, from the colors of the walls to the furniture. If you're bringing the kids or a group, the Plymouth Inn has two-bedroom suites. Open every day in season, weekends only in the off season. $$–$$$.

Rose Garden Inn
609-398-4889
www.rosegardeninn.us
1214 Ocean Ave., Ocean City 08226

This Arts and Crafts Period seashore cottage has six guest rooms, some with private decks. For the best view, book the Ocean View Room, which is at a vantage point for sweeping views of the Atlantic Ocean. Not all rooms have private baths, so check before you book. Open in season. $$–$$$$.

Scarborough Inn
1-800-258-1558
www.scarboroughinn.com
720 Ocean Ave., Ocean City 08226

This AAA three-diamond-rated bed & breakfast has been welcoming visitors to Ocean City since 1895. The rooms are well appointed, but not overly fussy in the romantic décor. They have a few two-bedrooms, too, if your stay will be more platonic. Check out the family photos on the corridor that leads from the living room area to the first floor rooms and kitchen. Open in season. $$$.

SOMERS POINT

Pier 4 on the Bay
1-888-927-9141
www.pier4hotel.com
6 Broadway, Somers Point 08244

The Pier 4 is a four-story hotel that first popped up on the bay in Somers Point in 1972. It was recently renovated to bring it up to the standards of today's Jersey Shore visitor. Every room has a balcony, and the Pier 4 has a private pool and sundeck facing the bay. $$–$$$.

Residence Inn by Marriott
609-927-6400
900 Mays Landing Rd., Somers Point 08244

This all-suite resort is located smack between Ocean City and Atlantic City and typically caters to business travelers, but makes a great out-of-the-way place to stay at the Shore. Sport court, exercise area, and pool onsite. $$–$$$.

EGG HARBOR TOWNSHIP

Tuscany House at Renault Winery Resort & Golf
609-965-2111
www.renaultwinery.com
72 North Berman Ave., Egg Harbor Township 08215

Tucked back among the woods and the vineyards of Renault Winery, this boutique hotel is like a slice of the Old World in New Jersey. You're greeted in the lobby by a bubbling

fountain and murals that bring Italy to life. Each room is flavored with Mediterranean style and has a separate bedroom and sitting area. It's close to the activities of the Shore, but just steps away from the vineyards and golf course that could make Renault an all-in-one vacation spot. $$–$$$.

DINING

OCEAN CITY

Aunt Betty's Ice Cream Shack
609-398-4001
2100 Asbury Ave., Ocean City 08226

It's more Caribbean than Jersey Shore at this Ocean City ice cream stop, which isn't a bad thing, especially if you're a Jimmy Buffett or reggae fan. Check out the interesting ice cream concoctions, like Betty's Favorite Sundae, which adds pretzels to a host of other oh-so-tasty toppings; birthday cake ice cream, which mixes chunks of cake and whipped cream into the ice cream; and the Dune Dog Delight, which is a dish of ice cream with a dog bone on top for your four-legged friend. No credit cards. Open 1 PM–11 PM in season. $.

Bloom 'n Tulip
609-399-4953
1001 Ocean Ave., Ocean City 08226

A big part of Bloom 'n Tulip's charm is that it looks like it's been there forever—well, at least since 1976, and not much has changed. Coffee still comes in a carafe, and mugs are always on the table. I half expected someone to come out of the kitchen and call me "Hon"—it's that homey. The food consists of diner staples, like pancakes and BLTs. It's a cool spot near the beach to grab a bite to eat that doesn't involve a paper plate. Breakfast, lunch, dinner. $.

Brown's
609-391-0677
110 Boardwalk, Ocean City 08226

The doughnuts are the star attraction at this boardwalk-side eatery. They come hot out of the oven, and each one is dipped into whatever you like, whether it be vanilla, chocolate, cinnamon sugar, or a host of other sweet toppings. Or you could go with plain, but why be boring? They serve lunch, too, but the doughnuts are the reason behind the long lines (avoid them by being an early bird). No credit cards. Breakfast, lunch in season. $.

The Chatterbox
609-399-0113
500 Ninth St., Ocean City 08226

It's almost not a vacation in Ocean City without at least one meal at The Chatterbox. It's hard to miss, too—the building is big, bright, and pink. The retro pictures on the wall make things even more interesting. The food is classic American surf and turf with a lot of good sandwiches, a knockout burger, and breakfast items. Breakfast, lunch, dinner. Closed Mondays in the off season. $.

Dixie Picnic
609-399-1999
www.dixiepicnic.com
819 8th St., Ocean City 08226

Tracey Deschaine modeled everything at Dixie Picnic, from the food to the mentality, around picnics she and her brothers shared with their eccentric Southern relatives. She's also got food chops from time at the Restaurant School in Philadelphia, so the food at Dixie Picnic is prepared from scratch, not from tubs of premade goo. The dining room isn't air conditioned, but fans keep it cool, much as they would in a Southern home. I stopped by on a hot, humid day and had no complaints. You can

Trio of Treats

If you're going to limit your culinary indulgences while in Ocean City, make room for at least three boardwalk treats: pizza from Mack & Manco, caramel popcorn from Johnson's Popcorn, and a cone from Kohr Bros. I surveyed regular Shore-goers about what I had to write about in this book, and anyone who mentioned Ocean City suggested all three of these specialties. When you go for your slice of pizza, make sure you stick around long enough to watch the dough being tossed into the air.

And if you're worried about your caloric intake, you are walking the boards, after all.

also pick up Bette's Box Lunch to take the beach—it holds a sandwich, deviled egg, choice of potato, pasta, or fruit salad, and an upcake. Upcake? It's a Dixie Picnic special: a cupcake flipped upside down and iced on three sides. Get one fresh so it's warm and melting in your mouth. Breakfast, lunch, dinner in season. Breakfast, lunch Sunday, Wednesday, and Thursday, plus dinner Friday and Saturday in the off season. $.

Dot's Pastry Shop
609-399-0770
3148 Asbury Ave., Ocean City 08226

It's worth the wait at this take-a-number bakery for scrumptious desserts, delicious cookies, and rich cakes. Cash only. Open 7 AM–6 PM Monday through Saturday and 7 AM–2 PM Sundays in season. Weekends only in the off season. $.

Hobby Horse
609-399-1214
800 Ocean Ave., Ocean City 08226

This carousel-inspired ice cream shop scoops up 45 flavors of ice cream. They also sell soft-serve ice cream, sugar-free ice cream, nonfat yogurt, fat-free ice cream, low-carb ice cream, plus parfaits, waffles, and heaping sundaes. Bring your appetite. Open 2 PM–midnight in season. $.

Java Jake's
609-352-4620
java-jakes.com
910 Asbury Ave., Ocean City 08226

You'll find caffeine-infused drinks at this coffee shop, which is more funky and bright than the cool and sedate coffee spots you might be used to. It's also gallery space and connected to Denovum, a home-goods store as funky as Java Jake's. And, yes, you can drink and browse at the same time. Open 7 AM–7 PM Monday through Friday, 7 AM–9 PM Saturday, and 7 AM-3 PM Sunday. $.

Johnson's Popcorn
1-800-842-2676
www.johnsonspopcorn.com
1368 Boardwalk, Ocean City 08226

This isn't exactly movie theater popcorn—instead of salt, the kernels are doused in hot caramel. It's a treat that's been delighting Shore visitors for more than 40 years. Their flagship store is on the Ocean City boardwalk, though you can buy the popcorn in other establishments throughout the Shore region, and online. Open 10 AM–4 PM. $.

Katina's Gyro Restaurant
609-399-5525
501 Ninth St., Ocean City 08226

A Greek restaurant might seem out of place at the Jersey Shore, but Katina's feels right at home. They've been dishing up gyros and just about anything you can imagine on a pita for over 20 years. It's still family owned, and the dining room holds only about a dozen tables. It's charming—Greek music piped in through the restaurant, and

a full wall mural honors both Ocean City and Greece. The food might not seem like a typical beach lunch, but their specialties, such as falafel, shish-ka-bobs, and moussaka are perfect for a midday or evening stop. Lunch, dinner. $.

Kessel's Corner
609-398-1170
2760 Asbury Ave., Ocean City 08226

Sit at a leather booth with red and white check tablecloths, or eat in at the small counter. Either way, Kessel's is always packed in season. They offer takeout with desserts, too, like impossibly thick milkshakes and Breyer's ice cream. No credit cards. Breakfast, lunch, dinner in season. $.

Kohr Bros.
www.kohrbros.com
Five locations along the Ocean City boardwalk.

It's not the Shore without ice cream, and it's not the Ocean City boardwalk without a cone from Kohr Bros. The ice cream spot started in 1917 in York, Pennsylvania, when Archie Kohr bought an ice cream machine and included homemade ice cream with the family's home milk delivery services. Archie and brother Elton made some adjustments to the recipe, and the machine, and came up with a soft-serve product. The addition of eggs to the recipe stiffened the ice cream (which is why it's called frozen custard), and helped the sweet treat stand up in that swirl. Kohr Bros. custard is lower in sugar and fat than regular ice cream, and you can get it at five different spots on the Ocean City boardwalk. For the best of both worlds, try the vanilla chocolate swirl. Hours vary. Open in season. $.

Lickety Split Ice Cream and Internet Café
609-525-0030
825 Asbury Ave., Ocean City 08226

Mack & Manco

You can get sandwiches, soup, coffee and caffeine drinks, plus ice cream and other sweet treats at this combination café and internet stop. Open 10 AM–9 AM Monday through Saturday and 10 AM–7 PM Sunday in season. $.

Luna Sea
609-398-5750
301 East 10th St., Ocean City 08226

Luna Sea stocks food and goods for the vegetarian, vegan, or clean-living, and fresh fruit and vegetables right off the farm for everyone. Luna also sells gluten-free products, books, CDs, and organic pet food. Open 9 AM–7 PM Monday, 10 AM–5:30 PM Tuesday, 10 AM–7 PM Thursday to Saturday, and 10 AM–3 PM Sunday in season. Open 10 AM–5:30 PM Monday through Saturday in the off season.

Ma France Creperie
609-399-9955
506 9th Ave., Ocean City 08226

This new restaurant turns the concept of crepes on its head—it's not just a breakfast meal anymore. Try the seafood variety for dinner. It's an interesting mix. Breakfast, lunch, dinner in season. Call for off-season hours. $.

Mack & Manco
609-399-2548
758, 920, and 12th and the Boardwalk, Ocean City 08226

The most famous pizza on the Ocean City boardwalk came here in 1956 when Anthony Mack and Vincent Manco brought their tomato pie from Trenton to the Shore. Don't worry if you've got sandy feet—Mack & Manco is built for the beachgoer. Watching the pizzas being made is half the fun. Lunch, dinner, late night in season. The 12th Street location is open year-round. $.

Mallon's
888-880-BUNS
www.mallonsbakery.com

14th and the Bay; 14th and Boardwalk; 55th and Central Ave., Ocean City 08226

If you like sticky buns, then this is your spot—Mallon's makes 14 flavors of this gooey treat. They also sell other freshly made sweet breakfast treats, like homemade doughnuts, muffins, and crumb cake, plus bagels, cookies, and coffee. With three locations in Ocean City, there's always one nearby. No credit cards. Hours vary by location, but always serve around the breakfast and lunch hours in season. Weekends only in the spring and fall. $.

McGlades

609-399-5588
228 Bay Ave., Ocean City 08226

The New York Times called McGlades the "omelet queen." If you're not an egg fan, this bayside eatery also serves yummy lunch and dinner selections, like shrimp salad sandwiches, crab and tuna melts, and a sprout avocado burger. They do not have

---

Corson's Inlet State Park

609-861-2404
www.state.nj.us/dep/parksandforests/
    parks/corsons.html
Ocean City and Upper Township, Cape May
    County

Corson's Inlet is 341 acres of undeveloped oceanfront land. It was preserved in 1969, and good thing, too, as most of the South Jersey Shore is now developed to the max. Corson's is home to sand dune systems, shoreline overwash, marine estuaries, and upland areas—including all the critters and creatures that live therein. It's a great spot for birdwatching, too, especially in the spring and fall during migration seasons. Corson's Inlet also includes a boat ramp, hiking trails, tours, saltwater fishing and crabbing spots, and catamaran boat storage areas.

---

soda, so be warned. And if you really are an egg fan, they make those omelets until 2:30 PM on weekends. Closed Tuesdays. Breakfast, lunch in season. Dinner Wednesday through Saturday in season. $.

Monkey Bread Café

609-399-1885 and 609-391-0113
3339 West Ave., Ocean City 08226 and 972 Boardwalk, Ocean City 08226

Pick up and pick at an individually sized portion of Monkey Bread at this high-flying café, which looks as much like a jungle as you'll get in New Jersey (the umbrellas turned into treetops is a nice touch). If the doughy cinnamon treat isn't your thing, Monkey Bread Café also dishes up omelets from an omelet station, pancakes, french toast, and bagels. They do lunch and ice cream, too. No credit cards. Breakfast, lunch in season. $.

Ocean City Coffee

609-399-5533
www.oceancitycoffee.com
928 Boardwalk, Ocean City 08226

This doesn't feel like a typical boardwalk shop. That's because the wooden walls, decorated with burlap coffee bean bags, and the roaster in the showroom floor of Ocean City Coffee are more coffeehouse than boardwalk stop. Open 7 AM–11 PM in season; 8 AM–6 PM Monday through Friday and 8 AM–9 PM Saturday and Sunday in the off season. $.

Oves Restaurant

609-398-3712
www.ovesrestaurant.com
4th St. and the Boardwalk

Since 1969, Oves has been dishing up fresh, homemade cake doughnuts. It's a seafood spot, too, serving fresh fare in a casual boardwalk setting. On a cooler day, the homemade soups are a sure bet. Credit cards at dinner only. Breakfast, lunch, dinner in season. $$.

Promenade Food Court
609-398-4174
744 Boardwalk, Ocean City 08226

If you're not sure what you want, or are trying to satisfy a few picky eaters, stroll through this outdoor food court, where you can choose from pizza, gyros, pierogies, Tex-Mex, crab cakes, funnel cake, and more. They have both indoor and outdoor seating areas, and no one scoffs if you're bringing your sandy feet along. Breakfast, lunch, dinner in season. $

Rojo's Tacos
609-391-0970
www.octacos.com
601 Ocean Ave., Ocean City 08226

Rojo's is a taste of Mexico in Ocean City, serving up burritos, tacos, ensaladas, fajitas, and quesadillas, plus breakfast sandwiches. Breakfast, lunch, dinner. Closed Sunday. $.

Voltaco's
609-399-0753
www.voltacos.com
957 West Ave., Ocean City 08226

You'll find unforgettable Italian take out at this small box shop. The sandwiches rule at lunchtime, but it's the specials that will bring a bit of Italy to your dinner table: baked spinach ravioli, stuffed shells, manicotti, baked ziti—it's pure Italian goodness from Voltaco's. No credit cards. Open 10 AM–8 PM in season; weekends only in March through late May and early September through mid-October. $.

A different bar at the Clam Bar

The Inlet
609-926-9611
www.inletrestaurantnj.com
998 Bay Ave., Somers Point 08244

When restaurateur Marty Grims saw that Sails, a venerable Somers Point restaurant, was about to go up for sale, he jumped at the chance to make the restaurant his own.

"The businesses that I'm involved in tend to be extensions of things that would appeal to me as a customer," says Grims, a Stone Harbor, New Jersey resident and the man behind the Moshulu, a well-touted restaurant in Philadelphia, and two restaurants in Long Beach Island, New Jersey. "What we wanted to do at The Inlet is introduce dining trends that are happening in the major cities and bring those trends down the Shore," he adds. "However, we still wanted to respect the tastes that are down there as well and being a little bit more conservative in our menu."

That's how you wind up with steamed littleneck clams, crab cakes, and shrimp scampi sharing the menu with lobster grilled cheese (with an avocado salsa), tuna nachos, and pan-seared mahi-mahi. Grims's personal favorite is the surf and turf (and mine would be that lobster grilled cheese, in case you're wondering).

The building's still in the same bayside spot as Sails, but the sensibility and atmosphere have been reinvented. The dining style was taken from formal to casual, and placed into a more relaxed setting. The price points were also lowered to keep the consumer in mind, and making the restaurant more open to vacationing families than it had been before as Sails.

The restaurant also has a lounge and bar area if you're stopping by for a drink or to meet up with friends (yes, they do have flat-screen TVs, and, yes, some of them are tuned to ESPN). If you're out on the water, you're welcome to dock at one of the restaurant's 20 slips and come on inside for your meal or drink.

The best part about Sails—the view—hasn't changed. You can eat your meal inside if the weather is acting up, or out on the water at one of the 175 seats available to take in phenomenal views of Great Egg Harbor Bay. Anywhere you sit in the 400-seat restaurant has a water views—even inside. The lunchtime crowd is subdued, but at night, the place hops with live music. It's also an all-seasons restaurant, open seven days a week, all year long.

SOMERS POINT

Charlie's
609-927-FOOD
www.charliesbar.com
800 Shore Rd., Somers Point 08244

This hole-in-the-wall bar and restaurant is the kind of place where you want to have a cold beer and good conversation after a day on the water. The food is good, simple, and unassuming, and served in generous portions. The wings alone are worth the trip. No credit cards. Lunch, dinner. $–$$.

The Clam Bar
609-927-8783
910 Bay Ave., Somers Point 08244

Sure, you could eat inside the Clam Bar's dining room, but the best place to eat your fresh-as-can-be seafood is at the outdoor counter, where you can watch your seafood being prepared. Their specialty, of course, is the clams. Eat them raw, steamed, fried, or as part of clam chowder or clam burgers. If you're looking for a bite to eat before heading out on the water, the Breakfast Shop is located at the back of the building, overlooking the water. No credit cards. Breakfast, lunch, dinner in season. $.

The Crab Trap
609-927-7377
www.thecrabtrap.com
2 Broadway, Somers Point 08244

This seafood restaurant lives inside the Somerset Plantation, which was built in the 1700s by Richard Somers, son of John Somers, who happened to be one of the original settlers of Somers Point (hence the name of the town). It became a restaurant in 1967 and has been a hit since. Seafood rules, and even if I have a quibble about some of the crabs coming from Maryland, the food is beyond good, especially the combination platters, which bring you the best of a few staple Crab Trap dishes, like filet mignon, lobster tails, shrimp, scallops, and flounder. Lunch, dinner. $$–$$$.

EGG HARBOR TOWNSHIP

Chickie's & Pete's
609-272-1930
www.chickiesandpetes.com
6055 Black Horse Pike, Egg Harbor Township 09234

It's all sports, all the time at this Shore outpost of a popular Philadelphia-area eatery.

If you want to watch the game at the bar, especially if it involves a Philadelphia sports team, get there early to make sure you grab a seat. The food is heavy and loaded with all the good stuff your doctor doesn't want you to eat. Try the crab fries, which are doused in Old Bay Seasoning with optional cheese for dipping. The mussels are always a sure bet, even if the Philadelphia teams are not. Lunch, dinner, late night. $.

Mangia by the Greens
609-601-8369
www.mangiabythegreens.com
3016 Ocean Heights Ave., Egg Harbor Township 08234

Stop off here for your 19th hole celebration or for a quick bite to eat at this casual eatery, which is part of McCullough's Emerald Golf Links. They dish up surf and turf, sandwiches, wraps, and pizzas. Check their Web site for happy hour specials, and Quizzo and live music nights. Lunch, dinner. Breakfast Saturday and Sunday. Late night Friday and Saturday. $–$$.

The Gourmet Restaurant at Renault Winery
609-965-2111
www.renaultwinery.com
72 North Berman Ave., Egg Harbor Township 08215

Wired Beaches

In 2007, Ocean City announced that it was going high-tech with its beach tags in time for summer 2008. Visitors to Ocean City beaches will be required to wear wristbands that are connected to either their credit cards or bank accounts so that the prices of beach tags, food, and parking will be charged directly to them. Officials are saying that beach tag prices won't change.

As of press time, the changes had yet to be made, and a lot of people are making noise about not wanting someone to be able to track their purchases. I say avoid the entire situation by going to the beaches on Wednesdays, when they're free in season.

Ocean City officials also say that, as part of these technology updates, garbage cans will e-mail city officials when they're full, which leads me to one important question: How did Oscar the Grouch get a Blackberry before me?

Walking into the Gourmet Restaurant is a treat—you pass through a tunnel of three 105-year-old redwood wine casks to get to the dining room. Even a few of the booths at this restaurant, which is on the site of the country's longest-operating vineyard, are made of 100-year-old oak casks. The historic wine pieces and stained glass windows, antique furniture, stone fireplace, and gazebo in the middle of the room, which is where Renault's New Jersey Champagne used to be made, complete the romantic staging. Of course, the food helps—the chef recommends putting aside an hour or two for the complete experience, which is gourmet through and through and features eight entrees, specially prepared appetizers, soups, pastas, ice-cold sorbet intermezzo, gourmet salad, and two wine samplings to match. You can indulge in wine-based drinks, or anything Renault makes. Say hello to Alphonse, too—he'll serenade you through dinner. Dinner Friday through Sunday. Sunday brunch. $$$–$$$$.

ARTS & CULTURE

Bayside Center
609-525-9244
520 Bay Ave., Ocean City 08226

This 1.9-acre area is both history and ecology lesson. The Bayside Center includes The Bay Window Environment Center, which is part museum and also runs summer camps for kids. They also have a butterfly garden where you can eat lunch on one of the many picnic tables. Then there's the building itself, which was built in 1910 and is home to a museum. The grounds are a popular spot to watch the annual Night in Venice Parade, which is held in July each year, and for kayakers looking to paddle up for a break. Open 10 AM–4 PM from late June through early September.

Discovery Seashell Museum & Shell Yard
609-398-2316
www.shellmuseum.com
2721 Asbury Ave., Ocean City 08226

This museum might look small, but it holds more than 10,000 species of shells from around the world, and most of them are for sale. They also stock shell-themed items for sale, like lamps, jewelry, posters, and books, plus hermit crabs and hermit crab aquarium supplies. Open 9 AM–5 PM. Free.

Ocean City Pops
609-525-9245
www.oceancitypops.org

They'll set your summer to a tune, whether you like classical music, opera, big bands, Broadway hits, or patriotic tributes. This professional summer orchestra plays concerts June through September at the Music Pier and Ocean City High School. $$.

Ocean City Historical Museum
609-399-1801

www.ocnjmuseum.org
1735 Simpson Ave., Ocean City 08226

Learn about Ocean City's past at this museum, which features two permanent exhibits. "Sea View and Salt Air: A History of Ocean City" combines the town's timeline with artifacts, photographs, and storyboards to show and tell the town's history. The second exhibit is about the *Sindia,* a four-masted barque that grounded itself in Ocean City in 1901. The museum features temporary, rotating exhibits, too. Open 10 AM–4 PM Monday through Friday; 11 AM–2 PM Saturday. Free.

SOMERS POINT

Atlantic Heritage Center
609-927-5218
www.atlanticheritagecenternj.org
907 Shore Rd., Somers Point 08244

Part museum, part library, this is the place to go to explore the region's roots—or your own. The museum has more than 20,000 local historical artifacts, from shipbuilding tools to antique coins, and guided tours are free. The library is also open to the public and includes documents like diaries, ships' logs, wills, and school rollbooks, some dating back as far as the late 1600s. Open 10 AM–3:30 PM Wednesday through Saturday and 6 PM–9 PM the first Thursday of the month. Free.

Bayside in Ocean City

EGG HARBOR TOWNSHIP

Jersey Shore Children's Museum
609-645-7741
www.eht.com/childrensmuseum
6725 Black Horse Pike, Egg Harbor Township 082341

It's a land of make-believe at this interactive kids' museum, which is located inside the Shore Mall. Your tykes can give the weather forecast, play dentist, or create a puppet show. Open 10 AM–5 PM Monday through Saturday and noon–5 PM Sunday. $.

Renault Winery
609-965-2111
www.rcnaultwinery.com
72 North Bremen Ave., Egg Harbor City 08215

Renault Winery is the oldest continually operating winery in the United States (yes, even through Prohibition—check the sidebar for an exercise in extreme marketing creativity). You can explore Renault's rich history by taking a winery tour. It includes a visit to the Antique Glass Museum, which is home to priceless Champagne and wine glasses that go as far back as medieval times. Make sure to seek out the pieces that were used at the dedication of the Eiffel Tower. You'll also see how the wine is bottled, and, if you come in the fall, the grapes come in from harvest. You can also peek into the climate-controlled wine cellar and end up at the Wine Tasting Emporium for a few sips of Renault wines. Open 10:30 AM–7 PM Monday through Thursday, 10 AM–7 PM Friday, 10 AM–8 PM Saturday, and 10 AM–4 PM Sunday. $.

ATTRACTIONS, PARKS & RECREATION

Aquaport Arcade & Billiards
609-398-0072
3349 Asbury Ave., Ocean City 08226

Renault and Prohibition

Renault Winery is the longest continually operating vineyard in the United States. They started putting out their products in 1870 and haven't stopped since. But how could that be, when Prohibition took wine off the shelves for 13 years?

Renault's owners did it through a shift in product, and clever marketing. Renault obtained a permit to keep making wine for religious and "medicinal" purposes. The religious wine went to churches. The medicinal product was Renault Wine Tonic, which was supposed to soothe an ailing stomach. It also had an alcohol content of 22 percent (compared to the 9 to 14 percent that's typical of today's wines) and a label that warned if the tonic was chilled, it would turn into wine, which led to rather than detracted from sales. The Atlantic City even had "nurses" giving one-glass doses to Boardwalk patrons.

The boardwalk in Ocean City Kathy Caraballo

There are all kinds of things to do at this fun center. One room features five red, felt-top billiards tables, separate from the noise and lights of the video game and pinball room. Open 10 AM–10:30 PM Easter through October. $.

Gillian's Island Water Park
609-399-0483
www.gillians.com
728 Boardwalk, Ocean City 08226

Sometimes it's too hot for the ocean, or the kids think the waves are too small for a real adventure. That's where Gillian's Island Water Park comes in. It has four different water rides for slipping and sliding, plus a kids area and lazy river if your idea of relaxing is floating the day away while the slides tire the younger ones out. Gillian's also offers private cabanas to rent, each one including lounge chairs, lockers, bottled water, and ceiling fans. Open 9 AM–6 PM, weather permitting, in season. $$.

Glazed Over
609-398-8880
935 Asbury Ave., Ocean City 08226

You paint the pottery at this studio, or create mosaics if you so choose. The cool, airy space will foster the best of your creativity as you paint at what could easily be your dining room table—if it were surrounded by such great works of art. Open 10 AM–8 PM Monday through Friday, 10 AM–6 PM Saturday, and noon–5 PM Sunday in season. Call for off-season hours. $$–$$$.

Jilly's Arcade

609-399-2814
www.jillysarcade.com
1168 Boardwalk, Ocean City 08226

You'll find video game piers all over the
South Jersey Shore boardwalks, but Jilly's
is a classic. It's been keeping kids (and
adults, of course) entertained in the elec-
tronic way for more than 25 years. It has
the latest and greatest must-play games,
like Dance Dance Revolution, less techie
games like Skee-Ball and air hockey, and,
in the backroom, classic games like Ms.
Packman, Asteroid, X-Men, The Simpsons,
and pinball. Open 24 hours in season. Call
for off-season hours. $.

Kidz Creations at Butterfly Boutique

811 Asbury Ave., Ocean City 08226
609-399-9922

Keep your kids occupied at Kidz Creations,
which runs science workshops, parties, and
storytime at 11 AM. They also have activity
classes, including cupcake decorating and
bead art. $.

Ocean City Golf Course

609-399-1315
2600 Bay Ave., Ocean City 08266

Miniature Golf in Ocean City

Not up for a full course? Or just want to play
in a zany atmosphere, like on a ship or among
cartoon characters? Ocean City has plenty of
options.

Congo Falls Adventure Golf
609-398-1211
www.congofalls.com
1132 Boardwalk, Ocean City 08226

Gillian's Island Water Park Adventure Golf
609-399-0483
www.gillians.com
728 Boardwalk, Ocean City 08226

Golden Galleon Golf
609-398-1211
1124 Boardwalk, Ocean City 08226

Goofy Golf
609-398-9662
920 Boardwalk, Ocean City 08226

Tee-Time Golf
609-398-6763
642 Boardwalk, Ocean City 08226

Under the Sea Miniature Golf
609-398-0300
744 Boardwalk, Ocean City 08226

Bring the family to this 12-hole, par 37 course. Every hole has tight fairways and small
greens, and at par three for 11 of those 12 holes, this is more of a beginner and family
course than something to challenge your driver. $.

Ocean City Water Sports

609-399-7588
www.oceancitywatersports.com
232 Bay Ave., Ocean City 08226

You can sit back and relax or go for the thrill at Ocean City Water Sports. They run whale
and dolphin watching cruises, plus fishing tours, and can set you up for wakeboarding,
water skiing, and tubing. Open 6:30 AM–7 PM in season. Fishing year-round. $$–$$$$.

Pirate Adventures

609-398-7555
www.pirateadventuresoceancity.com
926 Palen Ave., Ocean City 08226

Arrrr, matey! Get in touch with your inner pirate on this treasure hunt cruise adventure. It's designed with kids in mind—unless you really want your face painted, too—and is interactive for parents as well, since you'll have to save the ship from enemies using water cannons. Reservations required. Open in season. $.

Playland's Castaway Cove
609-399-4751
www.boardwalkfun.com
936 Boardwalk, Ocean City 08226

> **Ocean City Division of Recreation**
>
> If you're looking for a little something extra to add onto your Ocean City stay, check out the Ocean City Division of Recreation. They sponsor arts and crafts, sports, camps, basketball leagues, and gymnastics and tumbling classes. They also rent out beach surf chairs and motorized wheelchairs. Call 609-525-9294 for schedules and locations.

This pirate-themed pier has 30 rides for kids, grown-ups, and those somewhere in between. They also have go-karts and mini golf for a well-rounded adventure, and their ride tickets don't expire from one season to the next. Open April through early October. Call for in-season hours—they vary depending on the day of the week and the month.

Still Waters Stress Center
609-525-2125
www.stillwatersstresscenter.com
801 Wesley Ave., Ocean City 08226

No, they won't cause you stress, but will help wipe it away with a full selection of massages, from hot stone therapy to prenatal treatments to classic Swedish massage. Their larger location is in Somers Point, but the Ocean City outpost has just the right services to relax you. Open 10 AM—6 PM Monday through Wednesday and Saturday, 10 AM—7 PM Thursday, and 11 AM—6 PM Sunday. $$–$$$

Wet-N-Wild Wave Runner Rentals
609-399-6521
www.wetnwildwaverunners.com
44 Bay Ave., Ocean City 08226

No boater's license is required to take out a wave runner in Ocean City's back bay. But you'll have to stay in the guarded area, which has more than enough room for you to zip and play. Open 9 AM—sunset, in season.

Wonderland Pier
609-399-7082
www.gillians.com
854 Boardwalk, Ocean City 08226

This ride pier is a longtime favorite, with thrills for the entire family. They have plenty of rides for the little guys (and gals) that won't put you to sleep, either, including Little Wheel, Wonders Lil' Express, Wacky Worm Roller Coaster, and, of course, the classic carousel, which has been delighting families since 1926. And if your older kids need a jolt, there's still the Runaway Train Coaster, Sling Shot, and Canyon River Falls. Open Palm

The Carousel

For most amusement parks, it's all about providing the latest and greatest thrill. How high can we fling you in the air? How fast can we push you? How far do you want to drop?

This is certainly the case on the Ocean City boardwalk. But Wonderland Pier still keeps an important piece of history secure on its grounds, one that offers a more sedate ride experience in a classic setting: the carousel.

The Wonderland Pier carousel was built in 1926 and offers three kinds of rides: the stationary carts, the stationary horses, and the moving horses, which move up and down as the carousel spins around and around. If you're on one of the outer horses, you can still try to reach out and catch the rings. Get the golden ring, and you win tickets. You must be strapped in, especially to reach for the rings, or you risk falling out into the crowd.

The carousel has been beautifully maintained, and you can hear its calliope music from the boardwalk. For people of all ages, it's worth its weight in tickets.

Sunday through mid-October. Call for in-season hours—they vary depending on the day of the week and the month. $.

SOMERS POINT

Duke O' Fluke
609-926-2280
www.dukeofluke.com
Higbee Ave. and the Bay, Somers Point 08244

Hop on one of the Duke's four-hour back bay fishing trips—he runs two a day. They also run nature tours on the 45-foot, twin-engine pontoon boat. $$.

EGG HARBOR TOWNSHIP

Harbor Pines
609-927-0006
www.harborpines.com
500 St. Andrews Dr., Egg Harbor Township 08234

Golf Digest rated this 18-hole course as one of the top three conditioned courses in New Jersey. One of its beauties is its hazards—12 ponds and 17 acres of water dot the path through the field of play. $$$$.

McCullough's Emerald Golf Links
609-926-3900
www.mcculloughsgolf.com
3016 Ocean Heights Ave., Egg Harbor Township 08234

This par 71 course, which was designed by golf course architect Stephen Kay, is based on Irish and Scottish golf courses. It's 245 acres, 18 holes, and 6,600 yards, if you're counting. The fairways are open, but winds can make the game more interesting. $$$$.

Storybook Land
609-641-7847
www.storybookland.com
6415 Black Horse Pike, Egg Harbor Township 08234

Every ride at this 50-plus-year-old amusement park is built at the speed of kids, especially if it's their first time to a park or on rides. You won't find any high-flying thrills here. The attractions, like the Happy Dragon, carousel, and whirly-bug are built for the smallest of patrons. Hours vary by the month. Closed October through March. $$.

Vineyard Golf at Renault
609-965-2111
www.renaultwinery.com
72 North Bremen Ave., Egg Harbor City 08215

This golf course is the new kid on the block. It opened in 2004 but is a fast climber. *Travel + Leisure Golf* named it one of the 30 best new courses in the world, and *Golfweek* named it one of New Jersey's best courses for 2007. The course is on 225 acres, 25 of which wind through Renault's grapevines and orchards. It's par 72 and clocks in at 7,213 yards. $$$$.

Storybook Land Peter Pelland/Pelland Advertising

Asbury Avenue

Asbury Avenue is a Main Street throwback. It's what it a lot of American downtowns looked like when there were no indoor malls, strip malls, four-lane highways through the middle of town, or online shopping.

Its location near the beach and relatively far from any mall has probably helped preserve its "Main Street" status, even if blue laws kept the shops closed on Sundays until the 1980s.

What will you find? Just about everything, including kids' clothes (Sea Oats), home décor (Denovum), ladies' fashions (Colette Boutique), stained glass goods (Glass Frog Studios), intimate apparel (Pretty Woman Intimates), antique stores (Yours, Mine and Ours), an independent bookstore (Sun Rose), and lots of places to eat. The stores are open year-round, too, unlike most places on the boardwalk, and make for great strolling on a spring or fall day as well as in summer.

This isn't to say that the Ocean City boardwalk doesn't have its share of great shops—it does. But it's not open year-round, and the stock leans more toward kid pleasers.

SHOPPING

Air Circus
609 399 9343
1114 Boardwalk, Ocean City 08226

If you see kites flying near the boardwalk, you're probably watching the best of Air Circus's wares on display. This boardwalk store sells kites of all stripes, from your basic high-in-the-sky models to stunt versions. They also stock anything you could need to make your beach time more creative, like Frisbees and juggling toys. Open 8:30 AM–midnight in season. Call for off-season hours.

All Campus
609-814-0576
1070 Boardwalk, Ocean City 08226

Big fan? Then stop in All Campus, which stocks all kinds of paraphernalia adorned with college and pro team logos, including blankets, mugs, and stickers. The biggest draw is the hat collection, which goes beyond college teams and into professionals, the military, and food and drink brands. If you're not into billed caps, All Campus Women, which is located a few shops up the boardwalk, has the same wall-to-wall of hats, but of the hip and straw variety (with a few sports ones thrown in for good measure). Open 9 AM–11:30 PM in season, weekends only October to New Year's Day. Closed January through mid-May.

B&B Department Store
609-391-0046
827 Asbury Ave., Ocean City 08226

You'll find clothes for the entire family at this large but packed store. Make sure you look up—well, you won't be able to help it with VW Beetles, critters, and other modes of transportation hanging from the ceiling. Open 9 AM–9 PM in season. Call for off-season hours.

Make sure you look up at B&B Department Store

Boardwalk Peanut Shoppe
609-391-2002
www.boardwalkpeanuts.com
986 Boardwalk, Ocean City 08226

Those roasters aren't just for show. The 100-year-old machines, which were originally used for coffee, still roast peanuts—in the shell—as they have since the 1930s, when they were in the original Atlantic City Boardwalk Planters Peanut Store. You can pick up the freshly roasted peanuts, or chocolate-covered strawberries and bananas. Open 10 AM– 11:30 PM in season. $

Bookateria Two
609-398-0121
1052 Asbury Ave., Ocean City 08226

You'll find new and used books at this small shop. Everything new is 15 percent off, and you can bring in your old paperbacks to use as collateral toward a new—or used—purchase. Open 9 AM–8 PM Monday through Friday, 9 AM–6 PM Saturday, and 10 AM–2 PM Sunday in season. Call for off-season hours.

Brianna's
609-391-9199
409 8th St., Ocean City 08226

Vintage, vintage, vintage at this quaint store. Pick from pins, charm bracelets, purses, earrings, necklaces, bracelets, and even vintage swimsuits. Brianna's has some new jewelry too. If nothing's catching your eye, ask to see what's in the back—there are more vintage items stored there. Open 10 AM–5 PM in season. Call for off-season hours.

Butterfly Boutique
609-399-9922
811 Asbury Ave., Ocean City 08226

It's part event planning, part kids' wonderland at Butterfly Boutique. The shop stocks stationery that's both sophisticated and whimsical, and is also home to Kidz Creations, which runs science workshops, parties, and storytime at 11 AM. They also have activity classes including cupcake decorating and bead art. Open 9 AM–6 PM Monday through Saturday, 9 AM–8 PM Wednesdays.

Cloud 9
609-399-8989
www.shopcloud9store.com
976 Boardwalk, Ocean City 08226

Of-the-moment fashions at only-good-for-one-season prices. They have one wall dedicated to jewelry, and another to funny T-shirts that go beyond what you'll see at every other boardwalk T-shirt shop. They stock sensibly priced beach accessories, too, like sunglasses and cover-ups. Open 9 AM–midnight in season, 10 AM–7 PM in the off season.

Colette Boutique
609-525-0911
900 Asbury Ave., Ocean City 08226

It's dress-up for grown-ups at this women's boutique. The fashions lean toward 1950s vamp, with sexy kitten heels and items from retro vintage line Stop Staring! They've also got puffy dresses meant for twirling, plus denim and bathing suits. Open 10 AM–8 PM Monday through Saturday and 10 AM–6 PM Sundays in season; 11 AM–6 PM Monday through Sunday in the off season.

Denovum
609-814-9084
908 Asbury Ave., Ocean City 08226

It's funky, eclectic, bright, and, at times, just odd at this home décor store, which has high ceilings and plenty of light to give it a big, airy, barnlike feel. They sell furniture and knickknacks, so you can fill your big or small need for the eccentric. Open 10 AM–8 PM Monday through Saturday and 10 AM–5 PM Sunday in season, 10 AM–6 PM Monday through Saturday and 10 AM–5 PM Sunday in the off season.

Dreamcatchers
609-398-6551
704 Boardwalk, Ocean City 08226

With the crowds and real estate development near the South Jersey Shore, it's easy to forget that most of these barrier islands were first populated by Native Americans. They haven't at Dreamcatchers, which sells Native American art, crafts, jewelry, and décor. Open 9 AM —midnight in season. Call for off-season hours.

Gabrielle & Co.
609-399-1008
www.gabrielleandco.com
810 Asbury Ave., Ocean City 08226

Anything a gal could ever want is sold at this rambling shop on Asbury Avenue. Gabrielle & Co. stocks romantic under- and over things, along with a few knockout gowns, gourmet foods, furniture, linens, and organic makeup. Don't skip the Christmas corner, either, if you're looking to trim a tree, or get into the Christmas spirit early. Open 9:30 AM–9 PM Monday through Saturday and 10 AM–6 PM Sunday in season. Call for off-season hours.

Glass Frog Studio
609-398-7510
920 Asbury Ave., Ocean City 08226

This little store started as a stained glass shop. Owner Lynda Mitchell-Marino still has her studio in the store, and her work is sold at Glass Frog Studio, but she's added accessories like hats and bags to give the shop a wider appeal. Open 10 AM–6 PM Monday, Tuesday, Thursday, and Saturday, 10 AM–8 PM Wednesday and Friday, and 10 AM–4 PM Sunday from Easter through New Year's Day. Call for off-season hours.

Grassroots Music and Books
609-398-6500
1059 Asbury Ave., Ocean City 08226

The front room of this store is stocked with guitars, both acoustic and electric, plus music gear, like drumsticks and guitar picks. They also sell records, both new and used, plus CDs and music-related books. If you like your music on vinyl, Grassroots is a must stop. They sell new and old albums, ready for your turntable. Open 10 AM–6 PM.

Island Beach Gear
609-399-2267
www.islandbeachgear.com
900 Bay Avenue., Ocean City 08226

Get all your beach gear, like chairs, bodyboards, sunscreen, and beach apparel at this one-stop shop. You can't miss the shop if you come into Ocean City on NJ 52—their beach chairs are in a miniature beach right in the parking lot. Open 9 AM–9 PM.

La Bottine Boutique
609-399-6400
1033 Asbury Ave., Ocean City 08226

Shopping here is like browsing through your best friend's closet—if she had exquisite taste and everything in your size. Owner Suzanne Matura stocks a fabulous mix of accessories,

Surfers Supplies
609-399-8399
www.surferssupplies.com
3101 Asbury Ave., Ocean City 08226

It's not often that you walk into a surf shop and see surfboards. Well, at least not right away. "In most places, they're in the back. They're the core of our business, so we put them right up front," says Greg Beck, co-owner of Surfers Supplies, a surf shop that has been in business since 1962. Beck and two partners bought the store from its original owner in 2004, but kept the vibe of the store—which is located in a building over a century old—much the same.

You can rent or buy a board here, and they will also repair and customize your ride. They stock an impressive selection of wetsuits, board shorts, and what Beck calls "après surf," meaning clothes with the surfer in style—like flip-flops, tanks, tees, and button-up shirts with a cool, casual feel.

If you want a lesson, they'll recommend three top guys to teach you how to hang ten. Beck, who's been working at the store since he graduated from high school, says the best waves are at Waverly Beach on the north end of Ocean City, but that the water can be packed during tourist season. His solution? Get a thicker wetsuit and surf in the off season. "If I didn't have to visit my family in Delaware, I'd be surfing on Thanksgiving and Christmas," he says.

Surfers Supplies

including shoes—oh, the shoes. They're not outrageously priced, but those shoes she stocks are funky, fun, romantic, or comfortable—whatever you need. Open 10 AM—5 PM Monday through Saturday and 11 AM—4 PM Sunday.

Only Yesterday
609-398-2869
1110 Boardwalk, Ocean City 08226

Step back into your childhood—or your parents' childhood—at this antique store. Their stock includes kitsch like Campbell's Soup bowls and 1950s-era Corning Ware, vintage clothes, and magazines. Of course you read them for the articles: Only Yesterday has *Playboy* magazines from the 1960s through 2000. They also have a store location at 1137 Asbury Avenue that's open Thursday through Saturday. Open 11 AM—11 PM in season, 11 AM—4 PM Saturday and Sunday in the off season.

Pretty Woman Intimates
609-398-6656
www.prettywomanintimates.com
939 Asbury Ave., Ocean City 08226

You'll find the sexy, sensible, and support for any kind of body at this lingerie shop. They stock just-for-brides wear, too, and offer custom bra fittings. Open 10 AM—6 PM Monday through Friday, 10 AM—5 PM Saturday, 11 AM—4 PM Sunday.

Sea Oats
609-398-8399
710 Asbury Ave., Ocean City 08226

For more than 25 years, Sea Oats has been supplying clothes, costumes, shoes, and toys for girls and boys. You can't beat the cute factor here, even if you don't have kids just waiting to be spoiled. Open 9:30 AM—8 PM Monday through Friday, 9:30 AM—5:30 PM Saturday, and 10 AM—5 PM Sunday in season. Open 10 AM—5:30 PM in the off season.

Separately Swimwear
609-398-2922
818A Boardwalk, Ocean City 08226

Not all ladies have bottoms perfectly proportionate to our tops, which is why you can buy your two-piece in two pieces at Separately Swimwear. Mix and match different tops and bottoms in your right size to create a bikini perfect for you—not some size guide at a designer's workshop. Open 8:30 AM—11:30 PM in season. Call for off-season hours.

Shriver's
877-668-2339
www.shrivers.com
Boardwalk at 9th Street, Ocean City 08226

Salt water taffy and fudge here since 1898, which makes Shriver's the oldest business on the Ocean City boardwalk—period. The best part about Shriver's (aside from the candy, of course), is that they let you see the taffy being made in the store. Watch as the the raw

The kids' section at Sun Rose Words & Music

materials are mixed and then pulled into long rows of taffy at a rate of 300 to 400 pieces an hour, to be cut, wrapped, and boxed. If you're not ready to commit to an entire box of salt water taffy, or want to make your box more peanut butter than licorice, check out the taffy bins by the back of the store—you can make your own box. Open 9 AM–10 PM in season. Call for off-season hours.

Rock out at the Surf Mall

Sun Rose Words & Music

609-399-9190
756 Asbury Avenue, Ocean City 08226

This is the kind of bookstore that makes you hate the big-box chain stores. It's independent and tailored to the needs of both Ocean City residents and tourists. Of course they have all the latest best-sellers, plus classics and good beach reads. But Sun Rose also stocks an expansive selection of local titles and is a hub of author readings and signings—all books about the Shore area—plus office supplies, music, cards, and drawing pads and pencils. The kids' section is a delight, no matter how old you are. Open 9 AM–6 PM Monday, Tuesday, Thursday, Saturday, and Sunday, 9 AM–8 PM Wednesday, and 9 AM–9 PM Friday.

Surf Mall

609-398-1533
1154 Boardwalk, Ocean City 08226

Whatever is hot that summer, whether it's accessories for Crocs, faux faded sweatshirts, or hair wrapping, is at the Surf Mall. It's not an actual mall, but a cavernous space where different vendors set up shop. The old standbys are the collectibles vendor, who leans heavily toward movie memorabilia and action figures; and the rock store—their music posters line the back wall and parts of the ceiling of the Surf Mall. The acts cover all genres, though they lean heavily, of course, on Jersey boy Bruce "the Boss" Springsteen. Open 9 AM–midnight in season.

Whatever

609-271-7231
817 Asbury Ave. Ocean City 08226

It's not whatever, but everything that's $10 at this bright store. The goods, which include bags, jewelry, wraps, sunglasses, and bags, don't look like cheap copies, but probably won't last more than a summer or two. They come in all kinds of colors if you have a hard-to-match outfit that needs just one more thing to make it complete. Open 10 AM–whatever (they close when the customers stop coming) in season. Call for off-season hours.

Yours, Mine and Ours Antiques

609-525-0270
957 Asbury Ave., Ocean City 08226

This winding, rambling store is full of the stuff you probably got rid of in a yard sale, and now regret losing—figurines, dishes, Christmas ornaments, Nancy Drew books, toys, furniture, and salvaged glass doorknobs are just a few examples of what's carried here. Make sure to take your time, and look up, or you'll miss something. Open 10 AM–5 PM in season, 11 AM–5 PM in the off season.

WEEKLY EVENTS (IN SEASON)

Monday

Picnics in the Park

609-525-9300
www.ocnj.us
9th St. and West Ave., Ocean City 08226

The activities change each week, but one thing's the same: bring your bag lunch for some afternoon entertainment, which can range from musical performances to chats with artists. 11 AM–1 PM. Free.

Tuesday

Market Days

609-525-9300
www.ocnj.us
Downtown Asbury Avenue

The boardwalk doesn't have all the action in Ocean City. Check out downtown at weekly market days, held on Asbury Avenue on Tuesdays and Thursdays during the summer. Tuesday events feature a string band, stilt walkers, life-size puppets, and sculpture balloons. 10 AM–1 PM. Free.

Ocean City Beachwalk

609-525-9300
59th St. & Central Ave. and the Ocean City and Longport Bridge parking lot

Get a guided tour of what lives along the ocean's edge at this twice-weekly tour, which starts in two different locations. The tour is an hour long and run by volunteers. $.

Wednesday

Evenings on Asbury Avenue

609-525-9300
www.ocnj.us
Downtown Asbury Avenue

Add a little music to your summer nights at this weekly concert series, which starts in mid-July and runs through August. 5 PM–8 PM. Free.

Ocean City Beachwalk

609-525-9300
59th Street & Central Avenue and the Ocean City and Longport Bridge Parking Lot

Get a guided tour of what lives along the ocean's edge at this twice-weekly tour, which starts in two different locations. The tour is an hour long and run by volunteers. $.

Thursday

Inn-to-Inn and Historic Tour

609-399-2639
7th Street and Central Avenue
Check out the historic sights and inns of Ocean City on this weekly trolley tour. Early July to late August. $$.

Market Days

609-525-9300
www.ocnj.us
Downtown Asbury Avenue

The boardwalk doesn't have all the action in Ocean City. Check out downtown at weekly market days, held on Asbury Avenue on Tuesdays and Thursdays during the summer. Thursdays feature puppet shows, face painters, magicians, pony rides, live music, and balloon sculptures. 10 AM–1 PM. Free.

Ocean City Beachwalk

609-525-9300
59th Street & Central Avenue and the Ocean City and Longport Bridge Parking Lot

Get a guided tour of what lives along the ocean's edge at this twice-weekly tour, which starts in two different locations. The tour is an hour long and run by volunteers. $.

ANNUAL EVENTS

January

First Day at the Beach
609-525-9300
Ocean City Boardwalk

Just because it's cold doesn't mean the beach is closed. Some people take this literally at the annual first dip. Don't worry—no one will cry foul if you just watch. Free.

March

Jazz at the Point
609-927-7161
www.somersptschools.org/jazz

This three-day event spreads jazz throughout Somers Point with performances from local and national artists. The festival also sponsors student workshops, and proceeds go to Foundation for Education, a nonprofit organization dedicated to improving local schools. $$.

April

Doo Dah Parade
609-399-1412
Ocean City Boardwalk

Salt water taffy sculpting contest from Weird Week Kathy Caraballo

Death and taxes might be two things you can't avoid in life, but you can kiss tax season goodbye at this annual funny parade, which features more than 500 Basset hounds parading down the boardwalk. Free.

Great Egg Hunt
609-398-4662
Ocean City Beach, between 11th Street and 14th Street

Ready, set go! Five age groups head out onto the beach in search of 20,000 eggs. Happy hunting! Free.

Woofin' Paws Pet Fashion Show
609-399-2629
Ocean City Boardwalk

Dress your pup in his or her Easter best for this annual parade.

May

Martin Z. Mollusk Day
609-399-1412
Ocean City Beach at Ninth St.

Forget that groundhog. It's a hermit crab in Ocean City that determines if spring is really on its way. Will he see his shadow at this bizarre event, which also involves a sea turtle, a llama, and an Elvis impersonator? Head to the beach to find out. Free.

July

Night in Venice
609-525-9300
Ocean City Bay

One of the world's largest boat parades is right in Ocean City. The effect is doubled as the houses along the parade route light up to match the procession on the water as it travels from the bay up through Tennessee Avenue. It's been an Ocean City tradition since the 19th century, though in its original form, it was less merriment and more a showcase-on-water for local debutantes. You can watch from the grandstands lined up along the parade route, finagle an invitation to a bayside house party, or watch from the Bay Center (for a small fee). Free.

August

Annual Baby Parade
609-525-9300
Ocean City Boardwalk at the Music Pier

How cute is your kid, really? Let him or her dazzle the crowd at this parade, which is one of the oldest baby parades in the country. Free.

Art of Surfing Festival
609-398-8887
www.sagemore.com
Ocean City Boardwalk at the Music Pier

This festival, which is combination art show, music jamboree, and celebration of all things surf, takes over the Music Pier for three days every August. Free.

Boardwalk Art Show
609-399-7628
www.oceancityartscenter.org
Ocean City Boardwalk

This annual art show is one of Ocean City's oldest annual events, and it changes every year depending on who's coming to display their wares. Free.

Miss Crustacean Hermit Crab Beauty Pageant
609-525-9300
Ocean City Beach at 6th St.

Watch as these beauties claw their way to the crown. The winner takes the Coveted Cucumber Rind Cup and showcases her beauty by crawling her way down a flowery runway. Stick around, because the day after the pageant are hermit crab races, also on the 6th Street Beach. Free.

Twins Contest
609-525-9300
Ocean City Boardwalk at the Music Pier

How alike are you, really? See how you match up at this contest, which judges twins for who looks most and least alike. Free.

Weird Week
609-525-9300
Ocean City Boardwalk at the Music Pier

They're not kidding when they call this Weird Week. You have to see it to believe how weird it can be. Events start at 11 AM every weekday of the entire week and culminate with the crowning of Mr. and Miss Miscellaneous. Free.

October

Hayrides on the Boardwalk
609-398-4662
Ocean City Boardwalk

That's right—you can get your hayride with a dash of salt air thrown in. They provide free pumpkins and face painting as well. Free.

Indian Summer Weekend
609-525-9300
Ocean City Music Pier

You'll stuff your stomach and empty your wallet at this three-day festival. Seafood vendors take over the Music Pier, and Asbury Avenue turns into a block party with foods, crafts, music, and plenty of stuff to see and do. Free.

December

First Night New Year's Eve Celebration
609-525-9300
www.firstnightocnj.com

Ring in the new year at this family-friendly (and dry) New Year's Eve celebration, topped off with midnight fireworks. $$.

EMERGENCY NUMBERS

In an emergency, dial 911.
Poison information: 1-800-222-1222
Non-emergency fire: 609-525-9182
Non-emergency police: 609-399-9111

HOSPITALS

Shore Memorial Hospital
609-391-8105
www.shorememorial.org
914 Haven Ave., Ocean City 08226

Shore Memorial Hospital
609-653-3500
www.shorememorial.org
1 E. New York Ave., Somers Point 08244

NEWSPAPERS

Ocean City Gazette
609-624-8900
www.oceancitygazette.com

Ocean City Sentinel
609-399-5411

The SandPaper Magazine
609-624-8900
oceancitygazette.com/sp

REALTORS

Ocean City Board of Realtors
609-399-0128
www.ocbor.com
405 22nd St., Ocean City 08226

TRANSPORTATION

Action Transportation
609-839-9797

C&C Cab Company
609-399-9100

Gerry's A-1 Transportation
609-399-7444 and 609-927-9140

Enterprise Rent-A-Car
609-390-1061
Enterprise.com

Just Four Wheels
609-399-2522
www.just4wheels.com

TOURISM CONTACTS

Ocean City Chamber of Commerce
609-399-1412
www.oceancityvacation.com

Ocean City Tourism Commission
1-800-BEACH-NJ
www.njoceancity.com

New Jersey Travel and Tourism
1-800-VISITNJ
www.state.nj.us/travel

3

Sea Isle City

Vacationers' Delight

Including Strathmere and Ocean View

When Charles K. Landis came home from an Italian vacation, he decided to recreate that same experience closer to home. So he bought the area that is now Sea Isle City, making it a borough by 1880.

Sea Isle City might not look anything like an Italian resort now, but a few of those 1880s buildings are still around (just look for the "circa" signs, mainly at houses and stores along Landis Avenue), and people still vacation here.

Sea Isle City is located on a small, narrow barrier island bordered by the Atlantic Ocean on the east and marsh on the west. The southernmost streets are popular with families who come to town to enjoy the beach, the water, and the excellent dining that Sea Isle City offers. You won't find many hotels, motels, or bed & breakfasts here (as you'll soon read) because most people rent a private house for their one- or two-week stay. Sea Isle City is also a popular spot for 20- and 30-somethings, largely due to the cluster of bars and restaurants around JFK Boulevard, the main thoroughfare into town. They don't come for the week, but tend to rent houses with 15 of their closest friends and use them throughout the summer weekends.

These two crowds—families and young people looking for fun—create a unique balance and mix of people in Sea Isle. You'll find plenty of family-friendly restaurants, from ocean-size pizza parlors to BYOB cafes, and activities. But you can also rock out to cover bands, sample fine whisky menus, and pick up "a slice" at 2 AM. It's all within blocks of each other, and doesn't necessarily collide. The bars and the people who frequent them are more laid-back than high-energy, more casual bar than nightclub.

Sea Isle City shares the island with Strathmere, which is due north. It's a slip of a town that has a handful of restaurants and bars and far smaller crowds than you'll find in Sea Isle City, especially in the summer. It's still a relatively unknown patch of the Jersey Shore, and has managed to stave off the overdevelopment you'll see on other parts of the island.

Whether you're that family or a young person looking for fun at the Shore—or both—Sea Isle City could have what you're looking for. No promises on a gondola running down Landis Avenue anytime soon, though.

The Colonnade Inn

LODGING

Coast Motel
609-263-3756
www.lacosta-seaisle.com
4000 Landis Ave., Sea Isle City 08243

This motel, which is just a half block from the beach and smack in the center of town, is a drop-your-stuff-and-go kind of place. You book the room for the convenience of its location, not any added extras. That's not to say it's a bad place to stay—not at all. The 33 rooms at the Coast are clean, well maintained, have their own kitchenettes, and are in the perfect spot to crash after a day on the beach. Open in season. $$.

The Colonnade Inn
609-263-8868
www.thecolonnadeinn.com
4600 Landis Ave., Sea Isle City 08243

When the Jersey Shore became "the" place to vacation back in the 1800s, the Colonnade Inn was one of the many resorts that catered to visitors. Today, this inn, which was built around 1883, is the only hotel from that era standing in Sea Isle City. In 2004, it was renovated back to its original splendor, which shows in each of its 19 lodging options, which come as one-, two-, and three-room suites. The Colonnade operates much in the way a bed & breakfast does, except that many of the rooms belong to private owners who rent out their space when they're not in Sea Isle City. Don't skip

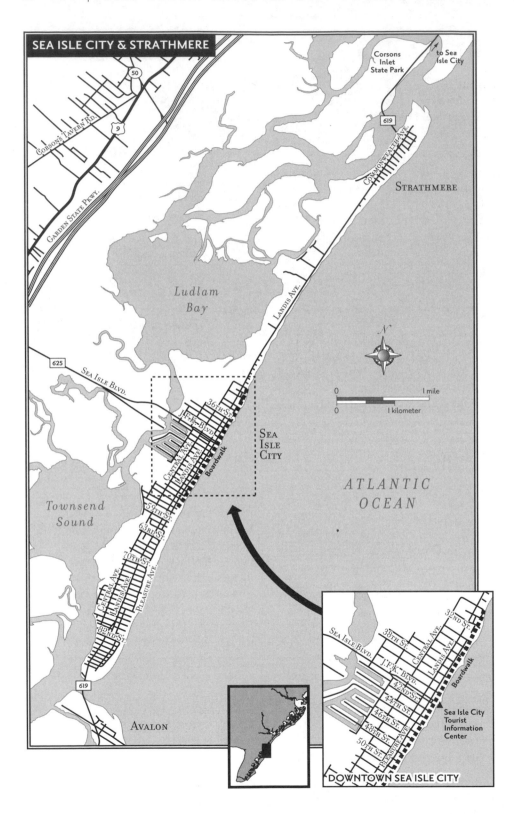

SEA ISLE CITY & STRATHMERE

Corsons Inlet State Park

to Sea Isle City

STRATHMERE

CORSONS' TAVERN RD.

GARDEN STATE PKWY.

Ludlam Bay

LANDIS AVE.

COMMONWEALTH AVE.

SEA ISLE BLVD.

36TH ST.

J.F.K. BLVD.

CENTRAL AVE.

LANDIS AVE.

Boardwalk

SEA ISLE CITY

ATLANTIC OCEAN

Townsend Sound

59TH ST.

63RD ST.

70TH ST.

CENTRAL AVE.

LANDIS AVE.

PLEASURE AVE.

82ND ST.

AVALON

N

0   1 mile
0   1 kilometer

SEA ISLE BLVD.

38TH ST.

32ND ST.

CENTRAL AVE.

LANDIS AVE.

J.F.K. BLVD.

42ND ST.

44TH ST.

46TH ST.

48TH ST.

50TH ST.

PLEASURE AVE.

Boardwalk

Sea Isle City Tourist Information Center

DOWNTOWN SEA ISLE CITY

the porch views—you'll see everything going on in the center of town. $$–$$$.

Sea Isle Inn

609-263-4371
www.seaisleinn.com
6400 Landis Ave., Sea Isle City 08243

The Sea Isle Inn is the largest motel on the island and offers efficiencies and suites for two to six people. Each room has a private balcony, and the motel has a miniature golf course and pool. Its pool is usually rocking, hosting live music throughout the summer. $$–$$$.

Centennial Guest House

609-263-6945
www.centennialguesthouse.com
127 39th St., Sea Isle City 08243

This house has a past. The Centennial Guest House was built in 1885 as a summer home for a wealthy Philadelphian, and during Prohibition it became a speakeasy. John and Madge DiGenni bought the house in 1980 and renamed it the Centennial Guest House in Honor of Sea Isle City's 100th birthday (in 1982). John DiGenni, the couple's son, now runs the guest house, which is a true guest house in the classical sense of the word. There is no breakfast (it's not a B&B), and the rooms don't have private bathrooms. But they are clean, charming, and feature air conditioning and wireless Internet. Make sure to bring your own towels, too. Open in season. $–$$.

OCEAN VIEW

Ocean View Resort Campground

609-624-1675
www.ovresort.com
2555 RT 9, Ocean View 08230

This campground's a big one—located on 180 acres of shaded woodland, including a freshwater lake that's swim-ready and stocked with hybrid striped bass and large-mouth bass. Each of the 1,000+ campsites comes with 20/30-amp service, water, sewer, and cable TV hookups, campfire ring, and picnic table. You can also rent cabins and trailers. To keep you and the kids occupied, they have a grown-up pool and a kiddie pool, activities building, tram, 18-hole miniature golf course, paddleboat rentals, and sports fields and courts. $–$$.

DINING

SEA ISLE CITY

Acme

609-263-9006
www.acmemarkets.com
63rd St. and Landis Ave., Sea Isle City 08243

This is the local outpost of a popular regional grocery store (no, not the place that sells all the cool stuff you see on Looney Tunes). It's like your regular grocery store but with more beach toys and supplies, which are set up outside. Sea Isle City beach tags are also sold by the entrance in season. Open 7 AM–11 PM Monday through Saturday and 7 AM–10 PM Sunday.

Braca Café

609-263-4271
www.bracacafe.com
18 JFK Blvd., Sea Isle City 08243

The Braca name was once stamped all over Sea Isle City, starting in 1901 when Lou and Madelena Braca moved here. A barber shop, grocery store, real estate company, theater, gift and card shop, ice cream store, and bowling alley all bore the Braca name. Many of the businesses were destroyed by storms, but Braca's Café still thrives in what used to be the Braca family home. The

Braca Café

menu offers surf and turf options with a hearty dose of pasta meals (usually with the surf items thrown in). If your appetite is more petite than monster, they offer half-size servings of the pasta dishes. Dinner. Lunch Friday, Saturday, and Sunday. $$–$$$.

Busch's
609-263-8626
www.buschsseafood.com
8700 Anna Phillips Ln., Sea Isle City 08243

This popular spot has been dishing up seafood for more than 125 years. Pick from the wealth of sea-themed meals, or try two at once, like baked deviled crabs and fried scallops, via Busch's combo entrees. The one thing you cannot skip is the she-crab soup. Owner Al Schettig makes it himself, by himself, to ensure that his recipe remains a secret. Kids eat free on Wednesdays. Dinner in season. Closed Monday. $$.

Commodore Club
609-263-4440
3700 Boardwalk, Sea Isle City 08243

The only way to get into the Commodore Club is to buy a membership or become friends—fast—with a member. And, yes, they are strict with that rule. But if you manage to get in and take a seat in one of the old, comfortably worn bar chairs, you'll enjoy boardwalk and ocean views, plus nightly food specials. It's not hard to have a sea view—the Commodore Club may be narrow, but it's long where it counts: facing the ocean. Dinner in season, weekends only in the off season. Memberships are $60 a year.

Dead Dog Saloon
609-263-7600
www.seaislenightlife.com
3809 Landis Ave., Sea Isle City 08243

They're not kidding about the dress code. Guys, if you walk in wearing a T-shirt, you are required to put a $10 deposit down on a Dead Dog Saloon collared shirt, which is why you might see a row of guys dressed alike when you walk in (and if you "forget" to return the shirt, it's yours, and they keep your $10). No baseball caps, either, in the evening hours. As for food, the menu is strictly bar food—but good bar food—with items like personal pizzas, coconut shrimp, and potstickers, which is shrimp or pork folded into a pastry with vegetables. The music and entertainment are usually low-key, even on the busier summer weekends.

Dinner plus lunch on Saturday and Sunday in season. $.

Dock Mike's Pancake House
609-263-3625
www.dockmikes.com
4615 Landis Ave., Sea Isle City 08243

The name here is a bit misleading. While Dock Mike's certainly dishes up pancakes in many different varieties, including sweet potato and "Mikey" Mouse, it's also a lunch spot and has more than 100 different items to try, including wraps, seafood samplers, and cheese steaks—all of which are listed on your placemat menu. No credit cards. Breakfast, lunch. $–$$.

Giovanni's Deli and Sub Shop
609-263-7684
4309 Landis Ave., Sea Isle City 08243

If you can't tell this is a true Italian deli by the tins of extra-virgin olive oil lined up in the window, you will when you walk in and are hit with that spicy meat-and-cheese smell. The hoagies here are the main attraction, though they also stock deli meats and cheeses, plus precooked meals and sides, including antipasto, salads, and Italian cookies. If you need the goods to make your own Italian masterpiece, Giovanni's also stocks anything you'll want, from the pasta to the sauce to, of course, that extra-virgin olive oil. Breakfast, lunch, dinner. $.

Mallon's
609-263-1280
www.mallonsbakery.com
5008 Landis Ave., Sea Isle City 08243

If you like sticky buns, this is your spot—Mallon's makes 14 flavors of this gooey treat. They also sell other freshly made sweet breakfast treats, like homemade donuts, muffins, crumb cake, plus bagels, cookies, and coffee. No credit cards. Hours

Wawa

Is it a convenience store? A gas station? A general store? Or a coffee shop with a lot of other items on the shelves?

It's all and none of the above. It's Wawa.

Wawa's deepest roots go back to 1803, when the Millville Manufacturing Company opened in its first farm in Millville, New Jersey. In 1902, Millville owner George Wood opened a small milk plant in Wawa, Pennsylvania, which started producing milk for home delivery. In 1964, the first Wawa Food Markets opened in Folsom, Pennsylvania. It was a way to save the company as manufacturing moved out of the area. But people still needed milk, and a lot of other items that the store offered. Wawa quickly expanded to include fresh fruit, produce, and a deli.

By 2001, Wawa had more than 500 stores in five states. On average, they sell more than 125 million cups of coffee, 35 million hoagies, and 92 million quarts of milk—every year. It's a staple, not just for commuters, but for just about everyone in the Philadelphia area. It offers convenience at grocery store prices, and one-person portions.

But one of Wawa's other strong footholds (or busiest spots in the summer, judging by the crowds) is the South Jersey Shore. They have locations in Avalon, Cape May, Cape May Court House, Galloway, Little Egg Harbor, Ocean City, Sea Isle City, Stone Harbor, Ventnor, Wildwood, and Wildwood Crest, sometimes with more than one location per town.

The best way to find one, at least in my experience, is to look for traffic jams. Most Shore Wawas weren't built to accommodate the popularity they would eventually achieve. But it's the best place to get anything you'll need while on vacation, things like the newspaper, lunch and breakfast sandwiches, snacks, ice cream, and coffee.

Oh, the coffee. It's nothing fancy like Starbucks, but it's not pricey, and you can't go anywhere on a Shore morning without seeing those paper coffee cups. You pick the blend of flavors that most suits your morning need.

"It's what people love at home," says Kelly Hennigan of Cherry Hill, New Jersey, a long time Wawa devotee who vacations in Sea Isle City. "There are certainly things people go to the Shore for, like sticky buns, but when it comes to coffee, people know what they like."

Especially that coffee. Me, I'm a half vanilla cream, half decaf kind of gal. At the Shore, I would stop by the Avalon Wawa for a cup and the morning paper to go with my breakfast, which was usually made perfect with Wawa milk.

"You trust the coffee, you trust the sandwiches. And it's cheap," says Hennigan. She's a 20-ounce-cup-of-regular-with-two-and-a-half-sugars person, both at home and at the Shore, in case you were wondering.

Today's newer Wawas, called "super Wawas," include gas stations, though you won't find many on the Shore's barrier islands because there isn't enough room. (One exception is in Wildwood—that's a fun Wawa, too, because it's done in Doo Wop style.) And if Wawa were to ever want to expand by adding gas in one of those small Shore locations, I would advise them to rethink what to do with that space and consider adding more parking spaces instead. It'll ease a lot of headaches for people who have not yet caffeinated themselves with a morning cup of Wawa coffee.

vary, but they always serve around the breakfast and lunch hours in season. Open weekends only in the spring and fall. $.

Mike's Seafood and Raw Bar
609-263-1136
222 Park Rd., Sea Isle City, 08243

Eat on the dock—literally—at this seafood spot. The dining area is covered with a thick green awning, but the sides are open to the water, just enough to give you that outdoor dining feel while staying cool. You can come in a large group and order your crabs by the pound (ready for you to crack and clean on your own if you so choose), or grab one of the smaller tables for two. It's BYOB and busy on the weekends, so expect a line around dinnertime (though you can have a predinner drink while waiting for your table). Lunch, dinner in season. $$.

Mrs. Brizzle's
609-263-2773
4411 Landis Ave., Sea Isle City 08243

The homemade cinnamon buns are only one prong to the missus's eat-in and take-out shop. She (or the college kids working behind the counter) also sells breakfast sandwiches, monster-size hoagies, and salads beyond the typical Caesar and garden varieties. There is select indoor seating, but the chairs are few and far between. Better to take your treat or meal home or right onto the beach. No credit cards. Breakfast, lunch. $.

Nickelby's
609-263-1184
8301 Landis Ave., Sea Isle City 08243

You won't find anything closer to an old-fashioned country store at the Shore than at Nickelby's, which sits on the meeting point of Landis and East Landis Avenues. You'll

Nickleby's

Where the Hell is Strathmere?

It's an old saying of some of the locals in Strathmere, which is stuck between Sea Isle City and Ocean City. It's even a bumper sticker, which you can buy at www.strathmere.net.

I e-mailed the woman behind the bumper sticker about where the idea came from. She didn't want to be identified, or talk over the phone, but she had a lot to say about Strathmere.

"It's an old joke around town, among some people," wrote the woman behind the bumper sticker—and www.strathmere.net—about the saying. "But some Strathmere people don't like the saying.

"Strathmere is a small, quiet, old-fashioned seaside town with old beach houses, a trailer park, and a few restaurants. Nothing touristy," she continued. "We've managed to hold off condo-nization and overdevelopment. It's a close community, and the quiet, quaint quirkiness is what people love about Strathmere."

I like the town now, too, much more than my first experience with its beach, which was after my junior prom. My classmates used it as a place to celebrate the prom on the day after, and not in the most legal ways (though I didn't participate—just watched).

Sure, there are houses in Strathmere, but the island is slim and offers little to no room for development—at least on stable ground. This keeps massive crowds out of town, or at least bound to the road on their way from Ocean City to Sea Isle City and vice-versa. Beachwise, you won't need a beach tag, and the crowds are much smaller than what you'll find at Strathmere's Shore neighbors, though there are lifeguards in season.

This doesn't mean Strathmere offers nothing in the way of civilization. Mildred's is a perennial favorite when it comes to dining. And the Deauville, which sits at the tip of Strathmere on the way to Ocean City, is a relaxing, casual restaurant and bar and a great place to stick your feet in the sand while having a drink. Almost like junior prom weekend—without the fear of getting arrested.

The town's been making noises about annexing itself from Upper Township. Their argument is that Strathmere is a Shore community paying taxes for inland problems, and that Upper Township is out of touch with Strathmere's needs, which residents say include more police patrols in season because of underage drinking (re: my prom story). A hinge point is the property taxes, which are so high that many people are having to sell houses that have been in their families for generations because they can't pay the tax bill.

I'm not going to wade into that debate, but I will say this: Strathmere looks nothing like an inland town. It looks like Sea Isle City without the noise. Maybe people will know where the hell it is now.

---

find a small selection of groceries, toiletries, hats, shirts, and toys, a deli and bakery, plus a coffee bar. Check out Flowers by the Sea by Nickelby's, which is located just outside the store, for fresh Jersey produce and, of course, flowers. Breakfast, lunch in season. $.

Ocean Drive
609-263-1000

www.theod.com
3915 Landis Ave., Sea Isle City 08243

It's not exactly the place where everybody knows your name. In fact, it's quite possible that no one will be able to find you in this always-packed Shore tradition of a bar. It's the place where the young 'uns go in Sea Isle City, and has been for the last 20 years. The drinks are cold and on special, and the cover bands are loud and play all the songs you know. It's not fancy, but no one will scoff if you come in right off the beach. In fact, the "OD" is regular host to the "No Shower Happy Hour"—you're *encouraged* to wear your bathing suit. Even if your 20-something years are long gone, you can stop in early to enjoy a drink and food specials, like mini-burgers, shrimp and clams, and tacos. Lunch, dinner, late night in season. $.

O'Donnell's Pour House

609-263-5600
3907 Landis Ave., Sea Isle City 08243

It's mostly fish and meat at this small eatery, but what really draws the patrons is the drink menu, specifically the whisky. Enjoy the likes of Jameson, Bushmills, Black Bush Special, and Midleton Very Rare, or try a few brands with the whisky sampler. The lamb stew is highly recommended—as are reservations. Lunch, dinner in season. $$.

Shoobies

609-263-2000
4003 Landis Ave., Sea Isle City 08243

Music rules at this retro diner on Landis Avenue. The restaurant is decorated in music paraphernalia, from the records that form a border along the ceiling to the posters, which celebrate everything from Doo Wop to '80s bands. If you're eating solo, sidle up to the counter and watch as sodas are served from the vintage 7-Up tap. Breakfast is heavy on the eggs, and varieties of pancakes and waffles (the peanut butter hotcakes are a real treat). Lunch and dinner are steaks and sandwiches, plus a monster sundae menu—if you can handle it. It's a kid-friendly, place too—placemats have kiddie activities built in, and TV characters regularly stop by to say hello and chat—well, mime—with patrons. Breakfast, lunch, dinner in season. Breakfast, lunch in the off season, weekends only. $.

The Carousel at the Springfield Inn

Springfield Inn

609-263-4951

www.thespringfieldinn.com

8 43rd St., Sea Isle City 08243

The Springfield, as it's more commonly known, isn't really an inn. Rather, it's a center for live music and cold drinks, skewing older in age than the crowd that flocks to Ocean Drive. The Springfield also has one of the few beach bars in the area—The Carousel, which also has live music (and not a carousel in sight). The view is more boardwalk than beach, but a seat at the under-cabana bar is relaxing just the same. Food comes from JB's, which is of the cheese steak and fries family. JB's also has a walk-up window on the beach if you're sticking to water or are underage. No credit cards. Open in season. Lunch, dinner at JB's only. $.

Sweet Pete's

609-263-1116

6116 Landis Ave., Sea Isle City 08243

It's hard not to feel cheery in this candy-striped ice cream parlor, which also dishes up yummy deserts for everyone and coffee drinks for the grown-ups (along with a Sunrise Parfait that's perfect if you're keeping your health in check while on vacation). It might take you a bit of time to take in all

they have to offer on the menu, which is written on blackboards that line the walls of this deep store, and includes ice cream, homemade waffles, gourmet desserts, brownies, milkshakes, and, of course, sundaes. No credit cards. Lunch, dinner in season. $.

Valarie's Place

609-263-5400

www.valariesplace.com

5900 Landis Ave., Sea Isle City 08243

Expect a good meal in a cozy atmosphere at this restaurant, which not only accepts kids but reaches out to them for breakfast, lunch, and dinner. The walls are decorated with colorful hand prints from kids who have visited Valarie's. There's even a play area for the younger patrons. The menu leans toward pasta and seafood, though the entrées also include un-Shore-like twists, including southwest chicken and grilled pork chops. BYOB. Breakfast, lunch, dinner. Call for off season hours. $$.

Vince's Restaurant

609-263-4567

www.vincesrestaurant.net

25 JFK Blvd., Sea Isle City 08243

Talk about luck. Vince and Annette Mollo knew they wanted to open a restaurant, but they didn't have the funds—that is until Vince won them in a poker game on his way back to the U.S. from serving in World War II. Vince's opened in 1953 and is still run by the family. Vince and Annette's grandson, Jim, is chef, combining his experience working in the kitchen with his grandfather plus time at the Academy of Culinary Arts and in the kitchens of a few Marriott hotels. Vince's has come a long way from the original sub shop and offers fine dining in a casual atmosphere overlooking the ocean. You'll find Shore regulars like mussels marinara and crab cakes, as well as menu items with flare, like ancho chili-rubbed

---

Miniature Golf in Sea Isle City

Teach the kids the fundamentals of golf—or the importance of patience—on one of these miniature golf courses.

Pirate Island Golf

609-263-8344

www.pirateislandgolf.com

3302 Landis Ave., Sea Isle City 08243

Pizza Putt

609-263-4663

9 42nd St., Sea Isle City 08243

mahi-mahi and broiled Brazilian lobster tail. Even the breakfast menu has a few flashes of culinary creativity, like the spinach and feta cheese omelet. BYOB. Breakfast, lunch, dinner. Call for off-season hours. $–$$.

Yum Yum's Ice Cream

609-263-2345
31 JFK Blvd., Sea Isle City 08243

You can get just about any kind of ice cream you want at this longtime Sea Isle City shop. You'll have to wait on the weekends, but it's worth it for the treat put at the bottom of the cone: a gum drop. It started as a way to keep ice cream from leaking out and has stayed because it gives your cone a little something extra when the goodness has come to an end. No credit cards. Open noon–10 PM in season (or later if the crowds keep coming). $.

STRATHMERE

Deauville Inn

609-263-2080
www.deauvilleinn.com
201 Williard Rd., Strathmere 08248

They say the sunsets are complimentary at the Deauville Inn, which straddles the border of Ocean City and Sea Isle. And they aren't to be missed, especially in the warmer months, when you can sit dockside for lunch, dinner, or a late-night snack, or enjoy your drinks on the sand (where the motto is "no shoes, no shirt, no problem"). As you'd expect at a bayside eatery, the menu is dominated by seafood. If you've got a monster appetite, or plan on sharing, go for the Captain's Platter, which features the best of what you can eat from the sea. Indoor seating is also available. Expect live music on the deck on Saturdays and Sundays, and a steel drum band Thursday nights in season. Reservations recom-

mended for dinner if you want to eat inside. Lunch, dinner, late night. $$$

Uncle Bill's Pancake House

609-398-7393
2 Ocean Drive, Strathmere 08248

Get your day going at Uncle Bill's, which packs in hungry patrons in just about every South Jersey Shore town (poor Atlantic City and Sea Isle City). The main attraction, of course, is the pancakes, but they also have plenty of egg options, as well as waffles and sandwiches. Expect long waits on the week ends in season. No credit cards. Breakfast, lunch in season. $

ARTS & CULTURE

Coffee.COMedy

609-263-JAVA
www.coffeedotcomedy.com
29 JFK Blvd., Sea Isle City 08243

No, this store isn't closed—the windows are just tinted to keep the interior cool, and to provide a better workspace for the stand-up comedians who regularly rule the roost in the summer. The acts aren't really top bill, but they almost always make you laugh. Coffee.COMedy serves an array of caffeine-infused drinks (it doubles as a coffeehouse during the day), along with breakfast bagels, sandwiches, and wraps. You can buy Internet time or hook up your laptop. It has plenty of workspace tables if you're dying to get some work done (though you might be laughing too hard at night to concentrate). Open 8 AM–11 PM. $.

Sea Isle City Historical Museum

609-624-7929
4208 Landis Ave., Sea Isle City 08243

There was a time when Sea Isle City wasn't overrun by beach rental houses, pizza shops, bars, and shoobies, which is what

Sea Isle City Promenade

The boardwalk in Sea Isle doesn't have any boards, and, as you've seen, it's not even called a board-walk (even if addresses along the Promenade are still listed as "Boardwalk"). It's not as developed as its counterparts in Atlantic City, Ocean City, and Wildwood but is far from empty. You'll find shops, casual eateries, and amusements along the Promenade, and where it intersects with JFK Boulevard is the host of a lot of activities, including live bands and performances. Biking and in-line skating are per-mitted from 5 AM–3 PM Monday through Friday and 5 AM–noon Saturday and Sunday.

If you're into people watching, the Promenade is an ideal spot to park yourself on a bench after dinner. Parents push strollers up and down the concrete (much more forgiving on the wheels than wooden boards), and couples stroll. I like getting an ice cream cone from Yum Yum's, which is right off the Promenade at JFK Boulevard, and taking a walk to check out the crowds while enjoying a few scoops of mint chocolate chip ice cream in a pretzel cone.

After the sun goes down, the crowd turns into more teenagers-too-young-to-get-into-the-bars set. They walk and strut, perfecting their flirting techniques. We didn't have cell phones—a must on the Promenade—when I was that age, but I was guilty of defying all fashion rules in hopes of looking cool and cute on the Promenade. Usually, based on pictures, I failed. I'm not sure many of the guys and girls strutting down the Promenade, which my brother calls the Cretewalk, pass either. But at least their parents will have something to hold over their heads a few years down the line, as my mom does with me.

The beach at Sea Isle City

the locals call summer-only Shore visitors. Those times are reconstructed and celebrated at the Sea Isle City Historical Museum, which stocks an impressive selection of memorabilia and photos from over 100 years of Sea Isle City history. Open 10 AM–3 PM Monday, Wednesday, and Friday and 10 AM–1 PM Tuesday, Thursday, and Saturday during the summer; 10 AM–1 PM Saturdays September through December and April through June. Special appointments also available in the off season.

ATTRACTIONS, PARKS & RECREATION

SEA ISLE CITY

Hardbodies Gym & Fitness
609-263-6500
hardbodiesgymandfitness.com
4411 Landis Ave., Sea Isle City 08243

Stay in shape (or work off last night's dinner and ice cream combination) at this two-story gym, which provides treadmills, rowing and elliptical machines, and weight machines, plus free weights. They have daily and weekly rates for vacationers. Open 7 AM–10 PM Monday through Friday, 7 AM–7 PM Saturday, and 7 AM–5 PM Sunday in season. Call for off-season hours. $$.

Red Dog Bait & Tackle
609-263-7914
104 42nd St., Sea Isle City 08243

Charter your next fishing trip on their 31-foot Bertram. They'll provide the bait and tackle, too. It's for small groups only—they take out up to six at a time to fish for tuna, bluefish, sharks, marlin, flounder, and stripers on inshore, offshore, and canyon trips. $$$$.

Sea Isle Parasail
609-263-5555
www.seaisleparasail.com
86th St. and The Bay, Sea Isle City 08243

Even if you are flying high above the ocean, parasailing is far from a roller coaster ride, which is why it's open to kids, adults, and seniors (the youngest they've flown here was five years old). Fly solo or with a pal—either way, it's a great way to take in the sights of the Jersey Shore. In season. $$$$.

Sea Isle Watersports Center
609-263-9100
www.seaislewatersports.com
329 43rd St., Sea Isle City 08243

For some extra fun on the water, head here to rent a wave runner or kayak. They also provide a separated wave running area, plus guided back bay tours. Sea Isle Watersports

Center stores and winterizes wave runners, and also services, repairs, and sells used ones, too. Check their Web site for rental coupons. Open 7 AM–sunset in season. $$$.

Uncle Al's
609-263-7485
35th Street & the Boardwalk, Sea Isle City 08243

Test your luck and wooden-ball-throwing skills at one of Uncle Al's 10 Skee-Ball lanes. If this isn't your game, you can also try other ticket-winning amusements, like slot machines, or play pinball or video games. Ticket points are doubled on "Double Ticket Tuesdays" between 10 AM and 4 PM, and Skee-Ball tournaments are held every Thursday at 10:30 AM in season. The prizes you get in exchange for your ticket winnings aren't always top of the line, but it's the journey that's the most fun here. Open 10 AM–10 PM in season. $

STRATHMERE

Frank's Boat Rentals
609-263-6913
www.franksboatrentals.com
100 S. Bayview Dr., Strathmere 08243

Venture out on your own by renting a fiberglass boat from Frank's. They come in at just under 16 feet, are equipped with 8-horsepower Yamaha motors. Great for beginners, or if you're bringing children out onto the water for the first time. You can rent fishing and crabbing equipment, or buy bait at Frank's, too. Open 7 AM–5 PM Monday through Friday and 6 AM–5 PM Saturday and Sunday in season. $$$$.

OCEAN VIEW

Shore Gate Golf Club
609-624-TEES
www.shoregategolfclub.com
35 School House Ln., Ocean View 08230

Golf Digest rated this par 72 course the second best public course in New Jersey—twice. It's located on 245 acres of forest with 88 bunkers and seven water hazards. And you thought you left the sand and beach behind you when you went inland. $$$$.

SHOPPING

Bath & Body Boutique
609-263-9401
www.bathbodyboutique.com
3700 Boardwalk, Sea Isle City 08243

Everything a gal could want for pampering is at this intimate store. They sell bath and body items, like soaps and lotions from the likes of Camille Beckman, Archipelago Botanicals,

Chrissie's Boutique

and the Little Egg Harbor Soap Company, and lingerie for comfort, or for play. Open 10 AM
–10 PM in season; 10 AM–5 PM Saturday and 10 AM–4 PM Sunday in the off season.

Book Nook

609-263-1311
3500 Boardwalk, Sea Isle City 08243

This boardwalk bookstore is an ideal place to get your beach reading material. They have
magazine racks in the front and back of the store (the front is more "greatest hits" of what's
popular to read on the beach), plus the mysteries, thrillers, and deep reads that keep you
anchored to your beach chair. They've also dedicated a chunk of the store to children's
books and activity books to keep the younger members of your clan occupied. Open 10
AM–11 PM in season.

Chrissie's Boutique

609-263-3509
3806 Landis Ave., Sea Isle City 08243

You'll find dresses of all kinds, from floaty cotton sundresses to bombshell satin halter-
top gowns at Chrissie's. The shop is nearly as charming as the dresses themselves—clothes
are displayed on the porch and draped inside this green and pink 19th-century building.
Open 9:30 AM–9:30 PM in season.

Dalrymple's
609-263-3337
20 JFK Blvd., Sea Isle City 08243

It's okay if you can't pronounce the name of this shop—I still can't. It's part Hallmark gift shop, part bookstore with a dash of general store thrown in for all those beach extras you can't live without. The book section is most interesting, especially as it stocks a lot of local-interest titles, including publisher-published and self-published titles by Mike Stafford, president of the Sea Isle Historical Society. Open 7 AM—10 PM in season. Call for off-season hours.

Haven
609-233-5317
www.ihearthaven.com
4105 Landis Ave., Sea Isle City 08243

This boutique leans more toward comfy luxury than beach wear. The styles are very now and very hip for the 20- and 30-something set, but still casual enough to fit in at the local nightlife scene. They stock tanks, dresses, and jeans, as well as casual and comfy sandals and sneakers and jewelry. Open 10 AM—7 PM Monday through Thursday and 10 AM—8 PM Friday through Sunday in season.

Follow the Gull

The Garden State Parkway isn't the only path through the South Jersey Shore. For a more scenic (though, in season, slower and more crowded) route, follow the gull up or down Ocean Drive.

The 26-mile road starts in Ocean City and runs all the way down through Wildwood. It takes you through the heart of Ocean City, Strathmere, Sea Isle City, Avalon, Stone Harbor, and the Wildwoods.

For most of the drive, the road is called, not surprisingly, Ocean Drive, though things can get tricky when you're passing from Stone Harbor into Wildwood. The best way to stay en route is to follow the Ocean Drive signs, but also to look for the round "Follow the Gull" signs. They're red and blue and have a picture of a seagull.

You'll encounter a few tolls a long the way, so keep your dollar bills handy. If you want to get an up close and personal view of everything along Ocean Drive—and you can run 26.2 miles—you can also sign up for the Ocean Drive Marathon, which is typically held in late March. Check out the details at www.odmarathon.org.

Heritage Surf & Sport
609-263-3033
www.heritagesurf.com
3700 Landis Ave., Sea Isle City 08243

The talk here is all surf all the time—except when conversations about snowboarding or "where I went last night" are thrown in by the staff, who know their surf and know their boards. Heritage also sells surf-inspired fashions for men, women, and kids. Don't skip the upstairs "board room," and by board, they mean surf, snow, and skate. Group and private surfing lessons are available. Open 9 AM—9 PM in season and 10 AM—6 PM off season.

Jamaican Me Crazy
609-263-0330
4204 Landis Ave., Sea Isle City 08243

Sessoms Nautical Gifts

This all-in-one shop is packed to the ceiling—literally—with beach gear (and, for some reason, one antique sled). You'll need to ask for help to get your perfect beach chair from that high perch, but everything else is at ground level, including boogie boards, towels, tank tops, bathing suits, and toys. Make sure to squeeze your way to the back of the store, which is a wall of flip-flops, beach shoes, and sandals in all shapes, sizes, and fashions. Open 9 AM–10 PM in season.

Sands Department Store

609-263-3351
6208 Landis Ave., Sea Isle City 08243

This isn't a department store the way you'd think of something attached to a mall, but an all-in-one store with a focus on the Shore. They carry made-for-comfort shoes, along with everything else you'll need (or forgot), like suntan lotion, bed linens, and kitchen gadgets. If you fish, check out their impressive stock of tackle. Open 9 AM–9 PM.

Seasons of Color

609-398-8100
www.seasonsofcolor.net
26 JFK Blvd., Sea Isle City 08243

The clothes, like the store, are punches of bright color, whether you're looking for shirts, shorts, casual dresses, or beach cover-ups, including selections from the Fresh Produce line of sportswear. Their stock is for everyone, too—Seasons of Color has sizes XS to 3X. Open 10 AM–9 PM Monday through Saturday and 11 AM–6 PM Sunday in season; 10 AM–6 PM off season.

Sessoms Nautical Gifts

609-263-6088
3800 Boardwalk, Sea Isle City 08243

The only requirement for something to be sold at Sessoms is that it has to do with the ocean—whether it's the Atlantic or not. That's how you get all kinds of stuff jumbled together. Nautical flags, horseshoe crabs, decorative light rings, and shell chandeliers hang from the ceiling and are mixed in with wooden ships, Pacific island décor, replica pirate booty, and lobster buoys from Maine (with "Sea Isle" written on them). It's a wacky, seafaring delight. Open 10 AM–10 PM in season; 10 AM–5 PM Saturday and Sunday in the off season.

WEEKLY EVENTS (IN SEASON)

Monday

Free Summer Concerts Under the Stars

609-263-TOUR
Sea Isle City Promenade

Listen to some cool tunes (or hot beats) at this outdoor concert. Free.

TUESDAY

Guided Beachcombing
609-263-9643
Sea Isle City Beach at 29th St.

Let the Sea Isle City Environmental Commission show you the ecological wonders of the beach. $

Movies Under the Stars
609-263-TOUR
Sea Isle City Promenade

Check out a kid-friendly movie at this weekly event. Free.

Wednesday

Free Summer Concerts Under the Stars
609-263-TOUR
Sea Isle City Promenade

Listen to some cool tunes (or hot beats) at this outdoor concert. Free.

Thursday

Free Family Night Dance Parties
609-263-TOUR
Sea Isle City Promenade

Boogie on down to the Promenade for this weekly dance party. Free.

Guided Beachcombing
609-263-9643
Sea Isle City Beach at 29th St.

Let the Sea Isle City Environmental Commission show you the ecological wonders of the beach. $

ANNUAL EVENTS

February

Polar Bear Plunge
609-263-TOUR
Sea Isle City Beach at 41st St.

Crabbing

They're pinchy little buggers, those crabs that live in the back bays and inlets of the Jersey Shore. There's a lot of ways you can get them from the water into your stomach. Here's how, from easiest to most difficult:

1. Order them, prepared into a delectable dish, at a restaurant.

2. Order them cooked whole at a restaurant. This leaves the cracking and cleaning up to you. It's a science if you want to get every single little scrap of meat left inside. My aunt Margie would take everyone's leftovers and pick clean what the rest of us couldn't get to. She got at least another crab or two worth of meat out of our scraps. You can buy these kinds of crabs at most seafood shops, or at restaurants like Mike's Seafood and Raw Bar (609-263-1136, 222 Park Road, Sea Isle City 08243), where you can order them by the pound.

3. Buy live crabs, and prepare them at home. This is not for the squeamish, as you'll either have to boil the crabs alive, or kill them (usually by opening their backs) and clean them while they're still squirmy.

4. Catch them. There are two levels of this method, too: the easy way, and the right way. The easy way is to buy or rent crab traps. You bait the trap, put in the water, and wait for a crab to walk inside. The right way is to make your own baited lines using rope, chicken backs, and fishing weights. You throw your line in the water (tied off to a pier or boat), wait, and then check your line every five to 20 minutes, depending on how busy it is that day in the water. Then slowly, very slowly, pull up the line, at just the right speed so the crab doesn't jump off the chicken or know that he's moving. Lower a net under the crab-on-bait, and voilà. Dinner.

I spent more than a few August days out on a single-engine boat, lines in the water, waiting for a crab to bite onto that chicken back. Every year, when my grandparents, cousins, aunts, and uncles would join my family at the Shore, we'd rent boats from Landis Marina in Sea Isle City and catch dinner.

My grandfather, Anthony Verzella, taught me how to tie on the chicken back while weighing down the line, and how to time the net just right so that the crab wouldn't dance away. I've seen him pinched by a crab, too, and not even wince—he was a tough guy with the biggest hands I've ever seen. After hours on the boat, we'd bring our catch back to where we were staying and my mother, grandmother, and aunts would build a huge crab feast around pastas and garlic bread, salads, and maybe, if we felt like it, corn on the cob.

My grandfather passed away while I was writing and researching this book. He had been ill for a very long time, so we knew what was coming, but the grief of his death passed over me in waves as I put the book together. I almost had to leave the table while eating dinner at Mike's. That meal was only a month after my grandfather had passed, and seeing a bunch of people tearing apart just-cooked crabs, and knowing I'd never share that with him again, was too much for me to handle.

As I helped my mom clean out my grandparents' house, I came across an AAA guide from 1988 about RV and tent sites in Delaware, DC, Maryland, New Jersey, Pennsylvania, Virginia, and West Virginia. Tucked inside were newspaper articles he'd saved about where to go to catch the best crabs, and a placemat from a seafood joint that had step-by-step, illustrated instructions on how to best pick the meat from a crab. He always wanted to do everything the right way, whether it was building a sky-scraper, or cleaning a crab. I'll keep those newspaper articles as a reminder of that.

When my cousins grew up and stopped coming down the Shore every summer, my mom and aunts started buying the crabs instead—live—and creating the feast. It was cheaper, cleaner, and certainly quicker than renting boats. But I miss the chase and those lazy days on a boat with my grandfather, waiting for the next big catch.

If your idea of fun is jumping into the frigid ocean, this is the event for you. If not and you want to watch, check out the costume contest or toast the divers at the post-plunge party. $.

March

Ocean Drive Marathon
609-523-0880
www.odmarathon.com

Take in the Shore sites through this spring marathon, which starts in Cape May and ends in Sea Isle City. The course is all on paved roads or on boardwalk and is a qualifying course. If you're not quite up to 26.2 miles, you can also run a 10-miler, 5k (or 3.1 miles), or 1.5-mile fun run and walk. $$$$.

St. Patrick's Day Parade
609-263-4461, X-230
Landis Ave., Sea Isle City

Show off your Irish pride (or the love of the Irish) at this annual parade. Free.

April

Easter Program
609-263-0050
59th St. and Central Ave., Sea Isle City

Put on your Easter best for this annual parade. Free.

May

Paws on the Promenade Fundraiser
609-390-7946
Sea Isle City Promenade

If you think your dog is just the cutest thing in the world, let him or her stroll on the Sea Isle City boardwalk to show off his or her chops . . . er, paws. Free.

July

Beach Patrol Mascot Races
609-263-3655
Sea Isle City Beach

Little guys and gals who want to be lifeguards can take two days of classes with the Sea Isle City Beach Patrol, the culmination of which are the Mascot Races held every July. Free.

August

Captain Bill Gallagher Island Run
609-263-3655
www.lmsports.com/seaisle.htm
Sea Isle City Boardwalk and Beach

This annual 10-mile run, which stretches through Sea Isle City and Strathmere, is a flat course, 7 miles of which are on the beach. Feel your calves are up to it? Register online, or watch from the boardwalk. $$.

September

Fall Family Festival Weekend
Sea Isle City Promenade

Check out a hodgepodge of fun family events at this annual fall weekend event, which includes an antique car show, dance party, dance contest, and sand sculpting contest. Free.

December

New Year's Eve Fireworks
Sea Isle City Promenade
Kick your New Year's off with a bang at this fireworks display. Free.

EMERGENCY NUMBERS

In an emergency, dial 911.
Poison information: 1-800-222-1222
Non-emergency fire: 609-263-4311
Non-emergency police: 609-263-4311
Ambulance Corps: 609-263-8686

HOSPITALS

Cape Regional Medical Center
609-463-2000
www.caperegional.com
2 Stone Harbor Boulevard, Cape May Courthouse 08210

NEWSPAPERS

Sea Isle Times
609-967-7710
www.seaisletimes.com

REALTORS

Coldwell Banker/Laricks Real Estate
1-877-SIC-RENT
www.laricks.com
4110 Landis Avenue, Sea Isle City 08243

Landis Co., Realtors
1-888-Sea-Isle
www.landisco.com
6000 Landis Avenue, Sea Isle City 08243

Sea Isle Realty, Inc.
1-888-848-4948
seaislerealty.com
5906 Landis Avenue, Sea Isle City 08243

TRANSPORTATION

C&C Cab Company
115 13th Street, Ocean City 08226
609-399-9100

Enterprise Rent-A-Car
609-522-1119
www.enterprise.com

Yellow Cab
609-263-2225

TOURISM CONTACTS

Greater Sea Isle City Chamber of Commerce
609-263-9090
www.seaislechamber.com

New Jersey Travel and Tourism
1-800-VISITNJ
www.state.nj.us/travel

Sea Isle City Tourism Development Commission
609-263-TOUR
www.seaisletourism.org

4

Avalon & Stone Harbor

Cooler by a Mile

In 1722, Aaron Leaming bought the 7-mile-long barrier island that is now Avalon and Stone Harbor, two separate towns that are, in character, feel, and population, very much the same. He bought the island for about $380. Today, you couldn't buy a square of sidewalk for that price.

Avalon and Stone Harbor are a mix of the family friendliness of Ocean City with the nightlife of Sea Isle City and Wildwood. It's long been a vacation spot for the more tony families of the Philadelphia area—there's a reason the harbors are called Princeton, Yale, and Cornell. A lot of the homes were privately owned cottages for families to use on the weekends and maybe a few weeks through the summer for their annual vacations. Some, too, were rented out to families and packs of 20- and 30-somethings who filled the houses and the bars on summer weekends. The same remains true today, but prices are higher. When the real estate market exploded, the cottages were replaced by new and lavish homes. Some empty lots are going for around a million dollars, so you have to have serious money to own a property on the island. Some of the houses along the bay and on the dunes are more like exotic castles than those quaint—and sometimes non-air-conditioned—cottages ever were. Renting private homes is still popular, which is why I've included contact information for realtors at the end of this chapter.

Unlike other Shore towns, Avalon and Stone Harbor haven't completely shunned development. In a lot of ways, they've embraced it, which you can see in the new high-end shopping on Dune Drive in Avalon and on 96th Street in Stone Harbor. Sure, you've still got your bakeries, pastry shops, Italian restaurants, pizzerias, and corner bars, but also gourmet dining, boutique shopping, and a lot more designer labels than you ever saw on the island before.

That's not to say Avalon and Stone Harbor puts on airs. It's a haven for vacationers of all economic stripes, and still carries a laid-back feel. You'll see families riding bikes up and down Dune Drive, packed beaches, and hopping nightlife, usually of the jeans and T-shirt variety. The island is also a prime location—it's smack in the middle of the South Jersey Shore, putting you between both Atlantic City and Cape May if you're looking to explore all the Shore towns during your stay.

The inland areas of Avalon and Stone Harbor offer a lot of options, too, both through the scores of antique shops along NJ 9 and the campgrounds tucked back into the woods. Camping isn't always exactly rustic, though you can set up a tent and grill over the fire—or rent a luxury trailer with air conditioning, if you so choose.

LODGING

AVALON

Avalon Inn
1-800-45-AVALON3
www.avaloninn.org
7929 Dune Dr., Avalon 08202

The Inn is actually quite large. It has 44 units, heated and kid pools, sundecks and pool patio, and a lot of options, depending on the size of your party. It's a drop-and-go kind of place—nothing too fancy, but a clean and well-attended spot to make your temporary vacation home. Open in season. $$–$$$.

Beachcomber
1-800-462-9703
www.avalon-beachcomber.com
7900 Dune Dr., Avalon 08202

The Beachcomber is a condotel, meaning that the efficiencies and one- and two-bedroom suites are individually owned, but operated and maintained by the Beachcomber, which rents out the suites when the owners aren't there. Some suites have two bathrooms—a rarity at Shore vacation spots. The Beachcomber also has heated swimming and wading pools. Open in season. $$$–$$$$.

Concord Suites
1-800-443-8202
www.concordsuites.com
7800 Dune Dr., Avalon 08202

The Concord is the only all-suite hotel in Avalon. The rooms are spacious and certainly big enough if you're bringing the family along. The décor is a bit beachy, but nothing off setting. The Concord also has two pools and three sundecks if the sand isn't quite your thing, or if you're looking for a change of pace. Make sure to stop in the Concord Café for at least one meal while you're in town. It has some of the best bar food on the island. Open in season. $$$.

Golden Inn
609-368-5155
www.goldeninn.com
7849 Dune Dr., Avalon 08202

The Golden Inn offers an upscale place to stay on the 7-mile island. The décor is Shore without looking weathered. The Golden Inn also has ocean views, heated outdoor pool, and a private dune-front beach. The two restaurants on site—Golden Inn Dining Room and Luigi's Pasta & Vino—are worth checking out even if you're not staying at the inn. Their beachside bar is a popular summer spot. $$$–$$$$.

Sea Lark Bed & Breakfast
609-967-5647
www.sealark.com
3018 1st Ave., Avalon 08202

The Sea Lark is the only bed & breakfast in Avalon. It's certainly homey—the furniture has been passed down through the

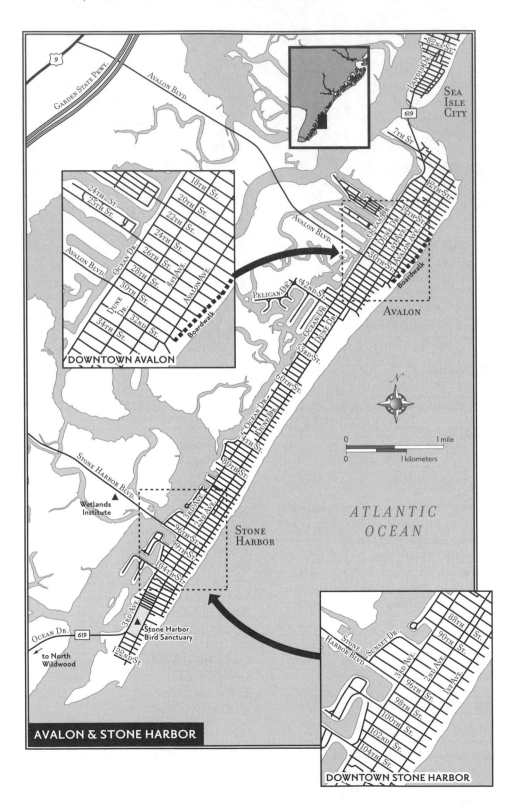

Colonial Lodge

innkeeper's family. Some of the available spaces are pet-friendly. If you're an art fan, rent the Artist's Loft, a third-floor room that is decorated with art from the owner's friend. It has a big deck if you're less into art and more into sun. Open in season. $$–$$$.

Windrift Hotel
1-800-453-7438
www.windrifthotel.com
125 80th St., Avalon 08202

The Windrift, a beachside staple in Avalon as a place to stay, eat, and dance the night away, recently gave its "place to stay" portion a facelift, making it one of the nicest places to book on the 7-mile island. The rooms range from efficiencies to three-bedroom condos. You can also eat and drink by the pool and sundeck. If you stay at the Windrift, you'll skip the cover charge at the bar. Open daily in season and weekends in March, April, and October. $$$–$$$$.

STONE HARBOR

Colonial Lodge
609-368-2202
www.stoneharbormotels.com/colonial.htm
9720 2nd Ave. Stone Harbor 08247

It's quaint and cozy at this brick-faced motel which, yes, does tip its hat to the colonial era, even if the building hasn't been around that long. The rooms are clean and cool—a great place to nap after your beach trip and before a night on the town. Or you can take advantage of the wide balconies and white tables and chairs on the sundeck. The folks at the Colonial Lodge also run a cottage house for rent. It's located next door to the motel. Open in season. $$–$$$.

The Dunes Motel
609-368-4121
www.stoneharbormotels.com/dunes.htm
9801 2nd Ave., Stone Harbor 08247

It's named after those things you're not allowed to walk on—the dunes—and keeps that seaside concept in mind throughout the motel, from your bedspread to the artwork in the lobby. It's right near the heart of Stone Harbor, the beach and, of course, the dunes. Open in season. $$–$$$.

Pebbles Guest House

609-368-2203
9400 First Ave., Stone Harbor 08247

Pebbles Guest House has that same Victorian charm that's made Cape May such a destination. It was built in 1909 and is just three houses from the beach and close to the center of Stone Harbor. The guest house has both room and apartments, but not all accommodations have a private bathroom—remember, it's a guest house, not a B&B, so choose your room carefully if this is a concern. $$–$$$.

Risley House Bed & Breakfast

609-368-1133
www.risleyhouse.net
8421 First Ave., Stone Harbor 08247

The Risley House is as tied to Stone Harbor as the name of the town. Reese Risley, one of the three brothers who founded and governed Stone Harbor, built the Risley House in the early 1900s. But the building isn't stuck in the past. In the late 1990s, the house underwent a major renovation to bring it up to modern sensibilities while still holding onto its Victorian appeal, especially in the rooms, which have that same charm but without the over-the-top Victorian fuss and muss that can turn off some travelers. If you look at the big green building with wraparound porches and say "Wasn't that the Holiday Manor Guest House?" you're right. That was the name of the place pre-renovation. Open in season. $$–$$$.

CLERMONT

Avalon Campground

1-800-814-2267
www.avaloncampground.com
1917 RT 9 N., Clermont 08210

Avalon Campground has been in business for over 40 years, and my family's been vacationing here since year one. They offer camping sites, no matter what level of "roughing it" you like. Pick from sites for your tent, RV, or trailer, or rent one of their trailers or log cabins. They have activities all summer long, including hayrides, craft days, and bingo, plus two pools and a game room for kids who might get a little restless on vacation. Open in season. $.

Driftwood Camping Resort

1-800-624-3743
www.driftwoodrvcenter.com
1955 RT 9, Clermont 08210

Avalon Campground

In 1966, Leonard and Connie Catanoso carved a campground from 80 wooded acres off NJ 9 in Clermont, New Jersey. At about the same time, my grandparents were looking for a place to take their family on vacation. They settled for the campground, rolling up with their trailer, eight kids, and a lot of camping gear in tow.

The family tradition of going to Avalon Campground lasted almost as long as the campground has. A lot of reasons factored into the decision to sell our permanent trailer at Avalon Campground, mostly my parents' divorce with a dash of leaky roof thrown in. In the years that followed, it was also easier and more convenient to rent a house in Sea Isle City or Avalon for a week than to hike back to the woods and cram everyone—including my siblings, aunts, uncles and cousins—into one small space.

In the course of researching this book, my mom and I stopped by Avalon Campground. So much and so little has changed. The roads are now paved, and the clubhouse has a wireless Internet café. The camp store's been redone, too, and you see fewer people using the pay phones. But much has stayed the same, too: two pools to play in, the big red barn that holds scores of events, families tucked back into the woods making their dinners over a campfire, kids racing their bikes down the street, and a lot of sandy feet inside that clubhouse. It's still a more affordable option than renting a house at the beach, and the campground offers kids a lot of activities to give them something else to do other than say they're bored. That was one reason my mother loved it—it kept us out of her hair, even if we did have to drive 20 minutes to the beach.

Leonard and Connie don't run the campground anymore—they retired to Florida, but two of their children, Marlene Testa and Lenny Catanoso, Jr., do. My mom was a kid when they were, and they ran around the campground together. My mom, Marlene, and I sat in that snazzy new Internet café (which is for 21 and up only, mind you) and caught up on what's been going on, chatting for about an hour. One of her brothers had passed away, as had my grandfather. I had written about Avalon Campground in New Jersey Monthly, and Marlene showed me where they'd displayed the article on the wall. We talked about this book, and she gave me a few tips about where to go and what to see, and invited me to their annual year-end barbeque that I'd never been able to go to before because of soccer practices.

Everything is always in flux at the Shore, but it's nice to know that at least in one pocket off NJ 9, a place that I hold dear, is relatively unchanged. I hope that if I'm lucky enough to have kids of my own, I'll be shooing them up to the pool so I can cook dinner over the open fire, or walking them to the big field—wearing bug spray, of course—to look up at stars against an impossibly black sky.

Brian's Waffle House

Driftwood offers all kinds of camping experiences on their 250 shady acres, including tent and trailer sites, plus trailer and cabin rentals. They've got perks, too, like a freshwater lake (and, yes, it's okay to swim there), swimming pool, tennis and basketball courts, plus a full range of activities. Open in season. $.

DINING

Avalon 29th Street Deli & Grill
609-967-DELI
2969 Dune Dr., Avalon 08202

This deli, which is attached to the Avalon Supermarket, is based on a classic Philadelphia Italian deli, but the added salad bar gives it a healthy angle. Expect sandwich staples as well as breakfast sandwiches. They'll deliver to you on the beach, too. Breakfast, lunch, dinner in season. $.

Avalon Anchorage Marina
609-967-3592
www.avalonanchorage.com
21st St. and The Bay, Avalon 08202

Boating isn't the only thing to do at the marina. They serve breakfast, too, right on the water, with unparalleled views of the boats going in and out of the bay. You can dine inside, too, if the heat's too much. Expect the usual egg and pancake fare along with house specials like homemade granola and blueberry muffins when the berries are in season. Breakfast in season. $.

Avalon Freeze
609-967-4141
23rd and Dune Dr., Avalon, 08202

Since the 1950s, Avalon Freeze has been capping vacationers' nights with something sweet. Soft-serve rules here, though they do have other ice cream and yogurt options. Open noon–11 PM in season. $.

Avalon Seafood & Produce Market

609-967-7555
www.avalonseafood.com
2909 Dune Dr., Avalon 08202

Get what's fresh from the land and sea at this combination seafood and produce market. On the produce side, they bring in whatever's coming in off the farms (the Jersey Shore is close to many of the places that put the Garden in Garden State), plus gourmet salads, dips, and salsa. Don't skip dessert, either—they have a pastry chef (as well as culinary chef) on site. On the seafood side, they stock the range of whatever you'd want from the sea, including scallops, fish, lobster tails, shrimp, crabs, and clams. Buy fresh or in one of their platters. It's all take-out. Lunch, dinner in season. $$.

Brady's Hoagie Dock

609-368-8213
6740 Ocean Dr., Avalon 08202

Don't know what a hoagie is? You'll learn at this shop, which is situated away from the buzz and crowds of downtown Avalon. You might call it a sub, or a hero, but here, it's all hoagie. Each sandwich is packed with provolone cheese, lettuce, tomatoes, and onions, then with whatever meat guts you like—tuna, Italian ham, roast beef, chicken salad—whatever. Just come hungry, as these sandwiches are for a working man's or woman's appetite. Brady's also sells wings, burgers, chicken, steak sandwiches, and salads. Lunch, dinner in season. Lunch in the off season. $.

Brian's Waffle House

609-967-3058
2408 Dune Dr., Avalon 08202

It's all breakfast all the time at this busy waffle house which, of course, sells other breakfast items, like pancakes, omelets, and cereal. Their multigrain waffles are surprisingly like the not-so-healthy variety—if you don't add the generous pats of butter that come with each entrée. Don't let the long lines outside deceive you. Brian's is bigger inside than it looks from the outside, and the wait is shorter than you'd expect, unless you're vying for one of the few outside tables. No credit cards. Breakfast, lunch in season. $.

Café Loren

609-967-8228
www.cafeloren.com
2288 Dune Dr., Avalon, 08202

This restaurant, which Zagat rates as one of the best at the New Jersey Shore, dishes up classic American cuisine in a casual setting (though they do ask that gentlemen wear collared shirts). You can go with the Café Loren tried and true, like the grilled lobster tail (as appetizer or entrée), grilled pork tenderloin, or grilled filet mignon, or try one of chef/owner Stephen Serano's daily menu additions. BYOB. Dinner in season. Closed Monday. $$$.

Circle Pizza

609-967-7566
www.avalonpizza.com
2108 Dune Dr., Avalon 08202

A popular pizza spot for over 40 years, especially with the late-night crowd looking for a post-bar snack. The menu, which is eat-in or takeout, leans heavily on pizza, of course, but also includes sandwiches and a surprisingly diverse salad selection, featuring oriental, house, garden, Greek, and Cobb salads, to name a few. Lunch, dinner. Late night in season only. $.

Circle Tavern at the Princeton

609-967-3456
2008 Dune Dr., Avalon 08202
www.princetonbar.com

Let's just get this out of the way: the Princeton, or the "P" as it's also known, is the place to end your night if you like to have a few drinks, and dance to rocking cover bands or top-40 hits with a few thousand of your closest friends. You either love or hate the crowds, the noise, and the high levels of alcohol intake. *But*—that's not to detract from the Circle Tavern portion of the Princeton, which is open year-round and does a good job dishing up quality lunch and dinner items that are reasonably priced. The Burger-Bomb, which is an apple-smoked burger with bacon, mushrooms, and cheese, is a tasty flip on an old classic. But if you're looking for a relaxing meal, you're best served getting out of there before 9 PM, which is when the nighttime and bar crowds start flocking in. Lunch, dinner. $.

Cheese! By Isabel
609-368-5055
2208 Dune Dr., Avalon 08202

You can pick up a salty or sweet snack at this cheese shop, but the main attraction at Cheese! By Isabel is the party platters. Packages come to serve six to a dozen people, and range from breakfast items to cheese trays, sandwiches, and desserts. If you're going in the store and looking for a price break, check out the "baked yesterday" items—just as good at a fraction of the price. They also have a bakery and café over at 225 Dune Drive called Isabel. Breakfast, lunch, dinner in season. $$.

Concord Café
609-368-5505
www.concordsuites.com
Concord Suites
7800 Dune Dr., Avalon 08202

This is where the locals go, and no wonder. The Concord's been voted best bar food and best burger in the *Gazette of Cape May County* for 10 years. Create your own burger to your personal perfection, or make a meal of the bar foods. The fries doused in wing

sauce and crumbled blue cheese is enough for two. It's a small place that's always packed in the summer, so prepare to wait, or grab one of the few seats at the bar. Lunch, dinner. $.

Cooper's Original Snowballs New Orleans Style
609-967-1350
2819 Dune Dr., Avalon 08202

It's not quite water ice, but not quite slushie. The snowball is somewhere in between. They'll make you this cool dish in over 70 flavors, including Splenda-sweetened varieties as well. Open 6 PM–10 PM in season. $.

Dining Room at the Golden Inn
609-368-5155
www.goldeninn.com
Golden Inn
7849 Dune Dr., Avalon 08202

For over 40 years, the Dining Room at the Golden Inn has been a Shore staple for fine dining with a casual feel. Their gourmet dishes comes in sizes for all appetites—they put both small and large plates on the menu, which Chef Ralph Sitero loads with surf and turf items like his signature crunchy Golden Inn jumbo shrimp and simple filet of beef with wild mushroom sauce. Reservations recommended. Lunch, dinner. $$$.

Maggie's
609-368-7422
2619 Dune Dr., Avalon 08202

The No Whining shirts aren't directed at you. It's Maggie's (the name of the owner) motto, and it's what she told her grandchildren, so they put it on the shirt. The dining is casual during the day, but the tables are draped with linens at night to class things up. Maggie's runs a free book swap, too. Breakfast, lunch, and dinner. $–$$.

Dunes are behind a fence for a reason.

Dunes: Keep Off

There's a reason walking or playing on the dunes carries such a heavy fine and possible jail time. They're a very important geographic feature all along the Jersey Shore, and they help control flood waters and are homes to important Shore ecosystems.

Dunes are what they look like: hills of sand. They're kept stocked by the wind, which, if blowing more than 10 miles per hour, will push sand up onto the hill. Some dunes are also manmade. But what makes the pile of sand a dune is the dune grass, which helps trap sand. Its root system keeps it in place, too, instead of letting it be blown away again by a sea breeze.

If you walk on the dune, you're breaking up that root system, and thus breaking up the dune and making already overdeveloped areas more prone to storm and flood damage. So stay on the paths (and maybe thumb your nose at the outlandish mansions built on dunes in Avalon—whose *first* home is that big?)

Mallon's

609-967-5400
www.mallonsbakery.com
2105 Ocean Dr., Avalon 08202

If you like sticky buns, then this is your spot—Mallon's makes 14 flavors of this gooey treat. They also sell other freshly made sweet breakfast treats, like home-made doughnuts, muffins, and crumb cake, plus bagels, cookies, and coffee. No credit cards. Hours vary, but they always serve around the breakfast and lunch hours in season. Weekends only in the spring and fall. $.

The Mouse Trap

609-967-3551
2301 Dune Dr., Avalon 08202

When the Mouse Trap moved to the other side of Dune Drive, not much changed except for their updated home—and that's a good thing. They still stock gourmet cheeses (both domestic and imported) as well as fresh bread, rolls, and party platters. I'll miss those mouse and cheese drawings in front of the old location, though. Breakfast, lunch, dinner in season. $.

Nancy Lynn Candies

609-967-4780
3289 Dune Dr., Avalon 08202

Call it a candy store with a lot of options. Nancy's sells your typical candies and sweets but also has a coffee bar, smoothie bar, and a cereal bar—pick from over 30 types of cereal, and feel free to mix and match, too. Open 10 AM–10 PM in season. $.

Oceanside Seafood

609-368-2114
2489 Dune Dr., Avalon 08202

It's an eatery in two parts—literally. You can pick up freshly made platters cooked to order with items like chicken, shrimp, oysters, scallops, flounder, crabs, grouper, and tilapia. Or eat in at the casual dine-in restaurant side, where the selection is very much the same but with an appetizer menu and pasta dishes added in. Sandwiches until 4 PM, too. If you're a DIY kind of person, or a chef in your own right, Oceanside Seafood has a fresh seafood market, so you can pick up your shrimp, scallops, clams, crabs, fish, or lobster to take home and cook as you please. Ice packing included. Lunch, dinner in season. $–$$.

Bobby Dee's Rock 'n Chair

609-967-3300
www.rocknchair.net
2409 Dune Dr., Avalon 08202

You don't get much more of a local tradition than dinner at the Rock 'n Chair. The food is upscale but in a casual setting. I highly recommend the tequila-marinated seafood martini, made with Titi shrimp, sea scallops, jumbo lump crabmeat, and mussels marinated in tequila, lime, and tomato salsa. It's an interesting way to mix seafood and alcohol. Upstairz at the Chair is one of the more upscale bars in the area, though the jeans and T-shirt crowd takes over on Sunday nights for Quizzo. The "little Cuban" sandwich goes perfectly with your trivia. Lunch, dinner. Rock 'n Chair: open year-round. Upstairz: open in season. $$–$$$$.

The Sea Grill

609-967-5511
www.seagrillrestaurant.com
225 21st St., Avalon 08202

There's no set menu at the Sea Grill—instead, check out what sea and land items are being offered that day by reading the blackboard, and tell the chef what you'd like and how you want it cooked. Don't skip over the artwork—all those funky paintings are from the owners' private collection. The Sea Grill also has an extensive wine list with nightly wine specials. $$$.

Sylvester's

609-967-7553
www.sylvesters-avalon.com
503 21st St., Avalon 08202

Eat your meal under the rolling awnings, or call ahead to take home seafood meals from this popular eatery. Sylvester's also carries pasta dishes, platters, and sandwiches. Lunch, dinner in season. $$.

Tonio's Pizza

609-368-5558
2475 Ocean Dr., Avalon 08202

Tonio's dishes up more than just pizza, even if that's the most popular item after midnight. The wings are some of the best on

Early evening rush at the Windrift outdoor patio

the island. For a double dose of Tonio's favorites, go for the buffalo chicken-topped pizza. Lunch, dinner. Late night in season only. $.

Tortilla Flats
609-967-5658
2540 Dune Dr., Avalon 08202

The Mexican food is authentic at this casual eatery that looks like a tiny restaurant in Mexico. The paper decorations hanging from the ceiling are particularly festive. Don't skip out on the warm tortilla chips brought to your table, and it's worth ordering a side of freshly made guacamole to go with them. Portions can be larger than life, so don't plan on needing to get lunch the next day. If you're eating on the go, Tortilla Flats has its own takeout kitchen up the street at 26th and Dune Drive, which is also open for lunch. Dinner in season. $$.

Uncle Bill's Pancake House
609-967-8448
3189 Dune Dr., Avalon 08202

Get your day going at Uncle Bill's, which packs in hungry patrons in just about every South Jersey Shore town (poor Atlantic City and Sea Isle City). The main attraction, of course, is the pancakes, but they also have plenty of egg options, as well as waffles and sandwiches. Expect long waits on the weekends in season. No credit cards. Breakfast, lunch in season. $

Via Mare
609-368-4494
2319 Ocean Dr., Avalon 08202

You'll find large portions of pasta and seafood favorites at this upscale restaurant on Ocean Drive. You can't miss with the frutti de mare—it dishes up the best of what the ocean—and Via Mare—have to offer.

Dinner. Closed late November through mid-February. $$$.

Windrift
1-800-453-7438
www.windriftbar.com
125 80th St., Avalon, 08202

This seaside spot has two distinct sides. First is the family-friendly restaurant area that serves a wide variety of staples, like egg breakfasts, sandwiches, and seven different burger varieties, as well as a "Shipmate's Menu" for the kids. The second is the nighttime hot spot, which features two big bars downstairs, one upstairs area that overlooks the water, and people—lots of people. They come for the atmosphere, the regulars, and the cover bands that play hits that reach back to the '60s. Wing night is on Tuesdays —the smaller kitchen in the bar portion of the Windrift will prepare thousands. Breakfast, lunch, dinner in season. $$.

Whitebriar Restaurant
609-967-5225
260 2nd St., Avalon 08202

Seafood is the specialty here, especially from the well-stocked and well-made selections at the sushi bar. Enjoy a drink or meal in the outdoor Octopus Garden seating area, or stick to the wooden indoor setting. The Mermaid Bar turns into a dance club at night, with overflow crowds spilling out into the Octopus Garden. Dinner in season. $$.

STONE HARBOR

Back Bay Seafood
609-368-2022
www.backbayseafood.net
8305 3rd Ave., Stone Harbor 08247

Back Bay's slogan is "Our fish slept in the ocean last night," and they aren't kidding— everything is as fresh as you can get. Pick up the uncooked stuff at 3 PM—no reservations required. But if you want the folks at Back Bay to make up their signature crab cakes, lobster tails, shrimp, scallops, and fish dishes, call ahead for a time slot or you'll be left without dinner. Dinner in season. $$.

The Back Yard
609-368-2627
220 81st St., Stone Harbor 08247

You might forget your Shore location at the Back Yard. It's set back within a magical garden setting that includes a grape arbor. The menu is small but sophisticated, and you can trust the chef's instincts. The shellfish jambalaya is divine. Reservations recommended. BYOB. Dinner in season. $$–$$$.

Bread and Cheese Cupboard
609-368-1135
246 96th St., Stone Harbor 08247

For over 30 years, this little shop with the orange awning has been luring customers inside with the sweet, syrupy smells that waft out the front door. Sure, they sell breads and cheeses, plus birthday cakes and coffees, but it's the sticky buns that are the prized menu item. Get them with raisins or walnuts—or without. Just don't skimp on the syrup. It's what puts the sticky in the sticky buns. No credit cards. Open 7 AM—7 PM in season. $.

Coffee Talk
609-368-5282
299 96th St., Stone Harbor 08247

Caffeinate yourself at this coffeehouse and restaurant. The décor is whatever they want it to be—it's mix and match, from the turquoise vinyl diner booths to the velour fainting chair. Tables come with cards and checkerboards. Open breakfast, lunch in season. Call for off-season hours. $.

How to Eat a Sticky Bun from the Bread and Cheese Cupboard

1. Do not let anyone pick them up for you. You need to be in control of all sticky bun decisions, and if you don't go yourself, you can't revel in the rich syrup and cinnamon scents that fill this Stone Harbor bakery.

2. Buy a half dozen, at least, even if only one or two people say they're interested. Sticky buns here have a way of changing people's minds.

3. Buy the sticky buns with raisins on top. It makes them much more interesting, and you can argue that you're eating the sticky buns for the fruit. No one, however, will believe you.

4. Once you return home with your package, set the box on the counter, open the lid, and smell. Even if you picked them up from the shop, one more hit of the sticky bun smell will properly whet the appetite.

5. Choose a bun from the middle, if possible. This will ensure that you get four sides of soft, sweet dough.

6. Using your hands, pick up a bun, and bite. Savor. Chew. Repeat.

7. Lick all remaining syrup off your fingers.

8. If possible, hide the remaining sticky buns in the microwave, and repeat steps 5 through 7 throughout the day. Do not let the buns sit overnight, and never, *ever* try to freeze them for later consumption. Fresh, right from the baker's oven, is best.

Green Cuisine

609-368-1616
302 96th St., Stone Harbor 08247

If you're a health nut, this is the place to go. The menu is hearty but healthy with a plethora of pita sandwiches, salads, and wrap options. The Greek pita is my favorite—the feta, olives, veggies, and sprouts stuffed into a whole-wheat pita hit the spot more than once. They have a smoothie bar in house, too. It gets crowded, so they have a stack of magazines to keep you occupied if the wait is too long. No credit cards. Lunch, dinner in season. $.

Harbor Pub

609-368-8800
261 96th St., Stone Harbor 08247

This bar and eatery, which is smack in the middle of 96th Street, has changed names a few times, but it's essentially the same—hearty bar fare during the day and evening, and a local hot spot at night. Kids free Tuesdays with a paying adult. Lunch, dinner, late night. $.

Henny's

609-368-2929
www.hennys.com
9628 3rd Ave., Stone Harbor 08247

This gray building might look a little weathered on the outside (which is true—it's in its fourth generation of family ownership, and the current location was "new" in 1935), but it's a Stone Harbor tradition and dishes up good food and drinks year-round. A big draw is the entertainment—Quizzo and live music are as regular here as Henny's deviled clams. Henny's is a popular breakfast option as well—it's served in season only. Closed Mondays in the off season. Breakfast, lunch, dinner in season. Lunch, dinner in the off season. $$.

Henny's

Kohr Brothers

www.kohrbros.com

609-368-5294

274 96th St, Stone Harbor 08247

This ice cream spot started in York, Pennsylvania in 1917, when Archie Kohr bought an ice cream machine and included homemade ice cream with the family's milk delivery services. Archie and brother Elton made some adjustments to the recipe, and the machine, and came up with a soft-serve product. The addition of eggs to the recipe stiffened the ice cream (which is why it's called frozen custard), and helped the sweet treat stand up in that swirl. Kohrs custard is

Fred's Tavern
609-368-5591
314 96th St., Stone Harbor 08247

It's all about the bar at this Stone Harbor staple. At Fred's, it's dark wood in a dark room with a rocking jukebox, plus live music in season. It's an early opener, too, if you're looking to start your night in the afternoon, or cool off with an ice-cold beer. You'll see plenty of Fred's T-shirts around town. It's that popular.

Why did I put this in a sidebar? Because Fred's isn't exactly known for its fine dining options—just good drinks and good company.

lower in sugar and fat than regular ice cream. For the best of both worlds, try the vanilla chocolate swirl. Open 7 AM–10 PM in season. Weekends only mid-September through late December. $.

Marabella's
609-368-5037
www.marabellasfamilyrestaurant.com
9426 3rd Ave., Stone Harbor 08247

Marabella's has been serving up homemade Italian food in Stone Harbor since 1972. The food, as you can imagine, leans heavily toward pasta and seafood dishes, but in an environment that welcomes the smaller members of your family. It's still family owned and operated. While they don't take reservations, you can call 30 minutes before you expect to arrive so that you can be put on the waiting list before you get there. You might still have a wait, though, once you arrive, especially on summer weekends. BYOB. Dinner. Breakfast Saturday and Sunday. $$.

Sea Salt
609-368-3302
www.seasaltstoneharbor.com
8307 3rd Ave., Stone Harbor 08247

Sea Salt is a local favorite for a gourmet meal in a casual yet romantic setting. Chef Lucas Manteca makes sure to use ingredients—from seafood to dairy to meats—from local farms, pastures, and waters. Manteca, originally from Argentina, has traveled the world, so influences from all over play into the menu, which changes frequently according to what's being delivered. BYOB. Dinner in season. Closed Tuesday. $$.

Stone Harbor Pizza
609-368-5454
315 96th St., Stone Harbor 08247

Eat in or take out from this bayside pizza parlor. The outdoor, shaded eating area with bay views is popular on nice days in the summer. Lunch, dinner. $.

Springers Homemade Ice Cream
609-368-4631
www.springersicecream.com
9420 3rd Ave., Stone Harbor, 08247

Yes, they do make their own ice cream (over 50 flavors) at this old-fashioned parlor, which has been in Stone Harbor since Prohibition. You can eat in, or take your cone, gelato, or sorbet to eat outside on one of the many benches. They'll make custom milkshakes, too. Expect to wait on weekends in the summer—the line can stretch out the door. Open 11 AM–11 PM in season. $.

Uncle Bill's Pancake House
609-368-8129
304 96th St., Stone Harbor 08247

Get your day going at Uncle Bill's, which packs in hungry patrons in just about every South Jersey Shore town (poor Atlantic City and Sea Isle City). The main attraction, of course, is the pancakes, but they also have plenty of egg options as well as waffles and sandwiches. Expect long waits on the weekends in season. No credit cards. Breakfast, lunch in season. $.

Ice cream at Springers

CAPE MAY COURT HOUSE

Karen & Rei's
609-624-8205
www.karenandrei.com
1882 RT 9 N., Clermont 08210

This Zagat-rated restaurant might be tucked away along NJ 9, but that doesn't mean the food is lacking in comparison to on-island dining. Chef Karen Nelson has created a New American menu that is a wonderful blend of tastes and textures, including a mahogany clam chowder, baked hazelnut-encrusted brie, and classic filet au poivre. For a different dining experience, choose something from the self-proclaimed "Eclectic Fare" portion of the menu. Reservations recommended. No credit cards. BYOB. Dinner. Closed Tuesday. $$$.

ATTRACTIONS, PARKS & RECREATION

AVALON

3206 Fitness
609-368-4242
3206 Dune Dr., Avalon 08202

This gym offers the usual cardio and weight machines, but also runs yoga classes and keeps some equipment in an outdoor area for a breezy workout experience. Open 7 AM–8 PM Monday through Friday; 7 AM–7 PM Saturday; and 7 AM–6 PM Sunday. Call for off-season hours.

Brian's Amazing Water Wars
609-967-3058
2438 Dune Dr., Avalon 08202

Cool off in competitive fashion. At Brian's you can launch water balloons at your not-so-unsuspecting prey. Open 9 AM–9:30 PM in season. $.

Hollywood Bicycle Center

609-967-5500

www.hollywoodbikeshop.com

2522 Dune Dr., Avalon 08202

Rent your ride at this bike shop, or look for something new. They also repair bikes and offer free air for your tires. Make sure to check out the collection of Simpsons, Pee Wee Herman, and Austin Powers toys that line the shop's ceiling. Open 8:30 AM–5 PM Monday, Tuesday, Thursday, Friday, Saturday, and 10 AM–5 PM Sunday. Open in season only.

Spa Avalon

609-368-3400

www.spaavalon.net

2488 Dune Dr., Avalon 08202

This sunny, sea-themed salon offers typical spa services, like massages and facials, along with salon treatments like manicures, pedicures, and makeup. To up the ante, go for one of their body wraps. The Detox Thallaso Wrap will help you rebound if you overindulged on vacation. Open 9:30 AM–5:30 PM Monday through Saturday and 10 AM–4 PM Sunday. $$$–$$$$.

STONE HARBOR

Harbor Bike & Beach

609-368-3691

9828 3rd Ave., Stone Harbor 08247

This venerable establishment has kept Stone Harbor on wheels for almost 50 years now. You can rent just about any kind of bike you'd want, plus surreys and tandem bikes. They also sell and repair bikes, inline skates, skim boards, and metal detectors. $–$$.

Stone Harbor Bird Sanctuary

11400 3rd Avenue, Stone Harbor. 08247

These 21 acres have been saved for the birds since 1965. Because the National Park Service has designated the sanctuary a National Natural Landmark, it won't be falling to condo projects anytime soon. What kinds of birds can you expect to find? The American, snowy, and cattle egrets are known to nest here, along with Louisiana, great blue, green, little blue, yellow, and black-crowned night herons, and glossy ibis. Free.

The Wetlands Institute

609-368-1211

www.wetlandsinstitute.org

1075 Stone Harbor Blvd., Stone Harbor 08247

Learn all the ecosystems around you at the Wetlands Institute. It's a water wonderland for the eco-friendly, with hands-on exhibits, a "terrapin station," nature trail, observation decks, and children's area with interactive exhibits. It'll make anyone think twice about dumping trash on the Shore—or even about the megamansions being built on the dunes. Open 9:30 AM–4:30 PM Monday to Thursday and 10 AM–4 PM Sunday in season; 9:30 AM–4:30 PM Tuesday to Saturday in the off season. $.

CLERMONT

The Pines at Clermont
609-624-0100
www.pinesatclermont.com
358 Kings Hwy., Clermont 08201

This nine-hole, Brent grass course is a quick play—a round averages under two hours. But it's a tick more challenging than the other short courses in the area, with holes split almost evenly between par three and four holes. $–$$.

CAPE MAY COURT HOUSE

Avalon Golf Course
609-465-GOLF
www.avalongolfclub.net
1510 RT 9 N., Cape May Court House 08210

If you've got a mixed bag—of players, not clubs—Avalon Golf Course is a good bet, as you can play one of four sets of tees to make your course between 4,924 and 6,325 yards. The course features a lot of water hazards, and even though it's inland, it's still close enough to the marshes and water to make wind a factor during play. $$.

Cape May Bird Observatory: The Center for Research and Education
609-861-0700
www.njaudubon.org/centers/cmbo/
600 RT 47 N., Cape May Court House 08210

This 8,600-square-foot center is the inland outpost for the Cape May Bird Observatory's Cape May location. Though inland, it's still surrounded by 26 acres of marsh and upland. Open 9 AM–4:30 PM. Free.

Bayside

If someone gives you an address that's something "bayside," like "21st Street, bayside," that means the location (probably a shore house) is located over the 21st Street bridge on a cluster of streets that's separated from the main Avalon island by the bay.

Most buildings on the bayside are private residences, many rented out to Shore vacationers, though here you will also find the Avalon Marina (great spot for breakfast) and Sylvester's (excellent crab cakes). It can be quieter than Avalon proper, though some of those Shore houses have rowdy parties at night on summer weekends. Police patrol regularly and stop too much zaniness before it gets out of hand.

Billy Bob's Family Fun Center

609-624-2500

2276 RT 9 N., Cape May Court House 08210

This roadside driving range has 24 tees for you and your favorite club, though you can borrow a course driver if you don't have your own. Billy Bob's also has batting cages, ice cream, mini golf, and video games, hence the "family fun center" part of the name. Remember your bug spray. Billy Bob's is built back into the woods, which makes for great vistas as you slice, shank, or drive, but also invites mosquitoes to feast on golfers. Open 9 AM–10 PM in season. $.

Miniature Golf Courses

If your idea of tee time is more putter than driver, check out these miniature golf options.

Club 18 Miniature Golf

609-368-4362

9505 3rd Ave., Stone Harbor 08247

Tee Time Green Rooftop Minigolf

609-967-5574

221 96th St., Stone Harbor 08247

Pirate Island Golf

609-368-8344

2738 Dune Dr., Avalon 08202

Cape May County Park & Zoo

609-465-5271

www.co.cape-may.nj.us

RT 9 & Crest Haven Rd., Cape May Court House 08210

The Cape May County Park & Zoo is worth visiting for a few reasons. First, it's free (though donations are greatly appreciated). Second, it's not just a zoo. It's a park, too, with picnic grounds, playgrounds, woods, a pond, gazebo, and now a disc golf course. Zoo open 10 AM–4:45 PM in season; 10 AM–3:45 PM in the off season. Park open 9 AM–dusk. Free.

A peacock at the Cape May County Zoo

Turtle Power

Sure, the Shore is busiest in the summer, but not just for humans—for turtles as well. Prime vacation time is also when female diamondback terrapins lay their eggs, and their nesting grounds just happen to be near the causeways that bring tourists from the inland areas to the Shore.

What can you do? To start, be careful when driving on the causeways.

If you see a turtle on the side of the road, stop and put him or her back into the salt marshes, or call the Wetlands Institute in Stone Harbor at 609-368-1211. They work through the nesting season to make sure turtles—and their nests—stay safe.

If you see a turtle that's been killed, that doesn't mean that it is a lost cause. The Wetlands Institute will take recently killed female turtles and harvest their eggs, incubate them, and then hatch the young. If you are willing to take a killed turtle to the institute, make sure that you wrap the body in plenty of towels and plastic—they can bleed profusely, but you'll be helping preserve an important part of the wetlands environment. Or call the Wetlands Institute, and they'll come out to collect the turtle.

Cape May Court House Historical Museum & John Holmes House
609-465-3535
www.cmcmuseum.org
504 RT 9 N., Cape May Court House 08210

Step back as far as the 17th century at the Cape May Court House Historical Museum, which is located in what was previously known as the John Holmes House. In 2005, the historical society hired Joan Berkey, a historic preservation consultant, to set the record straight on what the house had been, so the building's history has been completely rewritten—or rediscovered. For example, the house might be named after John Holmes, but recent research suggests that he didn't build the structure that stands today. In any case, it's still a nifty spot to check out the life and times of culture gone by, even if the past isn't too far away—the Military Room has artifacts from the Revolutionary through Gulf wars. Don't miss the stagecoaches and wagons that are housed in the barn. Open 10 AM—2 PM Tuesday to Saturday June to August; open 10 AM—2 PM Tuesdays in September. Call for off-season schedule. $.

Leaming's Run Gardens
609-465-5871
www.leamingsrungardens.com
1845 RT 9 N., Cape May Court House 08210

This private garden, which is the largest annual garden in the country, features more than 30 acres of gardens, ferns, lawns, and ponds. Leaming's has over 25 individually designed gardens to explore and enjoy, and plenty of benches are provided throughout the grounds. The best time to visit is in August, which is when the hummingbirds come back to town. Open 9:30 AM—5 PM in season. $.

Shopping

AVALON

Ciao Bella & Bellissima Boutique
609-967-4343
268 21st St., Avalon 08202

These two new connected shops in Avalon cater to those in the fashion know. They stock ultra-designer labels like Tory Burch and BCBG in Ciao Bella and high-end shoes like those from Christian Lacroix in Bellissima. Both shops lean heavily on very personal, one-on-one service. Plus, Bellissima has a section for any significant others who have to tag along—with magazines to fill their wait time. Open 10 AM–9 PM Monday through Saturday and 10 AM–8 PM Sunday in season. Call for off-season hours.

Antiques Etc.
609-967-5500
280 20th St., Avalon, NJ   08202

It's not just antiques in this big, rambling store. Different vendors sell new and antique goods, mostly in the home décor area, but you can also find purses, jewelry, and linens. Open 10 AM–6 PM in season; 10 AM–5 PM in the off season.

Bellissima Boutique Bellissima Boutique

A Note About Shop Hours

In season, most Shore shops have a set schedule. Off season is a completely different story. If I had tried to track every nuance of every off-season schedule, you'd be reading an encyclopedia—almost every shop is of the mom-and-pop variety, which means they can pick and choose when they'd like to stay open in the off season. Good for them. But it would have made for a messy guidebook.

In these cases, I've listed the in-season hours and a note if you should call for when the stores are open in the off season. Some are open weekends, some have weekday hours. Some open whenever the owner feels like it, so call ahead. Also, some shop owners told me that they'll close early in season if the weather's bad or if they're not seeing much foot traffic. So it's worth calling ahead anytime of year.

Armadillo
609-368-3000
www.armadilloltd.com
2761 Dune Dr., Avalon 08202

It's not easy to describe what Armadillo stocks because their selection is so eclectic—whatever strikes the owners' fancy is in the store. Their items range from fine art to casual décor. They also offer corporate and personal shopping, and a registry. Open 10 AM–4 PM Sunday through Friday and 10 AM–5 PM Saturday.

Closet Boutique
609-368-7400
2509 Dune Dr., Avalon 08202

Closet Boutique is the place to go for the stylish family. They sell men's and women's apparel (LeTigre, Penguin, and American Apparel for him; Park, Tibi, Ella Moss, and LaROK for her), plus cute items for baby. Open 10 AM–9 PM Sunday through Thursday and 10 AM–10 PM Friday and Saturday in season. Call for off-season hours.

It's All Good
609-368-0001
2307 Dune Dr., Avalon 08202

Pick up quality cotton goods, like T-shirts and sweats with your favorite Shore town (of course, they lean toward Avalon items) at this store. They also stock Margaritaville flip-flops. Watch out for that pot pot. Open 10 AM–8 PM in season. Call for off-season hours.

Pale Moon Boutique
609-368-1227
2488 Dune Dr., Avalon 08202

You'll find upscale fashions for men, women, kids, and tots at Pale Moon Boutique. It's also home to the Brendan Borek High Tides Memorial Fund, which raises money for area families who have children suffering from pediatric cancer. Memorial-related items, like sweatshirts, T-shirts, and onesies, sold in the shop raise money for the fund. Open 10 AM–9 PM in season.

Paper Peddler
609-967-4542
2538 Dune Dr., Avalon 08202

Paper Peddler sells books, magazines, and activity books for the family in this slip of a store that's been selling great reads since before you could read the news online. You might even be tempted to pick up a few titles for your post-vacation reading. They can order in books within two to three days if they don't have something that appeals to your taste, or if you need a specific title. Open 8 AM–10 PM in season.

She Be Surfing
609-967-3110
2516 Dune Dr., Avalon 08202

Surf-inspired gear for tweens, teens, and women with a knack for beachy fashions are sold at this elevated shop. They also offer surfing lessons taught by women for girls and women. Open 9 AM–10 PM in season. Call for off-season hours.

STONE HARBOR

Atlantic Book Shops
609-368-4393
261 96th Street, 106 Harbor Square Mall, Stone Harbor 08247

This is as close as you'll get to a bookstore chain at the South Jersey Shore. Atlantic has locations in just about every town in this book. They stock new titles, bargain books, maps, magazines, and items for the kids. Open 9 AM–10 PM in season. Call for off-season hours.

Barrier Island Trading Post
609-368-1415
www.barrierislandtradingpost.com
9501 3rd Ave., Stone Harbor 08247

Take a detour to this off-the-main-street used bookstore, and you're sure to score a bargain. Most books are priced between $1 and $5. They also stock rare first editions and collectible books, as well as select new titles and CDs. You can also trade in your books for store credit—but if it's a hardcover you'd like to trade in, it must have the dustjacket. Open 10 AM–10 PM in season. Call for off-season hours.

Shopping in Stone Harbor

Most of Stone Harbor's shops are located on 96th Street between 2nd and 3rd Avenues. But don't skip the shops on 2nd or 3rd—they range from a discount shoe shop to a used bookstore to an upscale, block-large boutique. 96th Street also has a lot of ice cream and sweets options, though most restaurants are located off the main strip.

96th Street in Stone Harbor

Barries Shoes

609-368-8200

www.barrieshoes.com

9501 3rd Ave., Stone Harbor 08247

Barries sells comfort shoes, including Naturalizer, Hush Puppy, New Balance, Sperry, and Minnetonka, at outlet prices. They stock narrow and wide sizes, too, plus flip-flops and handbags. Take note: the shoes are *not* irregulars, damaged goods, or so ridiculously out of style that it would be natural to see them priced so low. Open 10 AM–5 PM.

Bellanova

609-368-0606

218 96th St., Stone Harbor 08247

Check out beach wear and fashions for ladies who don't want to show too much skin. They also stock big floppy straw hats, reading sunglasses, and designer jeans. Open 10 AM–10 PM in season; 10 AM–5 PM weekends in the off season.

Calypso Nature & Nautical Shop

609-368-2002

268 96th St., Stone Harbor 08247

If it has to do with the beach, it's in this store, whether it's a miniature lifeguard stand made into a lamp, a shell jewelry box, or a boat wheel that's living its second life as a clock. They also have hermit crabs for the kiddies, plus Beanie Babies, shark teeth, and dolls. Open 10 AM–9:30 PM Sunday through Thursday and 10 AM–10 PM Friday and Saturday in season. Call for off-season hours.

Glassroots Gallery

609-368-8805

www.glassrootsgallery.com

9600 3rd Ave., Stone Harbor 08247

You'll see the eclectic at this shop, like sculptures, artwork, and paperweights made by glass artists from around the country. Popular items are wine, liquor, and beer bottles that have been flattened to form cheese plates and serving dishes. Open 10 AM–10 PM in season. Call for off-season hours.

The Happy Hunt

609-368-5734

9720 3rd Ave., Stone Harbor 08247

If you've got a daughter who likes horses, this is the place to go. You'll find a lot of horse wear—girl-sized, too—like sweatshirts, necklaces, and plush ponies. Happy Hunt also sells stuff for grown-ups, including fuzzy Stone Harbor sweatshirts and Charles River waterproof jackets and pants. Custom embroidery done on site. Open 10 AM–9 PM in season. Call for off-season hours.

Free Shop

609-368-5874
266 96th St., Stone Harbor 08247

For the fashionista with labels on her mind, this shop stocks denim from True Religion and Seven and Paige, plus cool, classic, and pricey looks from Juicy Couture and James Pearse. Don't skip the sunglasses collection, which is surprisingly affordable—I found a few pairs for under $10 a pair. Open 10 AM–10 PM in season. Call for off-season hours.

Frog & Toad

609-368-2800
9500 3rd Ave., Stone Harbor 08247

Anything goes at this spot, from silk floral arrangements to weathered frames to the perfect painted wooden letters for your daughter's bedroom. They carry items with a stamp of snark, too, like napkins emblazoned with the initials PMS. Open 10 AM–10 PM Call for off-season hours.

Jewelry Studio

609-967-4653
www.jewelry-studio.com
250 96th St., Stone Harbor 08247

You'll find a stunning variety of jewelry and watches in this store, which the Metzler family has owned and operated since 1982. You can gawk at or, of course, buy the engagement rings, diamond jewelry, watches, and precious stones. They also sell what you'll need to start, or add to, silver charm bracelets. Open 10 AM–5 PM.

Lace Silhouettes Lingerie

609-368-1259
www.lacesilhouetteslingerie.com
9504 3rd Ave., Stone Harbor 08247

Looking for a little something special for your romantic Stone Harbor stay? And I do mean little at Lace Silhouettes Lingerie, which sells romantic and sexy pieces. They also stock comfort staples, like fuzzy socks and robes. Open 10 AM–10 PM in season. Call for off-season hours.

Lighten Up

1-800-679-5747
www.lightenuponline.com
283 96th St., Stone Harbor 08247

You'll find toys for kids and grown-ups at this whimsical store, owned by the father-son pair of Todd and Shem Jenkins. They have a big selection of kites, windsocks, flags, toys, mind-bending puzzle games, and juggling equipment, as well as marbles. Make sure you visit the upstairs level—it's a high-flying adventure. Open 10 AM–10 PM in season; 11 AM–4 PM off season.

Hoy's vs. Seashore Ace

Hoy's and Seashore Ace are both stores in Stone Harbor that sell everything you could possibly need for your Shore vacation. But which is better for suntan lotion? A coffee maker? Souvenirs? Beach chairs? I asked a few Shore regulars (e.g., my parents, who between them have more than 80 years of Shore experience) where they'd go for what you forgot to pack:

Hoy's
609-368-4697
219 96th St., Stone Harbor 08247

Toys • Puzzles • Playing cards • Beach games • Books • Flip-flops • Suntan lotion • Hats • Postcards • Snacks • Cold drinks • Boogie boards

Seashore Ace
609-368-3191
260 96th St., Stone Harbor 08247
www.seashoreace.com

Cooking utensils • Cooking gadgets • Paper and plastic utensils • Beach chairs • Outdoor furniture • Beach towels • Tools • Hardware supplies • Sports equipment

Beach toys at Hoy's

Running at the Shore

While writing this book, I also kept up my four-days-a-week running routine (yes, I'm type A—how'd you guess?), which starts in Cape May and ends in Ocean City. Since I lived down the Shore during that summer of research, it meant that I needed to train, obviously, down the Shore.

But running here and running at home, which for me is the Philadelphia suburbs, are two different animals. You face different obstacles, from the weather to the tourists, and more running options. Here are a few tips on how to train by the sea:

1. Beware the sand. Sure, running on the beach might sound like a romantic idea in that "I'll be able to clear my mind" kind of way. But it can be hard on your calves and knees, especially if you choose to run on the hard-packed sand by the water's edge—it's on a slope. If you are going to give beach running a go, make sure you mix in some boardwalk or street time. Your legs will thank you. If you're a huge fan of beach running, you might want to try Captain Bill Gallagher Island Run, which takes places in Sea Isle City every August. Seven miles of the 10-mile course is on the beach.

2. Beware the tourists. Whether they're driving, walking, or biking, you need to be aware of the people around you because the streets are packed in season, and the last thing you want to do is get hit. Be especially careful in Ocean City if you're running in the streets because the combination of heavy traffic, narrow streets, and parked cars blocking views around corners can be dangerous. Do whatever you can to stay out of the bike lanes in Avalon—I've come close to accidents with a few bikers.

3. Check the wind. They don't call them ocean breezes for nothing—and a wind during your run can either push you along or hold you back. If you're going to run by the water, make sure that you run there in both directions. That way, you will be fighting the wind in one direction only. I tried to run up Dune Drive and down Ocean Drive in Avalon for one run. I had the ocean wind in my face on Dune Drive, but didn't get the same push back on Ocean Drive because it didn't have the sea breezes. It was not a fun workout.

4. Heat trap. Even if Shore towns are close to the water, they won't completely escape heat and humidity. I ran and researched on a few scorchers. So stay tuned to the weather forecast, and

Love the Cook
609-967-5252
www.lovethecook.com
272 96th St., Stone Harbor 08247

Did you ever know you needed an elephant teapot so badly? What about sea-themed barbecue tongs, or a cow oven mitt? You'll find what you never knew you were looking for at this kitchen specialty shop, along with spices, rubs, and gourmet coffees and teas. Open 10 AM–10 PM in season. Call for off-season hours.

Madame's Port
609-967-3332
www.madames-port.com
324 96th St., Stone Harbor 08247

make sure to check for the possibility of afternoon thunderstorms on those hot days. If you're spending a lot of time in the sun, or in the bars, you might want to recalculate your hydration. Both sun and fun can take a lot out of you, which could dehydrate you before a run.

5. Boardwalk bounce. I write about health and fitness and was told by one sports doctor that the absolute best place to run is on wooden boardwalks. Why? Because the wood gives, and since it's suspended on air, the combined effect is much more cushioning than running on asphalt, concrete, or sand. Atlantic City, Ocean City, and Wildwood have the most distance to offer on their boardwalks, but be careful about when you run, especially if you're going in season. Mornings belong to bikes and surreys, and nighttime brings crowds that can be difficult to navigate through just walking. I found that bright and early—like before 6 AM—is best in season.

6. Map your routes online. You don't need to use your car's odometer to measure how far you'll go. Go to www.gmap-pedometer.com and punch in the name of your Shore town. It's easier to see a bird's-eye view of where you're visiting, and where you'll be running.

7. Fun run. When I toured the Edwin B. Forsythe Wildlife Refuge, the first thing that the 8-mile continuous loop brought to mind wasn't birds or wildlife—it was running. The path is hard-packed sand, and the views are unforgiving in the summer since there's little to no shade, but makes a great distance run in the spring or fall. Make sure that if you're bringing a bottle of water or sports drink (there aren't exactly water fountains in the wild) that you carry it with you through the run. You wouldn't want to litter on the beauty you're running through.

8. Run the course. The spring, summer, and fall bring plenty of races—both running and triathlon—to the Shore, so check with the town chamber of commerce to see what kinds of 5ks, fun runs, and distance runs they have scheduled for the summer. The Ocean Drive Marathon, which is in March, is a great way to cap off a fall/winter/spring training season, and to kick off the summer. And what better way to take in the sights of the drive than by foot?

9. If you forgot your gear, or are looking for something new, Wave One (221 96th St., #225, Stone Harbor, 609-368-0050, www.waveonesports.com) and the Sneaker Shop (846 Asbury Avenue, Ocean City 609-391-5223) will have what you need, whether it's new shoes or summer running clothes.

Don't let the size of this shop fool you. It might look small, but inside, Madame's Port is a cool and soothing place to visit, even if all you want to do is browse. The inventory leans heavily toward wooden items, but in interesting forms, like watches and lamps. Make sure to look up at the parasols hanging from the ceiling, and to look down at the wooden inlay on the back half of the store. You'll find an inspiring message or two right in the floor. Open 10 AM–10 PM in season. Call for off-season hours.

Mimi's Shop & SunCatcher Surf Shop
609-368-3488
www.suncatchersurf.com
9425 2nd Ave., Stone Harbor 08247

Between Mimi's and SunCatcher, you'll be able to buy surf gear, surf wear, and upscale styles for the family. You might get a little lost winding from one section to the other, but they've got everyone from tweens to your grandfather covered. Expect a lot of surf and skate staple brands, like Billabong, Volcom, O'Neill, and Roxy. The women's section is more stately and upscale, with items from Nicole Miller and Vera Bradley among the stock. If you're a bargain shopper, check out the Attic, which is located next door. It sells whatever didn't quite move at the main shop. On Labor Day Weekend, they'll drop the price of everything to $20 per item, even if it started out as a $300+ cocktail dress. Open 10 AM–10 PM in season. Call for off-season hours. Attic open in season only.

Murdough's Christmas Shop
609-368-1529
256 96th St., Stone Harbor 08247

It's been Christmas at Murdough's for over 50 years—at least in the Stone Harbor location (they also have a store in Pennsylvania). Get what you need to trim a tree, or add to your Department 56 Christmas building collection. They also sell Advent calendars, Christmas cards, and even a few Halloween items. Make sure to say hello to the golden retriever who rests behind the counter, and check the "days left until Christmas" board as you leave. There's always a countdown. Open 10 AM–10 PM in season. Call for hours in the off season.

Paw Prints
609-368-3700
www.pawprintsofstoneharbor.com
281 96th St., Stone Harbor 08247

Spoil your dog or cat with items from this pet shop. They carry collars and leashes with summer and sports team themes, plus doggie Christmas cards and treats. Make sure to check out the second floor, which is where the sales are. Open 10 AM–10 PM in season. Call for off-season hours.

Pappagallo
609-268-6141
www.pappagallostoneharbor.com
237 96th St., Stone Harbor 08247

Get preppy at this longtime Stone Harbor shop. Along with tried-and-true classic polos, khakis, and sheath dresses, Pappagallo also carries prep accessories like multicolored headbands and embroidered totes. If you're around in winter, they have a blowout clearance sale on New Year's Day. Open 10 AM–10 PM in season. Call for hours in the off season.

People People
609-368-3355
9810 3rd Ave., Stone Harbor 08247

This shop is packed with clothes in all kinds of stripes and colors, favoring the Lilly Pulitzer set. They carry fashions for ladies of all ages, from the little tykes on up. Along with bathing suits and casual wear, People People also stocks cocktail gowns and items from Save2ndBase (www.save2ndbase.com), which raises money for the Kelly Rooney Foundation for breast cancer research. Open 10 AM–9 PM in season. Call for off-season hours.

Stone Harbor Bath & Body

Stone Harbor Bath & Body

609-368-4949
www.stoneharborbathandbody.com
270 96th St., Stone Harbor, 08247

This is the place to get the goods for pampering—for both men and women. The lotions, potions, and creams are in the front part of the store, along with candles and a claw-foot tub full of loofas. The back room carries soft, comfy nighttime clothes for women and a selection of racy lingerie from Betsey Johnson. Open 10 AM–9 PM Monday through Friday, 10 AM–9 PM Friday, 10 AM–10 PM Saturday, and 10 AM–4 PM Sunday. Call for off-season hours.

Talk of the Walk

609-368-0008
www.talkofthewalk.com
248 96th St., Stone Harbor 08247

This ladies' boutique has found a home in
Atlantic City casinos since 1979, and the
Stone Harbor outpost is the new kid in
their impressive block. Talk of the Walk
stocks racks of cocktail and evening
dresses, plus shoes to go with them, along
with more casual wear and designer sunglasses. Open 10 AM–10 PM in season. Call
for hours in the off season.

Wave One Sports

609-368-0050
www.waveonesports.com
221 96th St. #225, Stone Harbor 08247

Green Stone Harbor

While the ecofriendly and preservation band-
wagon didn't pick up steam until the 21st century (with a lot of help from Al Gore), Stone
Harbor has been working to preserve its natural wonders since World War II.

In 1947, the town created a bird sanctuary
and heronry, which is still on the island today
(between 111th–117th Streets). In 1970s, they
ran a "Save the Point" beach preservation
campaign, and the Wetlands Institute, which
saves terrapins from traffic (and even harvests
eggs from victims in season) and educates
about the ecosystems of the Shore, opened in
1972.

They don't sell just any old Shore gear at Wave One. Their items, which range from
embroidered sweatshirts to hats to T-shirts to sweat pants, are high quality and last for
years. (I have three sweatshirts older than my college diploma, if that says anything.) Look
out for the sale bin, which is where odds and ends are piled together, unfolded and ready
for sifting. The Stone Harbor location is larger than the Cape May outpost and also stocks
brand name sports gear from the likes of Nike and Body Armor, in the form of everything
from running shoes to soccer-ready shorts to sports bras. Open 9 AM–10 PM in season. Call
for off-season hours.

Wetsuit World

609-368-1500
www.wetsuitworld.com
9716 3rd Ave., Stone Harbor 08247

Buy or rent your perfect wetsuit, rash guard, or board at Wetsuit World. They've got gear to
protect your skin whether you're surfing, diving, jet skiing, wakeboarding, or kite surfing.
They also have snorkeling equipment, offer surfing lessons, and repair surfboards. Open
10 AM–6 PM Monday through Thursday, 10 AM–8 PM Friday and Saturday, and 10 AM–6 PM in
season. Friday, Saturday, and Sunday in the off season.

Victorious

609-967-9222
www.victoriousantiques.com
9718 3rd Ave., Stone Harbor 08247

Browse through new and estate jewelry and décor, nestled among bags and Victorian-era
items. Make sure to check out the mirrors lining the wall. They're re-creations of mirrors
from days gone by, but still gorgeous, heavy, and expensive. Most of the items in the Stone

Teaberry Antiques, Collectibles & Gifts

Harbor store are re-creations. If you're looking for estate jewelry, your better bet is the Cape May location in Congress Hall. Open 10 AM–8 PM in season. Call for off-season hours.

CLERMONT

Garden Greenhouse
609-624-1350
www.gardengreenhouse.net
1919 RT 9 N., Cape May Court House 08210

Sure, the Greenhouse Gardens does a lot of personal landscaping business, but any gardener, or at least someone who appreciates living things, will enjoy a stroll through their garden center. It's a special treat in the winter when Christmas gifts are added in, and Santa comes to town. Open 9 AM–5 PM.

Teaberry Antiques, Collectibles & Gifts
609-624-1700
1944 RT 9, Clermont 08210

Browse for hidden treasure among over 65 kiosks in this 15,000-square-foot, air conditioned building. It's not all antiques, though—vendors also sell gourmet foods, Christmas decorations (all year), home décor, furniture, and costume jewelry. There's even a vendor who sells old magazine advertisements, ready for framing. Teaberry is attached to Avalon Coffee, so feel free to grab a bite to eat in or a drink to sip on while taking a look at what Teaberry has to offer. Open 10 AM–6 PM.

EVENTS

May

Sail into Summer Weekend
609-886-8600, X-17
www.stoneharborbeach.com
95th St. Parking Lot, Stone Harbor

Preview the upcoming summer season at this annual festival, which includes boat and seafood shows. The Chowder Fest is worth its weight in clams. $.

June

Avalon Chamber of Commerce Craft Fair
609-967-3936
www.avalonboro.org

Check out the best of local wares at this annual craft show.

July

Stone Harbor Baby Parade
609-368-6101
96th St., Stone Harbor

You know your baby's cute—let the world know it, or check out the other toddling tots. Free.

August

Tour de Shore
609-967-3456
www.princetonbar.com

Tour de Shore is part Halloween party, part bike parade, and part bar crawl. Register your team, dressed in a theme, at the Princeton and then move en masse from one Avalon bar to another. Make sure you come up with something interesting to do on stage when your team is introduced to the crowd. The money raised is for charity, not just fun. Previous themes have included angels and devils; Roman legislature; future cougar bait; and five-year-old birthday party—it's only as interesting as your team makes it. $$.

September

Nun's Beach Community Day and Surf Invitational
111th Street beach, Stone Harbor

This surf festival is held at Nun's Beach in Stone Harbor, which is right by Villa Maria, a convent of IHM Immaculata. Yes, you could see a nun on a surfboard.

Wings & Water Festival
609-368-1211
www.wetlandsinstitute.org
Wetlands Institute

Celebrate (and support) the rich wildlife of New Jersey's coast at this annual event. Kids (and, okay, you) will enjoy the turtle release, touch tank, and retriever dogs in action.

The Brendan

In 1991, Brendan Borek lost his battle with Ewing's sarcoma, a rare pediatric bone cancer. He was only 16, and before he passed away, friends organized a surf competition in his honor. Since 1991, "The Brendan" has been held in his memory, but it's much more than a surf day now. The event is the cornerstone of a project that raises funds to support area families whose children are suffering from cancer. The fund, called the "High Tides Memorial Fund," pays for whatever a family needs—gas and tolls to and from hospitals (usually in Philadelphia), hotels, scholarships, groceries, utilities, mortgages, rent. They make gift baskets around the holidays and even give siblings of children with cancer gift certificates for back-to-school shopping.

"I didn't want other families to go through the experiences we went through as a family," Lydia Borek told me as we sat and chatted at the Pale Moon Boutique (2170 Dune Drive, Avalon, 609-967-0100). The shop is owned by Lydia's daughter-in-law and is also the offices of the High Tides Memorial Fund. Pale Moon stocks casual designer items, and also sells clothes, from T-shirts to onesies, with the Brendan Borek logo and, in some cases, Brendan's art, which also decorates the walls.

A big chunk of the money that the High Tides Memorial Fund pays out is raised during one week in August, a week that includes a fashion show, art show, skateboarding event, and restaurant days, when specific menu items purchased will go toward the fund. The crowning event is that surf competition, which kicks off bright and early at 6:30 AM on Saturday. It's followed by a homecoming party in town. It's a nice cap to a long week that's doing a great thing for local families.

For more information, visit www.brendansfund.org.

There are also boat rides, kayaking, a rubber duck race, crafting, jugglers, folk music, salt marsh safaris, and dune walks. The festival benefits the Wetlands Institute. $.

November

Christmas in Stone Harbor
609-368-6101

This isn't just any holiday pre-celebration. Along with traditional Christmas festivities like tree trimming and crafts, Thanksgiving weekend is a dog celebration in Stone Harbor. There's even a parade where you can dress up like a four-legged friend. Free.

NEWSPAPERS

Seven Miles Times
609-967-7707
www.7MileTimes.com

EMERGENCY NUMBERS

In an emergency, dial 911.
Poison information: 1-800-222-1222

AVALON
Non-emergency police: 609-967-8299

STONE HARBOR
Non-emergency police: 609-368-2111

HOSPITALS

96th Street Urgent Care
609-368-3500
www.96thstreeturgentcare.com
376 96th St., Suite 2, Stone Harbor 08247

Avalon Medical Center
609-967-3800
2355 Ocean Dr., Avalon 08202

Cape Regional Medical Center
609-463-2000
www.caperegional.com
2 Stone Harbor Blvd., Cape May Court House 08210

REALTORS

Avalon Real Estate
609-967-3001
30th and Dune Dr., Avalon 08202
www.avalonrealty.com

Century 21 Alliance
1-800-828-1521
www.theshorerentalsite.com
9821 3rd Ave., Stone Harbor 08247

Dillar Fisher
877-967-SOLD and 877-368-SOLD
www.dfrealtors.com
3101 Dune Dr., Avalon 08202 and 9614 3rd Ave., Stone Harbor 08247

MM Real Estate
609-967-3099
www.mmavalon.com
2743 Dune Dr., Avalon 08202

Tim Kerr's Power Play Realty
1-800-682-5940
www.powerplayrealty.com
2821 Dune Dr., Avalon 08202

TRANSPORTATION

C&C Cab Company
115 13th Street, Ocean City 08226
609-399-9100

Enterprise Rent-A-Car
609-522-1119
www.enterprise.com

Yellow Cab
609-263-2225

TOURISM CONTACTS

Avalon Chamber of Commerce
609-967-3936
www.avalonbeach.com

Stone Harbor Chamber of Commerce
609-368-6101
www.stoneharborbeach.com

New Jersey Travel and Tourism
1-800-VISITNJ
www.state.nj.us/travel

5

The Wildwoods

Honky Tonk Thrills

Including Rio Grande

The towns that make up what's collectively known as "The Wildwoods"—North Wildwood, Wildwood, Wildwood Crest, and West Wildwood—have seen their share of ups and downs. Today the Wildwoods are on another upswing that's celebrating this 5-mile island's kitschy past.

Explorers Henry Hudson and Robert Juet discovered the island in 1609. In the 1870s, the Wildwoods became home to offshore farmers, who let their animals graze on the land. The Hereford Inlet Lighthouse was built in 1874, and soon after, the Borough of Wildwood was born, incorporated in 1895.

The Wildwoods were sleepy barrier island Shore towns before the 1950s. It took the end of a war to bring Wildwood its boom. It was a major tourist destination for Philadelphians, especially in post–World War II America, when people had a little extra money in their pockets and could afford to pack up the family and spend part of their summer down the Shore. The Wildwoods also drew an A-list crowd and became the summertime home to the Las Vegas set because air conditioning hadn't yet been able to cool the dessert. Chubby Checker first performed "the Twist" at Wildwood's Rainbow Club (now Kahunas—there's a sign with the details outside the bar), and Dick Clark's first national broadcast of *American Bandstand* was from the Starlight Ballroom on the Wildwood Boardwalk in 1957. The nightlife boomed, and so did construction, especially of motels, which were then a new concept. You didn't have to check into a hotel and walk down long corridors to get to your room—just drive up and go into your room.

But prosperity and fortunes shifted. The motels showed their age, Vegas got air conditioning, and Atlantic City made gambling legal. Wildwood didn't swing the way it once had, and many of the family-friendly spots in town converted over until the Wildwood boardwalk became a place you didn't take your kids anymore because of the prevalence of seedy T-shirt shops and piercing and tattoo parlors.

The Wildwoods' fortunes have been shifting again, this time back to the upswing. It took a group of concerned citizens to save one of the things that made Wildwood special—Doo Wop architecture—in the form of the Doo Wop Preservation League. Instead of thinking these funky buildings were passé, the town celebrated its kitsch and worked to

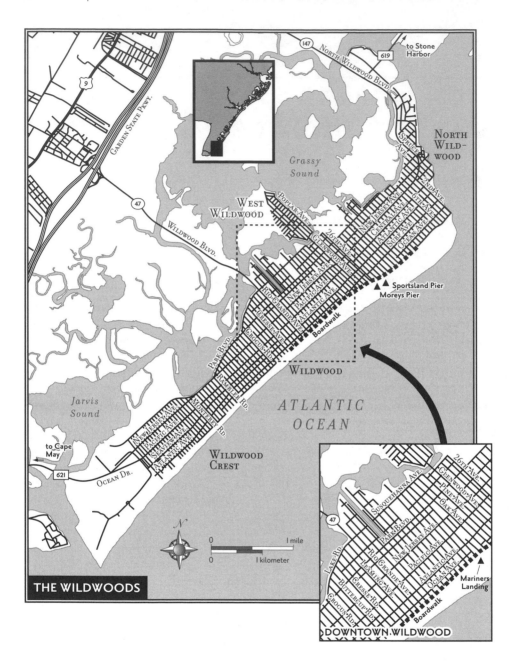

preserve their unique corner of history. Wildwood has more than 50 of these vintage motels and the largest concentration of Doo Wop motels in the country. Without the Doo Wop League, there'd be far fewer specimens—Wildwood had 100 such mid-20th-century buildings until 2000, which is when developers went demolition crazy and knocked down motels, putting up condos and duplexes in their places. You'll find most of the survivors on a 2-mile stretch between Atlantic and Ocean Avenues in Wildwood Crest.

Wildwood Beach Greater Wildwoods Tourism Authority

Today, the Wildwoods have what still attracts families to the Shore: a boardwalk, amusement rides, nightclubs and, of course, the beach. The Wildwoods have long beaches, too—up to 1,000 feet wide in some places—and they're free. The boardwalk is no longer one long strip of boarded-up shops, though you'll still find a few of those T-shirt shops and piercing parlors. The boardwalk also has rides—lots of them, more than Disney World. The towns have also worked to bring a variety of events to the island that are attracting visitors year round. The Fabulous '50s and '60s weekends, Irish Fall Festival, and Roar to the Shore attract tens of thousands of visitors. The construction of a new convention center has given the town the room and the ability to rebuild its tourism base year round.

Even though all four towns on the island work together to promote change and tourism, each has a distinctive feel. North Wildwood is more residential and has the widest beaches on the island (yes, there is a shuttle for a small fee), and the nightlife leans to the cozy, quaint Irish pub scene. Wildwood is what sizzles with the bulk of the boardwalk action, from the rides to the games to the sights. Wildwood Crest is home to many of the island's Doo Wop buildings, and has lakefront areas that offer sunset views. West Wildwood is so small that you could blink and miss it — which is why a lot of the people who live there love their small corner of the shore.

Wherever you plan to stay, you're close to everything the island has to offer—it is, after all, only 5 miles long.

Doo Wop Stop

Take that, Cleveland! "Wildwood is the birthplace of rock and roll," says Ben P. Rose, director of marketing for the Wildwoods Convention Center. In 1955, Bill Haley and the Comets performed "Rock Around the Clock" at the HofBrau Hotel in Wildwood and, folks in Wildwood say, this is the reason that their town deserves the "birthplace" distinction.

And now, more than 50 years later, the Wildwoods are well on their way to restoring and celebrating their rich mid-20th-century history. In 2007, the Doo Wop Experience, an interactive museum that pays homage to the Doo Wop music and buildings that put the Wildwoods on the map, opened in town.

"Doo Wop is more than just architecture, just music," says Dan MacElrevy of the Doo Wop Preservation League, which is the nonprofit organization that works to build awareness and appreciation of pop culture from the 1950s and 1960s and also to preserve Wildwood's Doo Wop architecture. "It's a heritage in Wildwood."

The Wildwoods was the major tourist destination for Philadelphia residents, especially in a post–World War II America when people had a little extra money in their pockets and wanted to spend their summers at the Shore.

Combined with America's fascination with space and promises of what science would bring in the future, plus the country's optimism as a world power, and you have Wildwood's unique collection of what is now officially known as Doo Wop and included a range of themes, such as Modern (like the Jetsons' house), PuPu Platter, Chinatown Revival, and Phony Colonee. No matter what the theme, it is bold, brash, and very brightly colored. You can see the best examples in Wildwood at motels like the Lollipop, Shalimar, and Caribbean.

The Doo Wop "experience" itself was once the Surfside Diner, a Wildwood Crest Doo Wop–style restaurant that was on the demolition list before it was donated to the Doo Wop Preservation League on the condition that they move it to another site. So they disassembled the restaurant, stored it, then put it back together once Betty Fox donated space for their museum across the street from Wildwood's Convention Center.

LODGING

NORTH WILDWOOD

Candlelight Inn
1-800-922-2632
www.candlelight-inn.com
2310 Central Ave., North Wildwood 08260

Sure, Wildwood is a Doo Wop town, but it does have a few Victorian-era buildings. The Candlelight Inn is one of them. Set inside a Queen Anne–style building, this bed & breakfast has eight rooms and two cottages to choose from—the cottages have whirlpools if that's what you're after. Every room features antique wooden beds, period antiques, and those extras that make the experience an individual one, like robes, chocolates, and fresh flowers. The wraparound veranda on the main building is the perfect place to relax. In the off season, the Candlelight Inn hosts murder mystery weekends for groups of 12 or more (don't worry if your group has fewer than 12—they'll match you up with others. $$$.

Lollipop Motel
609-729-2800
www.lollipopmotel.com
2301 Atlantic Ave., Wildwood 08260

You can't miss the Lollipop, or if you do, you might want to have your eyes checked.

Of course, it's not a diner anymore—the original interior is gone, and an interactive history of Doo Wop—both music and architecture—in Wildwood has been built in its place. Even though the space itself is smaller than your typical museum, the designers maximize every possible square inch. Doo Wop–style lamps and chairs are showcased in floor-to-ceiling columns, and vintage signs hang from the ceiling. You can even eat in Doo Wop style at the Jitterbug Malt Shop and Café, or take in the brighter Doo Wop sights at the neon garden outside—those buzzing vintage signs that hung all over Wildwood have been taken out of storage, cleaned up, restored, and put out for display.

Even the wood grain paneling installed on the interior walls is vintage. "We salvaged Brazilian rosewood paneling from a local car dealership," says Chuck Schumann, a board member of the Doo Wop Preservation League and the captain behind *Captain Schumann's Big Blue Sightseer*, which is, not surprisingly, a retro 1950s boat. "This is wood that's not even available anymore. You couldn't find anything like it today." The league saved many of the items displayed inside the Doo Wop Experience. Every time a building was knocked down, the league would save what they could, and many of those items are part of the display.

Along with the Doo Wop Experience, new buildings in town are going retro. Wildwood's Wawa, Commerce Bank, Harley-Davidson dealership, Pizza Hut, and the interior of the McDonald's are all built in Doo Wop architectural style, and the Starlux is a new hotel with vintage feel. In fact, the Wawa in town is the only Wawa ever built to deviate so radically from the company's corporate design.

The focus on Wildwood's place in musical and architectural history has not only helped boost tourism in town, but also preserved a unique chunk of Americana.

"Recent history is one thing that disappears much more quickly than ancient history," says Rose. "This is our little part of history."

As for that title of birthplace of rock and roll, Ernie Troiano, Jr., Mayor of Wildwood, did a send a letter to the mayor of Cleveland challenging their claim. He hasn't heard back yet.

The exterior is graced with a giant, 50-year-old lollipop (no, it's not actually candy) and the faces of two very happy kids. The bright, candy theme follows to the multicolored doors and eye-popping poolside umbrellas, but inside, the rooms are more what you'd find in a modern motel. Open in season. $$–$$$.

New England Beach Condos

856-547-9192
nebeachresort.com
104 W. 11th St., North Wildwood 08260

Bringing Fido along? These beach condos, which are privately owned but can be rented out, are pet-friendly. The condos are in a more residential area than most Wildwood stays, but still close enough to the beach, boardwalk, and restaurants around town that it's not an inconvenient place to use as your vacation headquarters. It also has two pools. As of publication, a few units were still up for sale, if you really like the area. $$$.

Summer Nites

1-800-ROC-1950
www.summernites.com
2110 Atlantic Ave., North Wildwood 08260

Sheila and Rick Brown have turned the B&B concept on its head with Summer Nites. Sure, the building might look like

The Elvis room at Summer Nites Summer Nites

your typical Shore home, but the classic car parked outside is a hint about the goodies inside. Elvis and Marilyn are in the building—plus rooms dedicated to '50s television and movies, the '60s, and the '70s, among others. Each room is meticulously decorated, from the custom, hand-painted headboards and murals to the *Grease*-decorated light switches to the gold lamé couches in the Elvis room. In typical B&B fashion, guests are provided with breakfast which, in typical Sheila Brown fashion, is served by Brown herself in a poodle skirt. Her mother, who lives a few blocks away, makes the meal every morning. Guests can also play tunes on the jukebox or pick up a bottle of Coke from a vintage, working Coke dispenser (dimes are provided as well). If you're a big fan of the King, Summer Nites has two Elvis weekends, plus a New Year's Eve party. No children allowed. $$.

WILDWOOD

AA Heart of Wildwood Motels
1-888-522-2248
www.heartofwildwood.com
3915 Ocean Ave., Wildwood 08260

This AAA three-diamond-rated motel is in the perfect spot, with more than half the rooms on the boardwalk, and those rooms are well appointed, beautifully decorated, and clean. AA has heart, and two pools. Open in season. $$–$$$.

Blue Palms Resort
1-800-2-HAV-FUN
www.bluepalmsresort.com
3601 Atlantic Ave., Wildwood 08260

Blue palm trees weren't exactly the Blue Palms Resort's original Doo Wop theme, but when the owners renovated the building, plastic blue palm trees fit. They've taken the '50s style to the extreme here, with Jetsons-style furniture and, yes, blue palm trees. They also have designer family suites, which are built for families of five. $$.

Brittany Motel

1-800-31-MOTEL
www.mybrittanymotel.com
3710 Atlantic Ave., Wildwood, 08260

A piece of France in Wildwood? Sure—anything could work as a theme in the Doo Wop motel, and the Brittany is one of the originals. Your stay includes pool and even babysitting services if you want a meal out without the kids. $$–$$$.

Nantucket Motel

1-800-832-6888
www.nantucketmotel.net
4100 Occan Ave., Wildwood 08260

Sure, it's located in the mid-Atlantic, but remember what I wrote about Doo Wop architecture? Anything goes. In the case of

Wildwood Crib Rental

609-522-2724
4903 Pacific Ave., Wildwood 08260

Take care of those extras that didn't fit in the car by renting them through Wildwood Crib Rental. They've got more than just cribs, too—baby gates, strollers, car seats, plus wagons, beach wheelchairs, canes, and scooters. $–$$$$.

the Nantucket Motel, that's a cheery blue and yellow, and beachy décor inside. The Nantucket offers standard efficiencies and apartments for rent. It's also a block from the beach and boardwalk. Open in season. $$–$$$$.

Sea Gull Motel

1-800-8222-2670
www.seagull-motel.com
5305 Atlantic Ave., Wildwood 08260

Blue Palms Resort

Starlux Hotel

This AAA two-diamond-rated motel offers everything from one-room efficiencies to four-bedroom apartments—even a four-bedroom townhouse if you're bringing a lot of people. Like most motels in Wildwood, the Sea Gull has an outdoor pool, plus it's close to the beach and boardwalk. Open in season. $$–$$$.

Starlux Hotel

609-522-7412
www.thestarlux.com
305 E. Rio Grande Ave., Wildwood 08260

The Starlux might not be one of Wildwood's original Doo Wop motels, but it pays homage to the best of the era in a brand new way. The rooms are groovy cool with a Jetsons vibe, but with luxury more befitting Mr. Spacely. Make sure you check out the boomerang-themed pool. You can also rent an on-site Airstream trailer for a uniquely Wildwood and still luxurious experience. $$$–$$$$.

WILDWOOD CREST

Acacia Beachfront Motel

609-729-2233
www.acaciabeachfrontmotel.com
9101 Atlantic Ave., Wildwood Crest 08260

This AAA, two-diamond-rated motel is close to the beach, but, like most motels in town, also has on-site pools. It's clean, efficient, and a good place to stop and drop on your way to vacation fun. Open in season. $$–$$$.

Adventurer Motor Inn

609-729-1200
www.adventurerinn.com
5401 Ocean Ave., Wildwood Crest 08260

Three diamonds from AAA for this ocean-front vacation spot. It's a big one, too, offering more rooms than the motels in town. The Adventurer offers the typical efficiencies and apartments, plus penthouses if you're looking to up the ante on your Wildwood vacation. Open in season. $$–$$$$.

Ala Kai Motel

609-522-2169
www.alakaimotel.com
8301 Atlantic Ave., Wildwood Crest 08260

Polynesian kitsch rules at this beach-block spot, which is one of the original Doo Wop–style motels in Wildwood. The vintage bamboo-lettered neon sign was recently refurbished so that the hula girl could shine her brightest. The tiki theme continues to your room, where the beds are adorned in wildflower-printed bedspreads. Ala Kai has a pool, and you can rent one-room suites, or one- and two-room efficiencies. Open in season. $$–$$$.

Caribbean Motel

609-522-8292
www.caribbeanmotel.com
5600 Ocean Ave., Wildwood Crest 08260

The Caribbean, which opened in 1956, was one of the Wildwoods' original and most popular Doo Wop motels. In 2004, George Miller and Carolyn Emigh bought the

motel, which had declined from her original splendor, and worked to bring her back to life. They call the décor "a reinterpretation of classic 1950s kitsch," which means you can expect bright colors (Caribbean-themed yellow and green, for the most part). You'll also see a lot more samples of hallmark Doo Wop features, such as crescents, spaceship lighting, and plastic palm trees. Open in season. $$–$$$.

Sand Dune Resort Motel

877-726-3835
www.sanddunemotel.com
6905 Atlantic Ave., Wildwood Crest 08260

The Sand Dune is an all-in-one kind of place—they have a pool and miniature golf course on site. Tropical beaches are the theme at this Doo Wop, 1960s motel, from the palm trees to the light, beachy, pastel décor in your room. Every room has an ocean view. Open in season. $$.

VIP

609-522-2550
www.wildwoodcrestvipmotel.com
6505 Atlantic Ave., Wildwood Crest 08260

Ala Kai Motel

Here, VIP means "vacation in paradise" (though they won't quibble if you want to be treated like a very important person). They have lots of non-beach things to do, if you're looking to keep the kids occupied, like Ping-Pong, shuffleboard, horseshoes, and, like most motels in the area, a heated pool. The playground with pirate ship is a big kiddie draw. Open in season. $$–$$$.

DINING

NORTH WILDWOOD

2nd Street Annie's
609-729-9100
www.2ndstreetannies.com
101 Olde New Jersey Ave., North Wildwood 08260

Annie's doesn't offer that big a menu, just enough to go with your drinks, because it's the nightlife that's the real attraction here. Like pianos? They duel at 2nd Street Annie's, which also features cabaret shows. The Tramp Bar is outdoors and is frequently home to entertainment from barbershop quartets and string bands. If you're a night owl, 2nd Street starts serving a special BBQ menu at 1 AM Saturday and Sunday mornings. Dinner, late night. Lunch Friday, Saturday, and Sunday. $.

Claude's
609-522-0400
www.claudesrestaurant.com
100 Olde New Jersey Ave., North Wildwood 08260

Ooh, la-la—yes, there is French dining in the Wildwoods, and you'll find it at Claude's. The husband and wife chef/owner pair put their culinary savoir-faire into the menu—Claude Pottier takes care of the cuisine, preparing savory items like pork, duck, and lamb, and Mary Pottier handles the desserts, like the triple berry pie.

Oh, Canada

If you think it's a coincidence that you're hearing a bevy of French conservations at the Shore, think again. Canadians—especially from Quebec—have long been Jersey Shore tourists, especially in August. In fact, Cape May County estimates that 25 percent of the 19 million visitors who played along the Jersey Shore in 2007 came from Canada, up from 15 percent in 2006.

Why? To start, Cape May County had and still has a heavy marketing presence in Canada, and many Canadians got two or three weeks of vacation in August (all at the same time). So they'd fill up the Jersey Shore with accents and Speedos (sorry, guys, it had to be said). Many stayed in Avalon Campground, which is where I spent my summers. Through August in the early 1990s, I probably heard more people speaking French than English while riding my bike around the campground.

That changed in the late 1990s, when the Canadian dollar's value plunged, at one point coming in at just 51 cents per United States dollar.

That two- to three-week vacation time for Canadians isn't all at the same time anymore, but the increased value of the Canadian dollar (95 cents to the United States dollar in 2007) has brought them back to the Shore. Nostalgia also plays a role in bringing kids back to where they vacationed when they grew up, the same mechanism that keeps people from the Philadelphia area coming back every summer, year after year—shorter drive, but same pull.

Reservations recommended. BYOB. Dinner in season. $$$.

Cool Scoops
609-SAY-COOL
www.coolscoops.com

1111 New Jersey Ave., North Wildwood 08260

Visiting Cool Scoops isn't just about good food—it's an experience. They serve up grub in 1950s style—they've got car booths, a black and white checked floor, vintage TV shows on the tube, pinball and video games, and a jukebox. The main attraction is the ice cream, especially the sundaes. Cool Scoops also serves up hot dogs, snacks, a Doo-Whopper, and classic fountain drinks, like a Brooklyn Egg Cream and a Black Cow. Open May through late November. Dinner starting at 3 PM. $.

Keenan's Irish Pub

609-729-3344
www.keenansirishpub.com
113 Olde New Jersey Ave., North Wildwood 08260

Yes, they do serve food at Keenan's, even if this spot is more known as a haven for cover bands and drink specials. The place rocks at nights during the season. Lunch, dinner in season. $.

Owen's Pub

609-729-7290
www.owenspub.com
119 E. 17th St., North Wildwood, 08260

Good food, good drinks, and good music—what else could you ask for at a local pub? The dining room is set aside from the bar area, though you'll find flat screen TVs in both. The best night to go (and the most difficult night to get a seat) is during the weekly "name that tune" competition. Lunch, dinner. $.

Piro's Restaurant

609-729-0401
1901 New York Ave., North Wildwood 08260

Since 1955, Piro's has been cooking up gourmet Italian and seafood dishes in

Tully Nut

What exactly is a Tully Nut? If I knew, I'd tell you, but the recipe's a secret, and has been since Mark Tully spent the winter of 1969 creating this drink. What I do know is that it has five kinds of liquors and is a favorite at #1 Tavern (1st and Atlantic Ave., North Wildwood 08260, 609-522-1775, www.supertullynut.com). This red, slushy drink is a kicker, though, so one Tully Nut is probably enough if you'd like to be able to walk home under your own power.

North Wildwood. To stick with the classics theme, try Piro's original Sunday gravy. There's a reason it's been on the menu since the place first opened. Reservations recommended. Dinner. $$$.

Star Diner Café

609-729-4900
www.stardinercafe.com
325 W. Spruce Ave., North Wildwood 08260

Philadelphia Magazine named the Star Diner Café the best diner at the Shore, and it's not hard to see why. The Star Diner Café has been serving up big portions of hearty diner foods for 40 years. And I'm not just talking burgers and fries, but full-size dinner meals, like chicken Napoleon and baby back ribs. The waffles are an excellent breakfast treat. It's right on your way on and off the island via NJ 147, which makes it ideal for saying hello or goodbye to the Wildwoods. BYOB. Breakfast, lunch, dinner. $.

Tony's Island Café

609-522-1821
www.tonysnw.com
2505 Delaware Ave., North Wildwood 08260

Sure, you could go for one of the seafood selections at Tony's, but the real highlight is

Bikes on the Boardwalk and One Golden Nugget

Obviously, I spent a lot of time on the Wildwood boardwalk while researching this book. But it wasn't until the very end of the summer, a week before I was to deliver the manuscript to my publisher, that I enjoyed it the way most people do: as a tourist.

My dad wanted to ride bikes on the Wildwood boardwalk, so I said I would go. A strong love of Wildwood runs in his family. His great-grandmother asked to be taken to the Wildwood boardwalk when she realized that she was in the last days of her life. The family took her to the boards, where she sat and watched the scene of people and ocean go by. She died the next day. My parents walked the boards, rode the Golden Nugget, and went to the movies on the boardwalk as teenagers. They even honeymooned in Wildwood Crest.

They brought me and my siblings to the boardwalk, too, though the last trip we took together was in the early 1990s. By that time, the boardwalk had turned less family-friendly and had more tattoo parlors and T-shirt shops. I remember thinking that the boardwalk here didn't look anything like the one in Ocean City, which was and is a bright, colorful, and happy place, or so it seemed to me. Even as a preteen, I could see that Wildwood's boardwalk was getting much the worse for wear. My father hadn't been back since, and neither had I until I started writing this book.

We made it to the beach early and parked by the Wildwoods Convention Center. I could see flocks of bikes already wheeling up and down the boardwalk. After renting two bikes, my dad ignoring the owner's warning not to ride the bike up and down the ramp, we pedaled away.

It was a Sunday, and not nearly as packed as a Saturday morning would be. Along the way, my dad told me what used to be where, like the movie theater, or the rides he remembered at what pier. I saw families taking a walk, runners, and a few people who looked like they hadn't slept the night before. The amusements and games were just coming alive, and people waited in line for a breakfast sandwiches from the Hot Spot restaurant. I saw a lot of bathing suits, boogie boards, and beach bags on people crossing the boardwalk to the beach. Sure, I saw a few of those unsavory T-shirt shops, but also candy stores, restaurants, and people selling Wildwood shirts without also offering the less G-rated options.

We had just passed a go-kart track when I saw my father do a double take and abruptly stop his bike. "It's the Golden Nugget!" he shouted, and promptly turned his bike around, rode back to the pier, past the go-karts, and right up to a fence that blocked us from riding back to a building on the pier.

The Golden Nugget was *the* highlight of the Wildwood boardwalk. The ride was built in the 1950s and, for 40 cents, you could zip through an indoor "abandoned mine" roller coaster. It might seem tame now, looking at the low, squat brown building at the end of the pier, especially when you look at the heights and spills offered by other Wildwood roller coasters, but my father says it was the ultimate thrill when he was a kid.

The Golden Nugget is still in Wildwood, though it's not operating. The ride is owned by the Morey Organization, which runs all the amusement piers in Wildwood, and you can see it, as my father and I did. You can still read where the name of the ride was, and see where the carts zipped in and out of the enclosed coaster.

It didn't take us long to ride the boards—the boardwalk's only 2 miles long—and then it was back to the car for bottles of water and air conditioning. We spent the rest of the morning driving around town so he could see how the place had changed, and what remained.

"It's better than it used to be, much better than when you were a kid," dad said as we headed up Ocean Drive toward Stone Harbor. "Much better than when I was a kid, too." Except for the Golden Nugget being out of commission, of course.

What's left of the Golden Nugget

the ribs. Full rack or half rack, they're big, messy, and worth diving into. Tony's is also a late-night hot spot—it's open until 3 AM in season. Lunch, dinner, late night. Live entertainment, including karaoke nights, in season. $$.

Westy's Irish Pub

609-522-4991
101 E. Walnut Ave., North Wildwood 08260

It might be an Irish pub, but they do wings right at Westy's. If you're into a less messy meal, try The Westy, which combines chicken, roasted peppers, jack cheese, and honey mustard on a baguette. It's a popular late-night spot, too, with live entertainment year-round, plus Quizzo and wing nights. Breakfast, lunch, dinner. $.

WILDWOOD

Alumni Grill

609-523-1111
www.alumni-grill.com
3421 Pacific Ave., Wildwood 08260

Get your food and go from this corner shop. Sure, they have your typical sandwiches and burgers, but they also dish up wraps, salads, and vegetarian fare. If you're eating in, try to snag the front corner table, which is decorated with newspaper reprints. Lunch, dinner in season. Lunch in the off season. $.

Banana's Ice Cream Parlor Café

609-622-5577
400 E. Lincoln Ave., Wildwood 08260

It's all about ice cream in this restaurant which is—not surprisingly—painted banana yellow. Go for a straight-up cone, or one of Banana's big banana splits. The Big Banana comes with 10 dips, two split bananas, choice of six toppings, plus whipped cream and cherries. Best enjoyed shared. Lunch, dinner, late night in season. Weekends only in May and June. $.

Beach Creek

609-522-1062
www.beachcreek.net
500 W. Hand Ave., Wildwood 08260

You'll find casual elegance at this waterfront restaurant, which not only boasts an oyster bar, but also sunset views (and drinks to go with it, which is why it's called the Sunset Martini Bar). The menu is broad, ranging from seafood classics to classics with a twist, like scallops Santa Fe and Kyoto steak and shrimp. They have a kids' menu as well, if you're bringing the tykes along. Dinner in season. $$.

Boardwalk Bar & Grill

609-522-2431
www.boardwalkbarandgrill.com
3500 Atlantic Ave., Wildwood 08260

Think you're hungry? Test your appetite with Boardwalk Bar & Grill's Kahuna

Burger, which weighs in at a pound of beef. If you complete your task, they'll put your picture on their Web site. But they're not just burgers—Boardwalk Bar & Grill also serves up sandwiches, salads, and a lot of fried finger foods. Live entertainment in season. For a Wildwood-themed drink, try the Tram Car. Lunch, dinner in season. $.

Boathouse

609-729-5301
www.boathouseonline.net
506 W. Rio Grande Ave., Wildwood 08260

Have your dinner on the water—literally. The entire building is over the water, though you can opt to eat indoors and still enjoy the sunset view. If you're itching to be closer to the water, set yourself up at the marina deck. The menu is mostly surf and turf, with pasta selections as well. The appetizer menu is a highlight and can easily be turned into a meal: Cajun popcorn shrimp, clams casino, oysters, clams, fried calamari—it's a spicy delight. Live music in season. Lunch, dinner. $$.

Doo Wop Diner

609-522-7880
www.doo-wopdiner.com
4010 Boardwalk, Wildwood 08260

Get a taste of history and the boardwalk at this diner. The menu isn't stuck in the past, though—you can get wraps as well as burgers at the retro diner counter or in a booth. Breakfast is popular here, too, as are the impossibly thick milkshakes. Breakfast, lunch, dinner in season. $.

Duffer's Restaurant & Ice Cream Parlor

609-729-1817
www.dufferswildwood.com
5200 Pacific Ave., Wildwood 08260

You'll find big portions at this AAA-rated, family-friendly spot that has a train running through it (a small one, of course—

Hot Spots

If you're looking for a quick bite to eat, but aren't sure what that bite should be, head to one of the many Hot Spots in Wildwood. Yes, I used capitals for H and S because Hot Spot is the name of several Wildwood eateries.

The original is at 3401 Boardwalk, with sequels in Wildwood and North Wildwood. All the Hot Spots dish up filling and, depending on what you order, greasy-but-good foods like burgers, gyros, and sausages.

it's along the ceiling). It's part restaurant, part old-fashioned ice cream parlor, and part activity center—Duffer's also has an arcade, miniature golf course, and souvenir shop on site. Breakfast, lunch, dinner in season. $.

Gia
609-729-5959
www.giawildwood.com
3001 Pacific Ave., Wildwood 08260

If you're looking for a more city-slick dining experience, Gia could fit the bill. This restaurant shirks white linens for red tablecloths and black napkins, and adds dashes of new American cuisine—like orange salad and New York strip steak—to its mostly Italian menu. If you're eating as a group, make sure to order the Salad Bella Mia to share. BYOB. Reservations recommended. Dinner. $$.

Groff's Restaurant
609-522-5474
www.groffsrestaurant.com
423 E. Magnolia Ave., Wildwood 08260

This Zagat-rated restaurant is a Shore institution. In 1918, Earl M. Groff moved to Wildwood and operated games for Wildwood vacationers. In 1925, he added a hot dog stand and kept expanding, until we have Groff's as it is today—and it's still family-owned. The menu is classic American with influences from Earl Groff's native Pennsylvania Dutch. Don't skip the pies, which are built to please. Groff's now sells them now for the holidays, too, if you're craving a bit of Wildwood with your turkey and ham. Dinner in season. Call ahead for pies in November and December. $$.

Idaho Sweets
609-729-9200
www.idahosweetsbbq.com
100 W. Andrews Ave., Wildwood 08260

You'll find real wood pit barbecue at this AAA one-diamond-rated joint. Don't skip the sweet potato fries. Lunch, dinner, late night in season. $.

Juan Pablo's Margarita Bar
609-729-6500
www.juanpablosmargaritabar.com
3801 Pacific Ave., Wildwood 08260

It's a good thing that the Mexican dishes served at Juan Pablo's come in big portions, because the margaritas, which is what most people come for, are strong. The platters are good for sharing, though we recommend that you do not take their advice when they say "Don't drink the water," if you want to make it out of the restaurant on your own two legs. For an extra swanky experience, dine in the side room, which features heavy doses of leopard print and a pool table. Lunch, dinner, late night. $$.

Kelly's
609-522-6817
4400 Atlantic Ave., Wildwood 08260

It's easy to blow your diet at Kelly's. The appetizers, like pierogies and potato skins, could be meals in themselves. The lunch menu features sandwiches, wraps, and burgers, and dinner adds in bigger, heartier fare, like New York strip steak and filet. Outdoor entertainment on the new patio in season. Lunch, dinner in season. $.

La Piazza Cucina
609-522-8300
4600 Pacific Ave., Wildwood 08260

The menu at La Piazza Cucina points out that Piazza means "the square," and indeed it's where a lot of people in Wildwood gather to meet, whether it's over drinks at the large bar, food in the dining room, or both, which is frequently set to the tune of live music. The food, of course, is classic Italian. What else would you expect in a

---

Two Mile Landing and Crab House

If you've been reading the Wildwoods dining section and wondering how I could possibly forget Two Mile Landing or the Crab House Restaurant, I had planned to write about both. Until one of them fell into the water.

On July 7, 2007—a very popular weekend at the Shore, since it was the weekend after the Fourth of July—diners at the Crab House Restaurant heard what sounded like gunshots. But it wasn't a violent attack—the floor was collapsing into itself and into the water below. A few people fell into the water, and nine were sent to the hospital. No one was killed, but the incident shut down the Crab House (obviously), and Two Mile Landing, which is the restaurant located next door on the same pier.

As of press time, both restaurants were closed. They very well could be open by the time you read this book—and hopefully so. Many visitors don't consider their Wildwoods vacation complete without a meal at either Two Mile Landing or the Crab House Restaurant.

---

restaurant and bar that features Rat Pack posters? Dinner. $$.

MagicBrain CyberCafé

609-729-8550 and 609-523-9000
www.magicbraincybercafe.com
4807 Pacific Ave., Wildwood 08260 and
2700 Boardwalk, Wildwood 08260

You can't help it—you've gotta be connected, even while on vacation. If you don't want to lug your laptop to the beach (or even if you do and need an Internet hookup), stop in here. It works as a standalone coffeehouse, too, with tasty drinks and Green Mountain Coffee Roasters coffee. The computers are speedy and let you make the most of whatever time you buy for the day or the week—you can keep coming back if you still have minutes left. Call for hours. $.

Marvis Diner

609-522-0550
4900 Pacific Ave., Wildwood, 08260

In 1965, two sisters from Saratoga, New York opened a diner in Wildwood. They got the business going, then moved on to other projects. They also got married, and each had a son. It's those sons who brought the Marvis Diner back into the family (the name Marvis is a combination of their mothers' names), and back to its former glory. Today it's a Doo Wop 1950s-style diner with plenty of shiny chrome and brightly colored booths. The food is mostly diner food with dashes of modern dishes thrown in, like Cajun grilled chicken, and the Marvis signature salad. The cheeseburger hoagie is a good bet if you can't decide between burger or sandwich. Breakfast, lunch, dinner in season. $.

Neil's Steak and Chowder House

609-522-5226
222 East Schellenger Ave., Wildwood 08260

If you're looking for a classic steakhouse, then check out Neil's, though it's more casual in setting and dress. Pictures of Wildwood from 1900 to 1982 ring the restaurant, giving it a vintage, old-time feel. The menu is surf and turf, with pasta dishes thrown in. If you've got a monster appetite, go for the 14-ounce Texas rib eye steak. The after-dinner drink and martini lists are worth a look, too. Dinner in season. $$.

Pacific Grill

609-523-1800
www.pacificgrillwildwood.com
4801 Pacific Ave., Wildwood 08260

BLT at Pink Cadillac

This seaside restaurant mixes California cuisine with local favorites. For example, the fish and chips come with ahi tuna tartare and plantain chips, and the crab cake is made with tomato-orange salsa, jasmine rice, and remoulade. BYOB. Dinner. Closed Tuesdays. $$$.

Pink Cadillac

609-522-8288
3801 Atlantic Ave., Wildwood 08260

Why's it called Pink Cadillac? Ask, and you'll be treated to the floor show, in which the servers do the Pink Cadillac Shuffle to the sounds of Bruce Springsteen's hit of the same name. The menu is classic diner fare nestled within the chrome and fun of this retro diner. It's very kid-friendly, too—see how many cartoon characters you can find hiding in the clouds painted on the ceiling. Breakfast, lunch, dinner in season. $.

Red Sky Café

609-522-7747
www.redskycafe.net
3601 Atlantic Ave., Wildwood 08260

It's a taste of Southwestern and Mexican cuisine at Red Sky Cafe. The quesadillas, chimichangas, fajitas, enchiladas, and burritos are hearty and spicy (unless you ask them to turn it down a notch, of course). Dinner in season, though their location in Seaville, New Jersey is open year-round. $$.

Rusty Rudder

609-522-3085
www.beachterrace.com

Schellengers

Beach Terrace Motor Inn
Oak and Atlantic Ave., Wildwood, 08260

It's no frills at this buffet, which is located inside the Beach Terrace Motor Inn, But it'll fill you up before you go about your day. The plates of hot, steaming food (sausages/ bacon/pancakes or pasta/seafood/beef/ ham) are hard to resist, especially when you can go up for seconds. Or thirds. Breakfast, dinner in season. $$.

Schellengers
609-522-0433
3510 Atlantic Ave., Wildwood 08260

The roof of Schellengers will catch your eye first—it's packed to the brim with sea scenes, like tugboats and a giant lobster hanging over the entrance to this seafood restaurant, which has been in Wildwood for nearly 30 years. The menu is huge and updated often, so ask your server what the latest and greatest may be. Or go with the tried and true, like the lobster bake, which mixes a whole lobster, clams, shrimp, crab, corn on the cob, and potatoes. Dinner in season. Dinner starts seating at 3 PM. $$.

Shamrock Café
609-522-7552
3700 Pacific Ave., Wildwood 08260

Believe it or not, the Shamrock does serve food courtesy of Diluzio's Kitchen. It's straight bar food fare because what keeps people at the Shamrock late into the night are the drink specials, the live music, and the crowds. They have outdoor seating and pool tables, too. Dinner, late night. Lunch Saturday and Sunday. $.

TLC's Polish Water Ice
609-846-0220
www.polishwaterice.com
Spicer, Juniper, Roberts, and the Boardwalk, Wildwood, 08260

Is it soft-serve? Is it water ice? It's both. Sort of. Polish Water Ice is a low-calorie dessert that uses no dairy, and has no fat and no cholesterol. But it's still sweet, yummy, and looks like frozen custard. They

have treats mixed with ice cream, but the original is still the best. Open 10 AM–midnight in season. $.

Uncle Bill's Pancake House
609-729-7557
4601 Pacific Ave., Wildwood

Get your day going at Uncle Bills, which packs in hungry patrons in just about every South Jersey Shore town (poor Atlantic City and Sea Isle City). The main attraction, of course, is the pancakes, but they also have plenty of egg options, as well as waffles and sandwiches. Expect long waits on the weekends in season. No credit cards. Breakfast, lunch in season. $.

Urie's
609-522-4189
www.uries.net
588 W. Rio Grande Ave., Wildwood 08260

Urie's has been a Wildwood tradition for over 50 years, though Urie's today has come a long way from its original incarnation, which was seasonal grub served on paper plates. Paper plates no more. Eat inside or right on the water (I highly recommend the latter) at this cool, casual eatery. If you're

Water, Water, Everywhere
Summers at the Shore can be hot, especially when the humidity ramps up. On one of these unforgiving days, I walked the Wildwood boardwalk, and I quickly drank the bottle of water I'd brought with me. I needed another if I was going to make it all the way down to the Wildwoods Convention Center. So I stopped at a pizzeria for a bottle.

"That'll be $2.25," said the clerk.

"Excuse me?" I asked.

"$2.25."

Sorry, not sold. So I headed into the $5 and Under Store (3514 Boardwalk and 2714 Boardwalk). Price? $1, same bottle, same size. It's the cheapest price I found on the boardwalk, and it was good and cold. So be careful where you buy water—I found similar markups at boardwalk eateries in Ocean City and Atlantic City, too. If you're wandering around town and looking for a great bottled water deal, the drug and convenience stores, like CVS and Wawa, are usually your best—and cheapest—bets.

not sure what to order, go for a Urie's staple: all-you-can-eat crab. Lunch, dinner in season. $$.

Wild Wings
609-846-WING
4500 Pacific and Davis Ave., Wildwood 08260

You'll find all kinds of wings and things at this spot, which is hard to miss, as it's painted bright yellow and orange. They've cooked up 15 different homemade sauces. But if wings aren't your thing, Wild Wings is also wild about shrimp and ribs, sandwiches, and milkshakes. No credit cards. Lunch, dinner, late night. $.

WILDWOOD CREST

Admiral's Quarters
609-729-0031
www.admiralsresort.com
Admiral Resort Motel
7200 Ocean Ave., Wildwood Crest, 08260

The Admiral bills itself as a house of pancakes and omelets—and, as far as I can tell, they're right. Plus, they serve breakfast until 2 PM if you're a late riser. The Belly Buster, which includes three eggs any style, two pancakes, sausage pattie and strip, bacon, and home fries, is a perennial favorite. And filling. Breakfast in season. $.

Carini's Restaurant
609-522-7304
www.carinis.net
9854 Pacific Ave., Wildwood Crest 08260

Eat in for a casual Italian meal at the restaurant portion of Carini's, or, if you're coming in off the beach, stop by the pizzeria side. Don't let the strip mall façade fool you—the food is for real—the Italian dishes, like chicken piccante, chicken parmesan, and linguini with mussels—are big and

hearty, and the pizza hits the spot after a day on the waves. BYOB. Lunch, dinner. $$.

Duffy's on the Lake
609-522-1815
7601 New Jersey Ave., Wildwood Crest

Get your breakfast or dinner with some of the best views in the Wildwoods at Duffy's, a longtime Wildwood favorite. You'll dine across the street from Sunset Lake while taking in a three-egg omelet, short stack of hotcakes, broiled filet, or roasted pork loin. Reservations recommended for dinner. Breakfast, dinner in season. $.

Fitzpatrick's Crest Tavern
609-522-1200
www.cresttavern.com
9600 Pacific Ave., Wildwood Crest 08260

Crest Tavern is your typical hometown, good-time bar, though with an added twist outside. The outdoor deck features not just tables and chairs for enjoying the evening air, but also classic video games. Lunch, dinner. $.

Marie Nicole's
609-522-5425
www.marienicoles.com
9510 Pacific Ave., Wildwood Crest 08260

The Artful Diner rated this as one of the top 10 Shore restaurants in New Jersey, and for good reason. Executive Chef Justin Barnabei has created a menu that focuses on the best of classic meals, like jumbo lump crab cakes, black angus filet mignon, herb-roasted chicken, and pan-seared halibut, but in gourmet fashion. Don't skip the wine. Marie Nicole's has an impressive and extensive stock. Indoor and patio seating available. Dinner in season. $$$.

Oasis Beach Grille
609-729-2121

View from Oasis Beach Grille

www.beaurivage-motel.com
Beau Rivage Motor Inn
9103 Atlantic Ave., Wildwood Crest 08260

This tiny restaurant is literally a few steps up from the beach, which makes it perfect for a break from a beach day, or to take in the view over your morning coffee. The utensils come in a beach bucket—fitting, considering how close you are to the sand. Breakfast, lunch in season. $.

RIO GRANDE

Dock Mike's Pancake House
609-889-6700
www.dockmikes.com
1603 RT 47, Rio Grande 08242

The name here is a bit misleading. While Dock Mike's certainly dishes up pancakes in many different varieties, including sweet potato and "Mikey" Mouse, it's also a lunch spot and has over 100 different items to try, like wraps, seafood samplers, and cheese steaks—all of which are listed on your placemat menu. No credit cards. Breakfast, lunch. $–$$.

Green Street Market
609-463-0606
www.greenstreetmarket.com
3167 RT 9 S., Rio Grande 08242

Organic? All natural? Vegan? Gluten-free? If you need a diet along any of these lines, or just prefer good-for-you foods, stop in at Green Street Market. They also sell body products, cleaning supplies, and plenty of supplements. Open 10 AM–7 PM Monday through Saturday and 10 AM–5 PM Sunday.

Arts & Culture

North Wildwood

Historic Hereford Inlet Lighthouse and Gardens
609-522-4520
herefordlighthouse.org
1st and Central Ave., North Wildwood 08260

This lighthouse, which was built in 1874, gives you 13 miles of viewing range on a clear day. It's still a working lighthouse. If you're not up for the climb to the top, then visit the gardens, which are home to more than 200 plant varieties and go right up to the ocean wall. Open 10 AM–4 PM every day in season; open 10 AM–4 PM Wednesday through Sunday in the off season. Lighthouse: $. Gardens: Free.

Segway Tours
609-729-7766
www.segwaysolution.com
321 E. 17th Ave., North Wildwood 08260

If you're not up to walking the Wildwoods, sign up for a guided Segway tour, which takes about an hour and a half from a gliding start to finish. They run two a day in season. American Association of Retired Persons (AARP) and military discounts available. Must be over 16 to ride. No credit cards. $$$.

Wildwood

Casba Comedy Club
609-522-8444
www.casbacomedyclub.com/
Atlantic & Spicer Ave., Wildwood 08260

Get your yucks at this beachside comedy club. They put the laughs on for two shows a night. Reservations recommended. Open in season. $.

George F. Boyer Historical Museum
609-523-0277
www.the-wildwoods.com/history/museum.html
3907 Pacific Ave., Wildwood, NJ 08260

Peek into Wildwood's deep past (it goes beyond Doo Wop, you know) at this museum, which is an old house converted to hold the town's treasures, including photographs, artifacts, and memorabilia. It's also home to the National Marbles Hall of Fame. Open 9:30 AM –2:30 PM Monday through Thursday; 9:30 AM–2:30 PM and 6:30 AM– 9:30 PM Fridays; 10:30 AM–2:30 PM Saturday and Sunday in season; and 10:30 AM–2:30 PM in the off season. Free, but donations are appreciated.

Whaling Wall by Wyland

www.wylandfoundation.org
Boardwalk Mall
3800 Boardwalk, Wildwood 08260

The artist known simply as Wyland has painted nearly 100 wall murals of marine life, like migrating gray whales, breaching humpbacks, and blue whales. The goal is to raise awareness of the life that lives in the ocean. One of these murals, located in Wildwood, is of humpback whales, and since it's life-size, it stands at 30 feet high and 220 feet long. Free.

ATTRACTIONS, PARKS & RECREATION

WILDWOOD

3J's Wildwood Bowl & Sports Bar

609-729-0111
www.3jwildwoodbowl.com
3401 New Jersey Ave., Wildwood 08260

For over 30 years, 3J's has been setting 'em up for you to knock down—and keeping kids occupied on rainy beach days. If bowling's not your thing, 3J's also has pool tables and Nintendo Wii sports on a big screen. Tuesday and Thursday nights are turned over to Club 3J's, where the regular bowling lights are turned down and the music up. Saturday nights are Rockin' Red Pin nights, where prices drop to $20 per lane per hour for up to five people to the same lighting and music effects as Club 3J's. Open 2 PM–midnight Tuesday through Sunday. Closed Mondays unless it's raining. $$

Captain Schumann's Whale and Dolphin Watching

1-800-246-9425
www.doowopdolphin.com
4500 Park Blvd., Wildwood 08260

It's not called the *Big Blue Sightseer* for nothing. It's a 1950s-era boat (brought up to modern standards, of course) that's a perfect fit for Captain Schumann, who is also the a key member of the Doo Wop Preservation League. He offers three whale and dolphin watching cruises a day in season. The morning cruise is the longest in Wildwood. The evening Dolphin & Dogs Sunset Cruise offers sights plus free hot dogs and pizza. Open in season. $$$.

Mocean Wave Runners

609-522-3159
www.moceanwaverunners.com
560 W. Rio Grande Ave., Wildwood 08260

Zip through the water on a wave runner, available at Mocean. You don't need a license to go, but if you don't have one, you'll have to stay in the Mocean guarded area, which is the largest private riding area in Wildwoods. Open in season. $$$.

"Watch the Tram Car, Please"
609-523-TRAM
www.dowildwood.com

The Wildwoods Boardwalk Sightseer Tram Cars have been taking people up and down the 2-mile boardwalk since 1949. The recording that blares out of the bright yellow and blue cars—"Watch the tram car, please," was recorded by Floss Stingel and has been in effect since those original cars rumbled up and down the boardwalk.

The carts were created in 1939 for the World's Fair and bought by Gilbert Ramagosa for the Wildwoods boardwalk. Eight are in service—five originals from 1939—and give rides to about 500,000 people a year. The trams run continuous loops from Cresse Avenue at the Wildwood/Wildwood Crest border to 16th Street in North Wildwood, and stop at all the hot boardwalk stops. A ride will cost you $2 each way. The carts start rolling part time on Easter weekend and, in season, 11 AM–1 AM.

In 2007, new tram cars were added to the fleet—for the first time in 44 years—and they run the same route as those original cars from 1939 do. The new cars look the same but have better cushioning and tires. And who cut the ribbon introducing those new cars to the fleet on June 27, 2007? Floss Stingel, of course. And, yes, she did give a live rendition of her famous call.

Watch the tram car, please! Greater Wildwoods Tourism Authority

Morey's Piers

609-522-3900
www.moreyspiers.com
3501 Boardwalk, Wildwood 08260

The Wildwood boardwalk has more rides than Disney World, mostly thanks to the Morey family. They operate four different ride piers on the boardwalk—three of them of the non-water-park variety: Surfside Pier, Mariner's Landing, and Adventure Pier. Each one has thrills and spills for the family. If your idea of fun is screaming while your stomach flips somersaults, this is the place to go. Between the AtmosFEAR!, Great White, Screamin' Swing, Sea Serpent, and Great NorEaster, to name a few, you'll more than get your fill of the scary stuff. Just hold off on concessions until after you're through—for your own good and that of the guests below the rides you'll be enjoying. Yes, they have rides for younger kids, too. You can buy tickets for rides, or wristbands that are accepted in all three parks. If you're going to be doing the water park, too, you can combine them with ride packages. Hours vary per pier per month. Check the Web site for details. $.

Splash Zone Water Park

609-729-5600
www.splashzonewaterpark.com
Schellenger Ave. & the Boardwalk, Wildwood 08260

Zip down a speed slide, body flume, or giant water blaster, or spend your day floating along the lazy river at this boardwalk water park, which is part of the Morey's empire. For a thorough dousing, stand under the aptly named "Giant Bucket," which dumps 1,000 gallons of water every three minutes. Open 9:30 AM–6:30 PM in season. $.

Zombie World

www.zombieworld.net
3122 Boardwalk, Wildwood 08260

Yes, it's super cheesy and might not make you believe that zombies are actually walking around, but Zombie World is good, creepy fun. The premise is that the earth's population is split between humans and zombies after the final world war, with zombies outnumbering humans 1,000 to 1 (of course, there are atomic bombs involved). Your job—aside from not screaming—is to laser down the zombies. Not exactly for little kids. Open in season. $.

WILDWOOD CREST

The Starlight Fleet

609-729-7776
www.jjcboats.com
6200 Park Blvd., Wildwood Crest 08260

The ships of the Starlight Fleet offer dolphin and whale watching trips as well as fishing in Wildwood and Cape May. The *Starlight* (the boat) runs starlight trips (130 people maximum) and the *Twilight* runs—you guessed it—twilight trips (100 people maximum), while the *Atlantic Star* runs 12- and 16-hour, offshore wreck fishing trips (150 passengers) and also has a sundeck and upper deck seating. If you're more of a landlubber but still like fresh seafood, you can buy fresh at Starlight's fish and seafood market. $$$$.

Cape May Par 3 and Driving Range
609-889-2600
www.capemaypar3.com
29 Fulling Mill Rd., Rio Grande 08242

This course, which is designed with the beginner in mind, is a great spot to take the kids if they have an interest in playing golf beyond the miniature version (or if you're not so sure of your own skills). Every hole is a par 3, and playing 18 holes won't take the entire day. It's casual, too—no dress restrictions or requirements. $$.

SHOPPING

WILDWOOD

Douglas Fudge
609-522-3875
3300 Boardwalk, Wildwood 08260

They've been dishing up fudge at Douglas since 1919, and stepping inside their Wildwood location is like jumping back in time. The walls are still wood paneled, and the floor is patterned with the Douglas logo. Scottie dog animals are all around (it's the company mascot), and they even have a resting area if you'd like to take a break while enjoying your sweet treat. Open 9 AM—10:30 PM in season. Call for off-season hours.

Fame
609-729-3263
3001 Boardwalk, Wildwood 08260

This boardwalk shop is a little bit movies, and a little bit rock and roll. You'll find T-shirts, home décor, and tschotschkes dedicated to the stars of screen and radio, with a heavy dose of Grateful Dead—inspired items. Open 10 AM—12:30 AM in season.

Holly Beach Train Depot
609-522-2379
www.hollybeachtraindepot.com
4712 Pacific Ave., Wildwood 08260

All aboard! The Holly Beach Train Depot stocks anything a model train enthusiast could ever want (plus plenty of conductor's caps if that's your thing). The shop is named after the real Holly Beach Train Depot, which is what the section of the Wildwoods that is now known as Wildwood was called before the borough incorporated itself. The depot was located one block from where the store now stands. They buy trains, too. Open 1 PM—5 PM

Stacks of books at Hooked on Books

Wednesday, Thursday, and Friday, and 10 AM–4 PM Tuesday and Saturday. Closed Sunday and Monday.

Hooked on Books

609-729-1132
www.hookedonbooks.info
3405 Pacific Ave., Wildwood

If you're a book lover, browse through this used bookshop. The selection is as interesting as what people bring in, and the stock usually piles up on the floor, which is part of the charm. Open 9 AM–10 PM in season.

Lula

609-522-8002
4805 Pacific Ave., Wildwood, 08260

This boutique, which is owned by four cousins, features the latest fashions, from dresses to jeans. The accessories alone are worth the trip. One of the cousins makes purses, clutches, clothes, and accessories by hand. These are sold at the store, or online at www.curlyhairconspiracy.etsy.com. She'll make custom bags, too, if you're interested and can wait. Open 11 AM–7 PM Monday to Thursday, 11 AM–8 PM Friday and Saturday, and 11 AM–3 PM Sunday.

West Wildwood

If you've never heard of West Wildwood, you're not the only one. I surveyed more than a few Shore regulars, who all replied with something along the lines of "west where?"

West Wildwood is located over a bridge on West Glenwood Avenue in Wildwood. It's the only road on and off the island. Most of the area is residential, but it is its own borough with its own fire department, police department, mayor, and everything else a township needs, though it doesn't have any traffic signals. No need—it's that small.

The bar in town, Westside Saloon (770 West Glenwood Avenue, West Wildwood 08260, 609-729-1488) is the kind of place where everyone knows your name, and if they don't, they'll probably ask. West Wildwood is prone to flooding, which is why most of the houses look like they've been lifted up on cinderblocks. Some started on the ground but were raised. Residents take the flooding in stride—one pointed out two areas of higher ground where people park their cars until the water levels drop back down.

You won't find much in West Wildwood in terms of nightlife or action, which is why most people like it. It's close to the water and has the same benefits as the Shore, but without a lot of traffic, both of car and people variety, or noise.

Learn more at www.westwildwoodnj.com.

Sand Jamm

609-522-4650
www.sandjamm.com
2701 Boardwalk, Wildwood 08260

Get your surf gear at this boardwalk shop, which stocks surf-inspired wear as well. If your board is of the wheeled variety, check out the upstairs Skate Shop. They have a flip-flop shop if that fashion's up your alley. Open 10 AM—midnight in season. Call for off-season hours.

Silen's Shoes and Resortwear

609-522-2155
5000 Pacific Ave., Wildwood 08260

Dress your feet in style at Silen's. They stock Uggs for the family, plus other foot comfort favorites, like New Balance, Crocs, Teva, and Clarks. Don't forget the clothes—they stock workout gear as well as T-shirts that say where you went on vacation. The shoe clearance rack is impressive, too, though it might take some work to find your size. Open 9 AM—8 PM in season. Call for off-season hours.

Wildwood Harley-Davidson

609-522-7151
www.wildwoodharley.com
127 W. Rio Grande Ave., Wildwood 08260

Rev up, hogs. This Harley-Davidson outpost has everything a biker could dream of. They rent bikes if you're looking for a sweet ride on your Wildwood vacation. They have a service shop, too, if your bike needs some work while in town. Store open 9 AM—7 PM Monday through Saturday and 10 AM—5 PM Sunday in season. Call for off-season hours.

WILDWOOD CREST

Diamond Beach Bums

609-522-9552
10100 Pacific Ave., Wildwood Crest 08260

Get what you need for the beach and more at Diamond Beach Bums. It's a hodgepodge of stuff inside and out (some of the inventory is kept on the porch), like boogie boards, bags, umbrellas, T-shirts, and souvenirs. Open 9 AM–8 PM Monday through Friday and 9 AM–8 PM Saturday and Sunday in season.

RIO GRANDE

Winterwood Gifts

609-465-3641
www.winterwoodgift.com
3137 RT 9 S., Rio Grande, 08242

Winterwood *used* to be in a secluded spot on NJ 9. That was before Wal-Mart and other box stores cropped up just to the south. But that hasn't changed Winterwood's charm. This Christmas store is set in an old house and sells every type of Christmas ornament, decoration, or tschotschke you could want. Winterwood also sells beach-themed items and decorations for other holidays. (Halloween seems to be a popular runner-up to the big December 25.) You'll find two more Winterwood stores in the area (Wildwood and Cape May), but the Rio Grande one is still the best. Open 10 AM–9 PM Monday through Saturday and 10 AM–6 AM Sunday in season; 10 AM–5 PM in the off season.

WEEKLY EVENTS (IN SEASON)

Monday

Captain Ocean's Ecological Program

609-522-2919

Learn more about the ecology of the Jersey Shore at this weekly morning event. Free.

Crest Pier Free Concerts

609-523-0202

This summertime concert series is laid-back and casual—bring your own chair, borrow theirs, or forget chairs altogether and dance the night away. Free.

Irish Pipe and Drum Parade

609-523-1602
www.dowildwood.com

Drink in the luck o' the Irish at this weekly event, which runs from late June through late August. 7:30 PM–9 PM. Free.

Tuesday

Doo Wop Back to the '50s Tour
609-523-1958
www.doowopusa.org
Doo Wop Experience Museum

Can't get enough of that '50s vibe? Then catch the Doo Wop Back to the '50s Tour, which is a trolley tour through the Wildwoods that showcases the seaside town's spot in music history and examples of stunning mid-20th-century architecture. Tour starts at 7 PM. $.

Wednesday

String Band Performances
609-523-1602
www.dowildwood.com

See the string bands strut their stuff along the Wildwoods boardwalk. Free.

Thursday

Doo Wop Back to the '50s Tour
609-523-1958
www.doowopusa.org
Doo Wop Experience Museum

Can't get enough of that '50s vibe? Then catch the Doo Wop Back to the '50s Tour, which is a trolley tour through the Wildwoods that showcases the seaside town's spot in music history and examples of stunning mid-20th-century architecture. 7 PM. $.

Friday

Fireworks on the Beach
609-523-1602
www.dowildwood.com

Sign from the neon garden at the Doo Wop Experience

Movies on the Beach
www.sunsetcinemainc.com
Beach behind the Wildwoods Convention Center at Montgomery Avenue, Wildwood 08260

Who needs the movie theater when you've got the beach? First-run movies are shown on the beach behind the Wildwoods Convention Center at Montgomery Avenue every night at 8:30 PM in season. $.

It doesn't need to be the Fourth of July for fireworks to grace the Wildwood sky. Catch the show at 10:30 PM. Free.

ANNUAL EVENTS

March

St. Patrick's Day Celebration and Parade
609-522-7722

Enjoy the best that Ireland has to offer at this annual parade. Noon. Free.

April

Doo Wop Duathlon
609-374-6495
www.delmosports.com

Nope, not a triathlon—this race involves a 2-mile run and a 12-mile bike ride and ends with a big breakfast for everyone who ran and rode. 8 AM. $$$$.

Sensational '60s Weekend
888-729-0033
www.fabfifties.com

This three-day event features dance parties, concerts, contests, and a street fair, all in the name of '60s music. Concerts at the Wildwoods Convention Center sell out quickly, so book as soon as you know you're ready to rock out.

May

Boardwalk Craft Show
Boardwalk south of the Wildwoods Convention Center
609-522-0378

Check out the handmade crafts on display at this weekend festival. 9 AM–5 PM. Free.

Wildwoods International Kite Festival
609-729-9000
www.wildwoodsnj.com
Wildwoods Convention Center

They're flying high in the sky at this event, which is the largest kite festival in the U.S. Inside the Wildwoods Convention Center, you'll find kite builders, competitions, kite making workshops, and kids activities. Outside, of course, you'll find kites flying high in the sky. Make sure to catch the Friday night illuminated kite fly, which starts at 9 PM. Free.

June

Mummers Brigade Weekend
609-729-9000

If you don't know what a mummer is, you might be puzzled by these string bands dressed in detailed and sparkling costumes walking down the street. But it's a Philadelphia tradition that has found a home at the Shore. Free.

National Marbles Tournament

304-337-2764
www.nationalmarblestournament.org

For over 80 years, kids have been coming to Ringer Stadium for this national competition, which pits the best mibsters (aka marble shooters) from around the country against each other. Free.

North Wildwood Original Italian-American Festival

609-729-4533
www.kofc2572.org

Celebrate your Italian roots (or how much you love Italian food) at this annual, three-day event.

Polka Spree by the Sea

609-729-9000
www.polkaspree.com
Wildwoods Convention Center

Polka bands from around the world fill the Wildwoods Convention Center with music and dancing for three days of events. Free.

Skydiving Extravaganza

856-629-7553

You don't have to jump, but you can watch the skydiving exhibitions on the beach. Free.

July

Cape May County Lifeguard Championship

609-522-3825
www.wcbp.org

Watch as lifeguards from 10 Cape May County beach patrols compete to determine who's the best of the best. Free.

Co-Ed Beach Ultimate Beach Frisbee Tournament

856-696-9705
www.wildwoodultimate.com

It's not just a lazy summer game—Frisbee is serious business, especially at this annual ultimate Frisbee tournament, which is on the beach. Free.

The Wildwoods International Kite Festival Greater Wildwoods Tourism Authority

Midsummer Festival
609-522-5176
Wildwood Crest

Celebrate the height of the summer season at this two-day event, which showcases crafters, music, and food and includes kids' activities as well. Free.

NJ State BBQ and Blues

www.njbbq.com, www.angleseablues.com

Whether you like BBQ, blues, or both, this annual festival brings the best from around New Jersey to Wildwood. The BBQ part is the New Jersey State Barbecue Championship, which pits the best of the best from the entire state against each other—for your stomach's delight. The blues part is the Anglesea Blues Festival, which brings regional and national acts to Wildwood to set the right mood for your culinary feast. Many acts play in the local clubs and bars after fair hours as well. Free.

Wildwoods Baby Parade

609-729-4000
Wildwoods Convention Center

This tradition, which started in 1909, showcases the cutest of the cute on parade up the boardwalk. Free.

August

United Way of Cape May County Rubber Ducky Regatta

609-729-2002
www.moreyspiers.com
Raging Waters Water Park

It's quite a sight—more than 10,000 rubber ducks race toward the finish line of the Endless River ride at Raging Waters Water Park to raise money for the United Way. Free.

September

Boardwalk Classic Car Show

609-523-8051
www.thundermoto.com
Wildwoods Convention Center

Check out the best of rides gone by at this annual event, which is on the boardwalk and inside the Wildwoods Convention Center. Free.

Irish Fall Festival

1-800-IRISH 91
North Wildwood

This four-day event celebrates the best of Irish culture and includes dancing, music, food, and crafts. The Wildwoods are heavy with Irish pubs—expect them to be packed, and offering specials. Free.

Mummers String Band Weekend & Strutters Contest

609-522-7722

If you don't know what a mummer is, you might be puzzled by these string bands dressed in detailed and sparkling costumes walking down the street. But it's a Philadelphia tradition that has found a home at the Shore. Enjoy their music at this twice-annual parade. This weekend-long event includes strutting contests, a concert, and a string band parade. The events are held at different locations through Wildwood. Free.

Roar to the Shore
609-729-8870
www.roartotheshoreonline.com

Bring yourself and your bike to this annual motorcycle rally, which draws over 100,000 bikes (and bikers). Activities include a Biker Bash, pig roast, and Biker Babe competition. Free.

Super Sunday
609-522-3900
www.moreyspiers.com
3501 Boardwalk, Wildwood

Say goodbye to summer at this one-day event. Morey's cuts prices on wristbands, and also sets up special games, prizes, and entertainment. $.

October

Barbershop Quartet Weekend
410-384-7655
www.harmonize.com/MAD/
Wildwoods Convention Center

Old-fashioned barbershop quartets take over the Wildwoods Convention Center at this annual convention. Events include barbershop quartet harmony competition, quartet, and chorus performances. Free.

Fabulous '50s Weekend
888-729-0033
www.fabfifties.com
4501 Boardwalk, Wildwood 08260

This annual event celebrates the Wildwoods' place in music history. Expect dance parties, concerts, a street fair, and contests. The concerts sell out quickly, so get your tickets as soon as you can.

December

Wildwood Holiday Spectacular
609-522-2444 X-2246
Wildwoods Convention Center

Ring in the holiday season in style at this holiday bazaar and concert.

EMERGENCY NUMBERS

In an emergency, dial 911.
Poison information: 1-800-222-1222
North Wildwood, non-emergency police: 609-522-2411
Wildwood, non-emergency police: 609-522-0222
Wildwood Crest, non-emergency police: 609-522-2456
West Wildwood, non-emergency police: 609-522-4060

HOSPITALS

Cape Regional Medical Center
609-463-2000
www.caperegional.com
2 Stone Harbor Blvd., Cape May Court House 08260

NEWSPAPERS

The Wildwood Leader
609-624-8900
www.thewildwoodleader.com

TRANSPORTATION

Caribbean Cab Company
609-523-8000

Checker Cab Company
609-522-1431

Hertz Rent-A-Car
609-522-0049
www.hertz.com

New Jersey Transit
800-582-5946
www.njtransit.com

Yellow Cab Company
609-522-0555

Tourism Contacts

Greater Wildwood Chamber of Commerce
609-729-4000
www.wildwoods.com

Greater Wildwoods Tourism Improvement and Development Authority
1-800-WW-BY-SEA
www.wildwoodsnj.com

New Jersey Travel and Tourism
www.state.nj.us/travel
1-800-VISITNJ

6

Cape May

Victorian Enchantment

Including West Cape May, North Cape May, and Erma

Cape May is, in a word, beautiful. The "Queen of the Seaside Resorts" at the tip of New Jersey is one of the most quaint towns on the Shore, and also the most year-round, after Atlantic City. But Cape May and Atlantic City have almost nothing in common except the Atlantic Ocean. Instead of gambling and flash and noise, Cape May is a quiet, romantic step back in time. The town is almost 400 years old and, in its entirety, a National Historic Landmark.

Cape May plays up its Victorian history, even if its past stretches back before anyone could have guessed what Queen Anne or Gothic Revival style would look like. But a fire wiped out a chunk of the town in 1878—30 blocks. What sprang up in the wake of that fire are what you'll see around town today: expansive Victorian buildings, once vacation homes for the wealthiest of Philadelphia's citizens, that are now charming bed & breakfasts where the innkeeper always knows your name.

That isn't to say that Cape May doesn't bustle. Its nightlife is among the most exciting at the Shore. But it's not a place where you'll find bars that pack in thousands of 20- and 30-somethings. The scene is more elegant and sophisticated, but with a casual feel. You are by the beach, after all.

Cape May is a romantic spot, too. It's the third largest destination wedding site in the U.S., and the most popular in the Northeast. That romantic appeal stretches year-round and makes Cape May a destination when most Shore towns have shut down for the year. While summer is the busiest season—and kids are more than welcome—Cape May is also bustling in the spring and especially in the fall, when couples looking to get away turn to the quaint streets, romantic inns, and gourmet restaurants to celebrate being together, whether it's their first anniversary or their 50th.

It's also in a unique geographical position. Cape May is the southernmost point in New Jersey, and because it's here that the Atlantic Ocean meets the Delaware Bay, Cape May is home to rich ecosystems. It's also along the Atlantic Flyway and a popular resting spot for migratory birds. Scott Weidensaul, author of *Of a Feather: A Brief History of American Birding*, writes that "Cape May . . . may be the single best place in North American—perhaps the world—for birding." So don't be surprised to see a lot of people wandering the streets with binoculars around their necks in the spring and summer. You can also watch a sunset over

Kayaking in Cape May Craig Terry

the ocean at Sunset Beach at Cape May Point.

Most of Cape May's dining, shopping, and places to stay are in the heart of the city, what's known as Cape May proper. West Cape May, North Cape May, and inland Erma are more residential but offer their own delights.

LODGING

CAPE MAY

Abbey Bed & Breakfast Inn
1-866-884-8800
www.abbeybedandbreakfast.com
34 Gurney Street, Cape May 08204

You won't find any monks here, but you will be wrapped in a Victorian feel at this Gothic Revival mansion. The Abbey doesn't just use the Victorian era as a design inspiration to start from, but as the Bible of how it's fitted out, from furniture to antiques. Its location makes it popular with birders as it's close to birding sites. Open April through mid-December. $–$$.

Alexander's Inn
1-877-484-2555
www.alexandersinn.com
653 Washington St., Cape May 08204

Diane and Larry Muentz have been running Alexander's for nearly 30 years. It's one of Cape May's quintessential Victorian bed & breakfasts, from the décor to the antiques. The Inn has eight rooms as well as a recently restored 1868 cottage, located directly across the street from the main inn. It's a hot spot for romantics, given the Victorian essence of the place, and that children under 14 years old are not allowed to stay at the Inn. For an opulent dining experience, don't miss the restaurant, also called Alexander's, that's located within the inn—Diane is not only an innkeeper, but also the chef. $$$–$$$$.

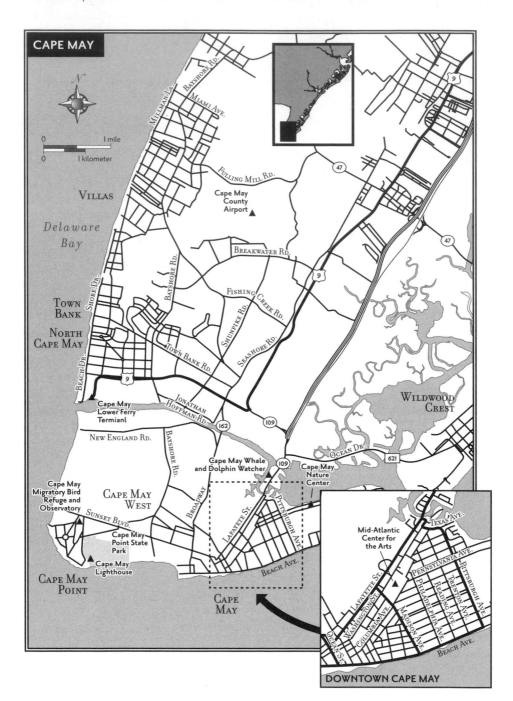

CAPE MAY

N

0 _____ 1 mile
0 _____ 1 kilometer

VILLAS

Delaware
Bay

TOWN
BANK

NORTH
CAPE MAY

MILLMAN LA.
BAYSHORE RD.
MIAMI AVE.

FULLING MILL RD.

Cape May
County
Airport ▲

BREAKWATER RD.

FISHING CREEK RD.

BAYSHORE RD.
SHUNPIKE RD.
SEASHORE RD.

TOWN BANK RD.

SHORE DR.

BEACH DR.

9

JONATHAN
HOFFMAN RD.

Cape May
Lower Ferry
Termianl

NEW ENGLAND RD.

BAYSHORE RD.

162

109

Cape May Whale
and Dolphin Watcher ▲

109

Cape May
Nature
Center

OCEAN DR.

621

WILDWOOD
CREST

Cape May
Migratory Bird
Refuge and
Observatory

CAPE MAY
WEST

SUNSET BLVD.

BROADWAY

LAFAYETTE ST.

PITTSBURGH AVE.

BEACH AVE.

Cape May
Point State
Park

▲ Cape May
Lighthouse

CAPE MAY
POINT

CAPE
MAY

47

47

9

DOWNTOWN CAPE MAY

TEXAS AVE.

Mid-Atlantic
Center for
the Arts ▲

PENNSYLVANIA AVE.
PHILADELPHIA AVE.
READING AVE.
TRENTON AVE.
PITTSBURGH AVE.

LAFAYETTE ST.
WASHINGTON ST.
COLUMBIA AVE.
MADISON AVE.

OCEAN ST.

BEACH AVE.

Angel of the Sea

1-800-848-3369
www.angelofthesea.com
5 Trenton Ave., Cape May 08204

The two buildings that make up the Angel of the Sea used to be one house (and, yes, that was one big house). The home was built in 1850 as the summer home for Philadelphia chemist William Weightman, Sr. After construction, Weightman decided that he'd rather have an ocean view, so he hired local farmers to move the house in the off season. The task proved to be more daunting than the farmers thought—when they got both halves of the house on the right location, they couldn't figure out how to put the two back together again, so they built walls on the open ends so that Weightman had two summer houses instead of one. You can still see where the two houses should have met to become one again. The building fell out of its glamorous beginnings and was abandoned when John and Barbara Girton literally climbed through one of the broken windows to see what was inside. They bought the property and renovated it. Since the building reopened as the Angel of the Sea, it's been recognized as one of the top 10 bed & breakfasts in the United States, and to step inside, you'd never dream that this gorgeous and inviting bed & breakfast was ever empty and vandalized. The building has 27 guest rooms, all decorated differently, all in Victorian style. $$–$$$$.

Billmae Cottage

609-898-8558
www.billmae.com
1015 Washington St., Cape May 08204

Want to bring Fido along? He or she is welcome at the Billmae Cottage, and might make a few friends, too, at this "B&D"—D stands for "doggie." The rooms have enough space for you, your family, and, of course,

Sterger's Beach Service

609-884-3058
www.eastcoastparasail.com/stegers.html

If you're not keen on buying all those thing that make the beach more enjoyable—beach chairs, umbrellas, body boards, surf boards—then Sterger's will bring them to you. They have 12 locations on the beach. You can even rent a storage box to keep everything together on a longer stay. Hourly, daily, weekly, monthly, and seasonal rentals available. $–$$$$.

your dog. They're decorated in country style and include a parlor, full kitchen, and bath. Remember, this isn't a B&B, so breakfast is not part of the package, but you can't miss out on "Yappy Hour" where the guest dogs, neighborhood dogs (and their owners, too) are invited to meet and hang out on the enclosed porch with innkeepers Bob and Linda Steenrod and their two husky/Lab/Ridgeback mixes, Jameson and Guinness. Bob and Linda also run the Billmae Cottage, which is a 1700s standalone house for a family (or up to nine people) to share. No cats allowed. $$.

Hotel Alcott

1-800-272-3004
www.hotelalcott.com
107–133 Grant St., Cape May 08204

The historic and the modern are mixed well at this 130-year-old hotel. Sure, you'll find an LCD television in your room, but it's surrounded by suites recently remodeled to reflect the building's rich Victorian history. A big draw is the veranda, with its white wood railings, rocking chairs, and ocean breezes. Why Hotel Alcott? Because Louisa May Alcott, author of *Little Women,* was a frequent guest. $$$–$$$$.

Yappy Hour at the Billmae Cottage

Carroll Villa Bed & Breakfast

877-275-8452
www.carrollvilla.com
19 Jackson Street, Cape May 08204

Locals and vacationers flock to Carroll Villa to eat at the Mad Batter, but those in the know are well aware of the gorgeous 22 rooms here—each one is beautifully decorated in Victorian style and, depending on the room, can also have a wicker sitting area. It's a quiet elegance. $$–$$$.

The Chalfonte Hotel

609-884-8409
www.chalfonte.com
301 Howard St., Cape May 08204

While most of the Victorian hotels in the area have updated themselves to 21st-century standards, the Chalfonte has held onto its classic charm. It doesn't have air conditioning or heat, and many of the rooms don't have private bathrooms. A lot of patrons don't see these as bad things, which is why the hotel is still in business, and thriving—it's a step back to a world uncluttered by technology, and many guests seek out that simplicity. The Chalfonte also offers single accommodations—a rarity in the area. Make sure you stop in at the hotel's King Edward Bar. "The Eddie" is a local's favorite (and is air conditioned). Open in season. $$–$$$

Inn at the Park

1-866-884-8406
1002 Washington St., Cape May 08204
www.innattheparknj.com

The Victorian charm is not lost at this bed & breakfast, which is right near the Emlen Physick estate. Enjoy a predinner cocktail hour by sampling from innkeepers Jay and Mary Ann Gorrick's extensive wine collection. This food here leans more toward the salty than the sweet—like a predinner appe-

The Fire

It might have happened more than 100 years ago, but people in Cape May still talk about "the fire." Why? Because it so radically changed the way the town looks.

Early on the morning of November 9, 1878, arsonists set a fire in Ocean House, a hotel that had been closed for the winter. It quickly spread to Congress Hall, and then from one wooden structure to another. Newspapers from the time say that the fire burned for over 11 hours, though it smoldered for much longer. In all, the fire destroyed more than 35 acres of Cape May. No one was killed, and the arsonists were never caught.

Of course the fire was devastating. But the destruction of so much property called for regrowth, and new building. If not for the fire, Cape May wouldn't have many of the Victorian bed & breakfasts that are such a draw today. If you read through the lodging section of this book, you'll see that most of the Victorian-themed buildings were constructed in the 1880s, many on the spots of the grand old (and very wooden) hotels that burned to the ground. Most residents think that a demolish-and-redevelopment craze that almost took over the town in the 1970s would have been much more devastating. And you know what? I think they're right.

tizer without having to order at the bar. The rooms are cozy with just a little bit of fuss—enough to enhance the sweet romantic vibe of the inn without going overboard. $$–$$$$.

Inn of Cape May

1-800-582-5933
www.innofcapemay.com
7 Ocean St., Cape May 08204

Congress Hall
888-944-1816
www.congresshall.com
251 Beach Ave., Cape May 08204

There might not be a "hotel" in the title, but Cape May's Congress Hall has been serving guests in luxury and style since 1816. Well, with a few slight interruptions, including fire, hurricanes, war, and scores of renovations. As it stands today, Congress Hall is a reincarnation of its former self with the most modern of amenities, offering visitors a first-class vacation with a laid back, almost Southern charm.

"When first built, the hotel was called the 'Big House by the Sea,' " says John Daily, general manager of Congress Hall. And it was—in 1816, it had 100 rooms, which made it one of the largest hotels in the country. Most people weren't sure how a seaside hotel would do. Congress Hall was, after all, the first such establishment. So the townspeople nicknamed the building "Tommy's Folly" after Thomas Hughes, who built Congress Hall. Where does the Congress part come in? From 1829 to 1833, Hughes served in Congress—and his building proved to be no folly.

The original building burned down in the great fire of 1878. Within a year, Congress Hall—this time built of brick instead of wood—was back in action. Since then, Congress Hall has been at the center of a bitter town feud, shut down, reopened as the site of the first post-Prohibition cocktail bar, and part of the Cape May Bible Conference. In 1995, Curtis Bashaw and Craig Wood brought the building back to how it looked, reopening in 2002. Many of the rooms still contain vintage pieces, like clawfoot bathtubs, but have the modern conveniences of a luxury hotel. Plus, if you're a guest at the hotel, they'll bring your lunch to your beach chair. The restaurants and bars at Congress Hall bustle all season long, and the line of rocking chairs outside are a popular meeting spot.

Want to change your life at Congress Hall? It's a great place to get hitched. "We do over 80 weddings a year now," says Daily. "And at every wedding, there's one or two potential brides who will say they want the same kind of experience." But book ahead—even though Congress Hall was once a folly, it's now a success, and very much in demand.

Congress Hall is also home to the Cape May Day Spa and pool, plus the Blue Pig Tavern (that, despite the swine-y name, is a decidedly sophisticated place to eat in Cape May) and two lounges. The Boiler Room is where its name implies—in the site of the hotel's former boiler room, and its mix of exposed walls plus stainless steel décor and live music creates a sophisticated nightclub experience underground. You can also sip swanky cocktails and relax in the Brown Room, which connects the lobby with the ballroom and dining rooms.

If you're a beer fan, especially microbrews, try the Blue Pig Tavern Ale. It has a light taste made for summer while still embodied with flavors—the folks at Congress Hall tell me it's Midwestern two-row malt, imported Munich malts, Mount Hood, and Magnum hops that I'm tasting. I just know that I liked what I tried, and what I saw at Congress Hall.

The Inn of Cape May started as a 60-room boarding house along the water in Cape May. That was in 1894, and the Inn is still welcoming vacationers today, though it's expanded from 60 rooms to one of the largest and most recognizable lodgings in Cape May. Every room is different, but most have wicker furniture and some have antiques. The veranda, set under bright purple awnings, is popular with guests and those waiting for a meal at Aleathea's Restaurant, which is located inside the Inn.

Open in season, weekends only mid-October through mid-December. $$$–$$$$.

La Mer Beachfront Inn
1-800-644-5004
www.capemaylamer.com
1317 Beach Ave., Cape May 08204

Not everything is Victorian in Cape May. One obvious example is La Mer, which offers 133 thoroughly modern rooms right across the street from the ocean. The inn also has a pool, sundeck, fitness center, business center, and the always fun Sand Bar Lounge. Closed January 3 to Valentine's Day. $$$–$$$$.

Mainstay Bed and Breakfast Inn
609-884-8690
www.mainstayinn.com
635 Columbia Ave., Cape May 08204

This inn, which was built in the late 1800s and designed by Philadelphia architect Stephen D. Button, started out as a private gambling club. From there, it changed hands and served as a summer residence, a guest house, and a bed & breakfast. A 1970s renovation brought the inn back to the way it looked when Lady Luck lived within its walls, and its well-appointed, lush rooms are decorated appropriately (in fact, some of the furniture could easily be showcased in museums). The Mainstay also includes a cottage, which is located next door and was built by the same architect as the original portion of the Mainstay. Open April through December, weekends only December through April. $$$$.

Mission Inn
1-800-800-8380
www.missioninn.net
1117 New Jersey Ave., Cape May 08204

This California Mission–style building looks out of place among the gingerbread houses throughout town, but that's why a lot of visitors call here first for a place to stay—not everyone likes the fussiness or florals of a typical bed & breakfast. Instead, the Mission's rooms are works of art of a different kind, with murals depicting seascapes or highly detailed headboards on the walls. They also have exquisite gardens and a solarium. If you're a classic film buff, the Mission Inn has pedigree—Tyrone Power, Errol Flynn, Diana Barrymore, and Gloria Swanson have all stayed at here. $$$–$$$$.

Poor Richard's Inn
609-884-3536
www.poorrichardsinn.com
17 Jackson St., Cape May 08204

It's not exactly a poorhouse, though innkeeper Harriet Sosson tries to keep prices in check so that you can enjoy a beachside vacation without emptying your savings account. The rooms are a hodge-podge of antiques, leaning toward country Victorian but not stuck in it. If you've got a cat allergy, you should know that a kitty lives on the premises. Closed January through mid-February. $$–$$$.

Queen Victoria Bed & Breakfast
609-884-8702
www.queenvictoria.com
102 Ocean St., Cape May 08204

It's not exactly one bed & breakfast at Queen Victoria—the complex is made up of four buildings. The Queen Victoria building, which has nine rooms, was built in 1881 and sold in 1889 to Dr. Franklin Hughes, who leased it to the Navy to use as a war camp community service building before the Hughes family took up residence in 1918. The House of the Royals has nine rooms and is the oldest structure on the property. It was built in 1776 by Charles Shaw, who also built the Chalfonte Hotel and Emlen Physick Estate. The Queen's Cottage is an 1888 building and is the cottage of choice for many vacationing couples. Prince Albert Hall has six rooms and five luxury suites, all with private whirlpool tubs. The rooms, like the building, are all Victorian. $$$–$$$$.

DINING

NORTH CAPE MAY

Harpoon Henry's
609-886-5529
www.harpoonhenrys.net
91 Beach Dr., North Cape May 08204

Like Teresa and Ed Henry's other Cape May restaurant, Henry's on the Beach, the view here is beautiful. Instead of beach sights, though, this Harpoon Henry's overlooks the Delaware Bay, hence the sunset views. Build your own burger, or try a basket of something good and fried, like shrimp or chicken. They have over 250 frozen drinks, too, so you can sip and toast as that sun slides down. Lunch, dinner mid-April through mid-November. Weekends only in spring and fall. $$.

Rainbow Palace Family Restaurant
609-886-9891
3718 Bayshore Rd., North Cape May 08204
If you want to take the kids out for lunch and maybe ice cream, or maybe miniature golf, head to Rainbow Palace because they've got all three, plus mini remote-control motorboats. The food is classic American, like burgers and chicken Caesar salad, with dashes of flair, like the Greek gyro and veggie wrap. The ice cream is the real highlight—Rainbow has dozens of sundae options and more than enough to make you want to golf off that extra scoop. Breakfast, lunch. $.

Uncle Bill's Pancake House
609-886-0066
3820 Bayshore Rd., North Cape May 08204

Get your day going at Uncle Bills, which packs in hungry patrons in just about every South Jersey Shore town (poor Atlantic City and Sea Isle City). The main attraction, of course, is the pancakes, but they also have plenty of egg options as well as waffles and sandwiches. Expect long waits on the weekends in season. No credit cards. Breakfast, lunch in season. $.

CAPE MAY

Alexander's
609-884-2555
www.alexandersinn.com
Alexander's Inn
653 Washington St., Cape May 08204

This Zagat-rated restaurant is nestled into the Alexander's Inn. It's well known as a romantic Victorian-themed spot, and for its elegance—don't be surprised by the tuxedoed waiters. The French food matches the décor. Caviar is a menu regular, as are escargots, roast half duckling, sautéed sweetbreads, soft shell crab, and twin lobster tails. If you stay at Alexander's Inn on a Saturday night, their superb five-course Sunday brunch is complimentary. Dinner. Brunch Sunday. $$$$.

Axelsson's Blue Claw
609-884-5878
www.blueclawrestaurant.com
991 Ocean Dr., Cape May 08204

This dockside restaurant comes with a five-star rating from the North American Restaurant Association. As you can imagine, the blue claw crab crab cakes (appetizer and entrée sizes) are a popular menu item, as are rich pasta dishes and the oyster bar. They have an impressive martini menu as well. Dinner. $$$.

Ballyhoo's
609-884-5611

www.grandhotelcapemay.com/ballyhoos
1045 Beach Dr., Cape May 08204

It's Caribbean cool at this popular Cape May spot. If you have a monster appetite, try the "Tornadoes of Beef," which includes two filets and jumbo lump crabmeat, or the all-you-can-eat seafood buffet on Thursdays. Happy hour is very happy at Ballyhoo's, especially if you're sipping from "The Beast," which is a concoction of spiced and dark rum and Ballyhoo's special tournament punch. Breakfast, lunch, dinner. Breakfast on weekends only October through April. $$.

Blue Pig Tavern
609-884-8422
www.congresshall.com
Congress Hall
251 Beach Ave., Cape May 08204

This restaurant isn't really a tavern, and, aside from the charbroiled pork chop, doesn't have much to do with pigs. Congress Hall's in-house restaurant was named after the first tavern to come to Cape May, which was located on what is now Congress Hall's lawn. The menu is a mix of surf and turf classics but with a new cuisine twist, like the Mediterranean summer salmon that features not just beefsteak tomatoes but also kalamata olives and couscous. I liked the baked macaroni and cheese—a grown-up spin on a childhood classic. Eat inside or outside. Breakfast, lunch, dinner. $$.

Carriage House Tearoom & Café
609-884-5111
www.capemaymac.org
1048 Washington St., Cape May 08204

The Carriage House, which is part of the Emlen Physick Estate, serves classic tearoom dishes, like fresh-baked tea breads, sandwiches, and soup du jour, plus desserts to go with the Harney & Sons teas. They also serve café selections like sandwiches and wraps if you're going more for the atmosphere. The meals are sold in packages and include several small courses. For the complete high tea experience, don one of the colorful and flowery hats provided by the Carriage House, and choose the Victorian Lunch Combination, which includes bread, soup, salad, sandwich, dessert, and, of course, your tea. BYOB. Lunch, afternoon tea in season. Call for off-season hours. $$.

Copperfish
609-898-0354
1246 RT 109 S., Cape May 08204

It's New American cuisine at this Zagat-rated restaurant. What's New American? How about pecan-encrusted salmon, peanut curry chicken, and New York strip steak? They stick local, too, and serve only New Jersey wines. BYOB otherwise. Dinner in season. Closed Monday. $$.

Cucina Rosa
609-898-9800
www.cucinarosa.com
301 Washington Street Mall, Cape May 08204

It's family-friendly at this well-priced Italian restaurant. Everything's homemade, including the cannolis, which are not to be missed. For the best people watching spot, sit on the outdoor patio. BYOB. Dinner. Closed Wednesday. Closed January through mid-February. $$–$$$.

Dock Mike's Pancake House
609-884-2855
www.dockmikes.com
1231 RT 109, Cape May 08204

The name here is a bit misleading. While Dock Mike's certainly dishes up pancakes in many different varieties, including sweet potato and "Mikey" Mouse, it's also a lunch spot and has over 100 different items to try,

Elaine's Victorian Inn & Dinner Theater   Bill Bader, www.capegraphics.com

like wraps, seafood samplers, and cheese steaks—all of which are listed on your placemat menu. No credit cards. Breakfast, lunch. $–$$.

The Ebbitt Room

609-884-5700
www.virginiahotel.com
Virginia Hotel
25 Jackson St., Cape May 08204

This gourmet restaurant has received kudos from all over the country, from *The New York Times* to Zagat, which rates it as one of the best restaurants at the Jersey Shore. It's *the* place to go in Cape May for a luxurious meal, or for a special occasion (more than a few engagements have been sealed at the Ebbitt Room). It's hard to go wrong with anything on the menu—oysters and caviar; steamed mussels; black sea bass with foie gras; pan-roasted free-range chicken—everything is gourmet, and good. The

cheese plates are knockouts, too. If you're not feeling up to the full luxury experience, you can sample bits of the Ebbitt Room menu, like Kobe beef sliders and pommes frites, in the Ebbitt Room Lounge. Reservations recommended. Dinner. $$$–$$$$.

Elaine's Dinner Theater

609-884-4358
www.elainesdinnertheater.com
513 Lafayette St., Cape May 08204

If you like a fright with your meal, check out Elaine's, which runs a variety of slightly frightly (not enough to ruin your appetite) shows to go with three-course meals. Elaine's has clout, too—the Food Network named it one of the top five dinner theaters in America. For a less theatrical yet still horror-ific dinner experience, opt for your meal in the haunted mansion, which keeps dinner interesting with funny illusions, special effects, guest ghosts, and deadly funny stand-up comics (pun intended). Closed January through March. $$$.

Gecko's
609-898-7750
31 Perry Street, Cape May 08204

Make sure you sit on the deck at Gecko's. The treetop canopy makes it a shady experience just close enough to the action of Cape May to keep the people watching interesting. Chef Randy Bithell has created a Southwestern menu, which also explains why you see so many people carry in Coronas for their meals. The three-sister quesadilla is a highlight, and might make you think that turning vegetarian isn't such a bad idea. BYOB. Lunch, dinner in season. $$.

Henry's on the Beach
609-884-8826
www.henrysonthebeach.com
702 Beach Ave., Cape May 08204

If you're worried you won't be able to grab a beachside seat at Henry's, don't worry—that deck is huge, and is what makes Henry's a draw. The food doesn't hurt, either—the Italian bake is a perennial favorite, as is the Key lime pie. If you're a late riser, Henry's has select breakfast items on the lunch menu. BYOB. Breakfast, lunch, dinner in season. $$.

Hot Dog Tommy's
609-884-8388
www.hotdogtommys.com
Jackson Street at Beach Ave., Cape May 08204

Sure, you could get just a hot dog here, but why not step out of norm and go for The Doc Dog, which has mustard, chili, and onions? Or the Buffalo Dog, which has buffalo sauce, onions, and blue cheese? Or a Tornado Dog, which has mashed potatoes, chili, cheese, salsa, banana peppers, and

sour cream? Hopefully you'll catch Tommy himself behind the counter. He and his hot dog hat are hard to miss. No credit cards. Breakfast, lunch in season. $.

Lobster House
609-884-8296
www.thelobsterhouse.com
Fisherman's Wharf, Cape May Harbor, Cape May 08204

Eat right on the water—literally on the deck of a schooner—at this popular seafood spot. If you don't quite have the right sea legs, don't worry—the bulk of the Lobster House's seating is indoors. Seafood is king here, both on the main restaurant menu and through the ever popular raw bar. The specialty? Lobster, of course, which comes in the form of lobster tails or whole lobster, steamed or broiled. Don't turn aside the house bread, either—it's incredible. Expect long waits in the summer, though there is a way around the line. I visited on a Saturday night in August and arrived right at 5 PM. The restaurant had just opened, so we early birds were put into a line and seated—no wait required. An hour later, though, a few dozen people hung around the bar and entrance to the Lobster House for what I heard was expected to be a wait of an hour or two. In this case, at least, the early bird gets the worm. Or the lobster. Breakfast, lunch, dinner in season. Call for off-season hours. $$–$$$$.

Lucky Bones Backwater Grille
609-884-BONE
1200 RT 109 S., Cape May 08204

Even though this restaurant has the same owners and executive chef as the Pelican Club, and even lives in the same building, Lucky Bones has lost the pomp and circumstance (and high prices) of its predecessor, which closed in 2005. The menu runs from thick-crust brick oven pizza to the Lucky Bones Burger—all 10 ounces of it. The late

Lobster House Spirit Catcher Photography

night menu features the greatest hits of the dinner menu, and the bar scene is packed—one of the busiest in Cape May year-round. Lunch, dinner. $$.

Mad Batter
609-884-5970
www.madbatter.com
Carroll Villa Hotel
19 Jackson St., Cape My 08204

New Jersey Monthly named Mad Batter as having the best breakfast and lunch in the state. And who can blame them? The breakfast menu takes American breakfast classics, like pancakes and French toast, and makes them gourmet. The Victorian brunch is a special treat, as is dinner at this hotel restaurant. The bar is a great place to

stop for a drink and a meal, too. Reservations recommended for dinner. Breakfast, lunch, dinner in season. Weekends only January through March. $$–$$$.

MagicBrain CyberCafé
609-884-8188
www.magicbraincybercafe.com
31 Perry St., Cape May 08204

You can't help it—you've gotta be connected, even while on vacation. If you don't want to lug your laptop to the beach (or even if you do and need an Internet hookup), stop in here. It works as a standalone coffeehouse, too—they pipe in cool tunes from the likes of Jamie Cullum and Amy Winehouse along with tasty drinks and Green Mountain

Coffee Roasters coffee. The computers are speedy and let you make the most of whatever time you buy for the day or the week—you can keep coming back if you still have minutes left. Call for hours. $.

Mario's Pizza

609-884-0085

7 Victorian Plz., Cape May 08204

Just because Cape May is full of gourmet restaurants doesn't meant that, sometimes, all you want is a slice of pizza. Mario's is a good bet in such instances. They also serve up hearty Italian dishes, like roma panini and parmesan if you're looking to eat in, but in a casual setting. BYOB. Lunch, dinner. Closed January and February. $.

Martini Beach

609-884-1925

www.martinibeachcapemay.com

429 Beach Ave., Cape May 08204

They've got martinis, and views of the beach. What more could you want? Food, of course, and Martini Beach was the first spot in Cape May to offer tapas, or small plate, dining. This way, you can taste the beef satay, seared sea scallops, baby lamb chops, and warm duck salad in one meal. They also offer regular-size meals if you don't want to share. You can't beat the view—Martini Beach is upstairs, so you can overlook the beach while you nosh or sip. Live music in season. Reservations recommended. Dinner, late night. $$.

McGlade's on the Pier

609-884-2614

722 Beach Ave., Cape May 08204

If you're an omelet fan, you must stop here. McGlade's has more than 20 varieties on the menu, and was named Omelet Queen by *The New York Times*. And the beach views are spectacular. If you're feeling adventurous, try the Mickey omelet, which has lump crab, sprouts, and avocado. If eggs aren't your thing, McGlade's has other menu options, like crab cakes and filet. Breakfast, lunch, dinner. $.

The Merion Inn

609-884-8368

www.merioninn.com

106 Decatur St., Cape May 08204

Philadelphia Magazine dubbed the Merion Inn the best place to get a martini in Cape May. The drinks (and dinner) start at 5 PM with nightly piano kicking in at 5:30 PM. The décor leans to the Victorian (the inn was built in 1885), but the food is very now, with items like a pear, walnut, and gorgonzola salad, deviled crab cakes, flounder franchese, and lobster tail. The no-frills seafood menu is a simple yet tasty option as well. If you're dining late, ask about the Night Owl prix fixe option. Dinner, late night. $$.

Peter Shields Inn & Restaurant

1-800-355-6565

www.petershieldsinn.com

1301 Beach Dr., Cape May 08204

The views are almost as good as the food at this oceanside restaurant. I say almost

St. Mary's by the Sea

What's that white and red building at the southernmost point in New Jersey? No, it's not a mansion, hotel, or luxury cottage. It's a convent.

St. Mary's by the Sea was the Shoreham Hotel and is now the summer retreat for the Sisters of St. Joseph. There were once four hotels at the point—Sea Grover House, Cape House, Centennial House, and the Shoreham Hotel—but the rest were lost to the sea.

Coincidence that the nuns' retreat is the only building left? That's for you to decide.

Married in Cape May

Cape May is the most popular destination wedding spot in the Northeast, and the third most popular in the country, behind only Las Vegas and Walt Disney World. In 1999, 185 couples registered for marriage licenses. By 2006, that number had jumped to over 400, and that's not counting vow renewals, which are also popular in town.

"Businesses in town have really catered to weddings. They've all gotten behind it and realized what a great business it is," says Bob Steenrod, president of the Chamber of Commerce of Greater Cape May—and a registered minister who performs some of those weddings.

The result is an economic force that is filling hotel rooms, bed & breakfasts, restaurants, shops, and many of Cape May's rental halls, which accommodate everything from small gatherings to big, blowout receptions.

"What really made it work, first, is that in Cape May, you can get married on the beach," says Catherine J. Walton, who started Weddings by the Sea, a wedding planning business, 10 years ago. Walton came to town before a Cape May wedding was the thing to do, and she's watched the wedding business turn into an economic bump that's spread across America's oldest seaside resort.

If you're looking to tie the knot in Cape May, the town offers plenty of rental spaces that can accommodate intimate affairs (Hotel Alcott) to large, elegant parties (Congress Hall). It's also one of the few Shore towns that features sunsets on the actual beach instead of the bays. At the aptly named Sunset Beach, couples can get married as the sun goes down. Cape May also has the Harbor View Park Pavilion, which provides a slightly indoor setting while including the sights and sounds that make the beach such a draw. Sunsets aren't mandatory—you can get married on the beach during the day, too. In fact, Cape May is such a popular wedding spot that couples now must register with the township for a beach time slot. This way, the nuptials aren't overlapping.

You can get just about everything you need for a wedding in Cape May—church, reception site, officiant, flowers, cake, decorations, invitations, and jewelry. The only thing not readily available are wedding dresses, and that's because most brides are coming from the Philadelphia, New York, Baltimore, or Washington, DC areas and bring their gowns with them.

"You can do as much or as little as you want," says Steenrod, who has performed weddings in everything from full Victorian formal garb to Hawaiian-themed outfits. When the daughter of Jay and Mary Ann Gorrick (the couple who own the Inn at the Park bed & breakfast) wanted a Victorian-themed marriage, they planned a simple reception on the grounds of the grand Victorian Emlen Physick Estate. Steenrod's also officiated second marriages, a Hindu-Catholic wedding, and happily includes dogs in ceremonies.

The most popular wedding months in Cape May are September and October, followed by June and May, then July and August, though Walton has planned beach weddings as early as April and as late as November.

because Chef Eric Hegyi has done a superb job creating a menu of New American cuisine with menu items like seafood tapas and rocket salad (a mix of baby arugula, toasted hazelnuts, sweet and sour beets, feta, and tomatoes) with seaside classics, like lobster crab cake and seafood risotto. No children or infants. BYOB. Dinner. Closed Mondays in the off season. Dinner. $$$.

Pilot House

609-884-3449
www.pilothousecapemay.com
142 Decatur St., Cape May 08204

The Pilot House is that hole in the wall with the good food, the worn bar, and the same cluster of guys at their designated barstools. Except the Pilot House isn't a hole in the wall but smack in the middle of Cape May. That doesn't take away from its locals-only feel, especially in the off season. The food is classic, simple, and good, with selections like seafood pasta, Cape May crab cakes, and London broil. They have a kids' menu, too, if you're bringing the tykes. Lunch, dinner. $$.

Ugly Mug

609-884-3459
www.uglymugenterprises.com
426 Washington St., Cape May 08204

The food is good and hearty at this longtime Cape May staple. No need to dress up—just come as you are, and enjoy. It's mostly American bar food, though the restaurant is family-friendly before 9 PM, so don't worry if you're bringing the kids. They won't be too corrupted. Every August, Ugly Mug hosts a froth blowing contest, which is exactly what it sounds like—a contest to determine who can blow the most froth out of their ugly mug of beer. Silly hats are optional. Lunch, dinner, late night. $.

Uncle Bill's Pancake House

609-884-7199
261 Beach Ave., Cape May 08204

Get your day going at Uncle Bills, which packs in hungry patrons in just about every South Jersey Shore town (poor Atlantic City and Sea Isle City). The main attraction, of course, is the pancakes, but they also have plenty of egg options, as well as waffles and sandwiches. Expect long waits on the weekends in season. No credit cards. Breakfast, lunch in season. $.

Washington Inn Bill Horan Photography

Washington Inn
609-884-5697
www.washingtoninn.com
801 Washington St., Cape May 08204

Washington Inn started as a plantation home in 1840. Today, it's one of the most elegant dining experiences in Cape May. While the main menu might tempt you to fill your stomach with the likes of herb-crusted New Zealand rack of lamb and five-spice grilled Long Island duck breast, leave room for dessert. In the spring and fall, Washington Inn also offers wine cellar dinners. What better place to hold them than at Washington Inn, which has over 10,000 bottles? Proper dress required. Reservations recommended. Dinner. Closed January through mid-February. Friday, Saturday, and Sunday only February and March. $$$.

WEST CAPE MAY

Black Duck on Sunset
609-898-0100
www.blackduckonsunset.com
1 Sunset Blvd., West Cape May 08204

This Victorian BYOB restaurant is rated by Zagat as one of the best at the Jersey Shore. It's tucked into a gray clapboard house, and even if the food is luxurious, the feeling of Black Duck is comfortable and like that home away from home. The black and white photographs that grace the walls add to that feeling. On the menu, you'll find fresh seafood dishes, meats, and the house special—the roast duck. BYOB. Dinner in season. Call for hours off season. $$$.

Mangia Mangia
609-884-2429
www.mangiamangiacapemay.com
110 North Broadway, West Cape May 08204

If you like pasta, and a lot of it, you'll want to make a stop at Mangia Mangia. For over a dozen years, it's been dishing up the best of the startchy stuff in proportions that'll fill you for a day, or more. The fried ravioli is a local favorite. BYOB. Dinner. $$.

Cape May–Lewes Ferry
1-800-643-3779
www.capemaylewesferry.com

Just because New Jersey stops in Cape May doesn't mean the country does, and an easy way to keep moving south is through the Cape May–Lewes Ferry. It's $9.50 each way and a cheap boating thrill to ride across from the tip of our state to Delaware. A trip takes 80 minutes. If you want to enjoy Delaware's tax-free shopping, you can also bring your car on board, though it'll cost you more to bring the car than a vehicle-free ride. A shuttle bus is also available on the Delaware side that includes stops at the Rehoboth Beach Outlet Centers. Make your reservations before you bring the car along, though. The ferry's car spots frequently sell out.

I've heard people complain about the recommended wait time pre-trip—the folks at the ferry suggest you get there an hour early, and you must check in a half hour before your scheduled departure time (make sure to bring a valid photo ID, and your passport if you're not a U.S. citizen). But terminals on both sides of the water now have eateries and shopping where you can nosh, browse, and even enjoy a drink or two (as long as you're not driving) before your voyage. The Cape May terminal is a great spot to enjoy a sunset, too, and is home to the festivals run by the Garden State Wine Growers Association. Again—only if you're not driving.

ARTS & CULTURE

CAPE MAY

Emlen Physick Estate
1-800-275-4278
www.capemaymac.org
1048 Washington St., Cape May 08204

In 1879, Emlen Physick built an 18-room mansion in Cape May, which was just starting to become a seaside resort. He liked it so much that he moved to Cape May from Philadelphia, bringing his mother and aunt along. The estate had fallen into disrepair until it was saved in 1970 by the Mid-Atlantic Center for the Arts, which is now located within the estate. They've restored the building, designed by famed Philadelphia architect Frank Furness, to just about how it looked with the Physicks lived there (though ask about the corner left untouched in the formal parlor—you can see what bad shape the building had been in). It's an ideal place to see how wealthy Victorians lived, and it's the only Victorian museum in town. Guided tours are available year-round. Children's tours are also available. Tour times vary throughout the year. Tours daily April through December and on weekends January through March. Call for tour times. $.

Cape May Fire Department Museum
609-884-9512
www.capemayfd.com/museum.htm
643 Washington St., Cape May 08204

Indulge your childhood fantasy about growing up to be a fireman at this museum. Like most things in Cape May, it's from the Victorian era, and inside is a 1928 American LaFrance fire engine. Open 8 AM–9 PM. Free.

Cape May Lighthouse
609-884-8656
www.capemaymac.org
104 Lincoln Ave., Cape May Point 08212

This still-active lighthouse is the third lighthouse at the tip of Cape May (two more were lost to erosion). This one was built in 1859 at just over 156 feet tall and 218 steps. You can walk up them all for unparalleled views from the southern tip of New Jersey, but be warned—it's a hike up to the top and back down, so if you're not looking to sweat on your trip, then enjoy the gift shop in the base of the light house, or visit when the keeper of the Cape May Lighthouse gives a half-hour talk about the lighthouse and what his job is like. Open daily April through November. Call for off-season hours. $.

Cape May Stage
609-884-1341
www.capemaystage.com
31 Perry St., Cape May 08204

Cape May Lighthouse

Classic, traditional, contemporary, and new theater productions all find a home at this professional Equity theater. The Robert Shackleton Playhouse is small and cozy, so you'll feel almost part of the action. The annual holiday shows are some of the most popular each season. Many of Cape May's restaurants participate in "Dinner and a Show," where you'll enjoy specials on ticket prices or food. $$.

Cape May Winery & Vineyard
609-884-1169
www.capemaywinery.com
711 Townbank Rd., Cape May 08204

An ideal setting to sip local wines: sit on the deck of the Cape May Vineyard headquarters, or take your picnic out on the lawn. You might not expect such variety at a New Jersey vineyard, but they produce top quality wines like Chardonnay, Riesling, Merlot, Cabernet Franc, and Cabernet Sauvignon. Wine making tours are also available. Open noon–5 PM daily May through December. Open noon–5 PM, Wednesday through Sunday, January through April. $.

Center for Community Arts
609-884-7525
www.centerforcommunityarts.org
712 Lafayette St., Cape May 08204

Camp isn't just for children. The Community Center for the Arts offers art camp for both adults and kids in everything from basket weaving to watercolor painting to floor cloth painting. Classes stretch over a few weeks or, if you're not in town long, back-to-back days. $$–$$$$.

East Lynne Theater Company
609-884-5898
www.eastlynnetheater.org
First Presbyterian Church
500 Hughes St., Cape May 08204

You'll see American classics and world premieres through this theater company, which performs at the First Presbyterian Church of Cape May. They also take their talents into the town by performing short stories on the porches and verandas of Cape May's inns and B&Bs. $$.

Flag Ceremony
Sunset Beach, Cape May Point
www.sunsetbeachnj.com

Take in the sunset at this beach, which is the southernmost point in New Jersey, and one of the few places in the state you can see the sun set (as opposed to rise) over the ocean. Flags flown here are only those from the graves of American veterans, and "God Bless America" is played every night as the sun sets. Free.

Cape May Winery Mid-Atlantic Center for the Arts (MAC)

Cape May Saved

The fire of 1878 almost did Cape May in. It destroyed about 30 blocks of the town. Cape May almost faced the same fate in the 1970s, but from a different source: progress.

Cape May wasn't always known as a center of Victorian architecture (which plays into the romance factor and tourist appeal in town). Just 30 years ago, the buildings were seen as old, worn down, and roadblocks to progress. Developers wanted to knock them down and put up what you'll see through most other Shore towns: bland, characterless condos and duplexes meant to draw vacationers for a week or two. But local citizens bent on saving these gorgeous buildings started to fight back.

The idea to save the unique history of the town germinated in 1959, when Cape May celebrated its 350th anniversary. The same year, the National Trust for Historic Preservation held their annual meeting in Cape May, giving an extra push to people who wanted Cape May to keep the buildings.

In 1962, a Nor'easter destroyed the boardwalk, Convention Hall, and a lot of properties in Cape May. In 1965, Cape May was awarded an Urban Renewal Grant to replace the boardwalk with a sea-wall and promenade, protecting many of the remaining Victorian buildings from the threat of flood or storm damage. The grant required that Cape May catalogue its historic buildings. Carolyn Pitts headed the Historic American Buildings Survey Team, and in 1970, Pitts, along with Edwin C. Bramble of the Cape May Cottagers Association, ensured that all of Cape May was made a National Historic Landmark, thereby saving the buildings that were left. They did so without the approval of Cape May's mayor, the local congressman, or the governor of New Jersey. But the decision couldn't be reversed, and many of the buildings that you see in Cape May were saved by the ruling. Also in the 1970s, a group of volunteers saved the Emlen Physick Estate and formed the Mid-Atlantic Center for the Arts (MAC). The tide had clearly turned against developers—Bruce Minnix, then leader of MAC, was elected the next mayor. Today, MAC runs most of Cape May's Victorian and cultural events and has offices inside the Emlen Physick Estate.

Many of those "worn down" buildings were soon converted to bed & breakfasts. They were more economically feasible operations than summer homes. While the Victorian homes are gorgeous, they are difficult to maintain, especially if you're using them only for three months a year, if that. The Victorian theme caught on so that the town started offering walking tours, then horse and carriage rides. Now you can't turn in any direction without seeing or hearing about some kind of Victorian-themed event.

Historic Cold Spring Village

609-898-2300
www.hcsv.org
720 RT 9 S., Cape May 08204

Don't roll your eyes—visiting Historic Cold Spring Village is *not* a boring history lesson. It can be a relaxing outdoor stroll (they have 22 acres of land here), an arts and crafts shopping spree (artists work in the village through the country store), or cooking trip (you can take in a 19th-century cooking demonstration and download recipes from the Historic Cold Spring Village Web site). Of course, you can make your visit a history lesson about life in the 19th century, but whether or not it's boring depends on you. Open 10 AM–4:30 PM

Historic Cold Spring Village   Historic Cold Spring Village

Saturday and Sunday, late May through late June; 10 AM–4:30 PM Tuesday through Sunday from late June through early September; 10 AM–4:30 PM on Saturday and Sunday until mid-September. $.

ERMA

Naval Air Station Wildwood Aviation Museum
609-886-8787
www.usnasw.org
500 Forrestal Rd., Rio Grande 08204

Check out World War II aircraft at this museum, which is located inside the Cape May County Airport. The airport itself used to be a naval air base during World War II, and it's where pilots learned to fly the SB2C Helldiver. You can check out the Helldiver, the F-14 Tomcat, the UH-1 Huey helicopter, and the T-33 Thunderbird, among others. Open 9 AM–5 PM in season; 9 AM–4 PM in the off season. $.

ATTRACTIONS, PARKS & RECREATION

CAPE MAY

Aqua Trails
609-884-5600
www.aquatrails.com
The Nature Center
1600 Delaware Ave., Cape May 08204

Whether you've got your own kayak or have no idea how to make the thing move, Aqua Trails can show you the way to touring the wetlands of New Jersey under your own manpower. They offer kayak rentals and lessons. Try a beginner's tour if you're new; or join up for a two-hour tour if you know your way around a paddle. The wetlands are beautiful enough, but try a full moon or sunset tour for the most brilliant viewing. Open in season. $$$.

Balance Pilates & Yoga Studio
609-884-3001
www.balancecapemay.com
318 Washington St., Cape May 08204

Keep up with your routine or start another at this Zen-like studio. Group and private classes are available, as are summer classes on the beach. If you want someone else to help you relax, ask about A Touch of Heaven Massage Services, which also operates out of the studio. $$.

Horseshoe Crab

They certainly look strange, nasty, and dangerous—no horseshoe crab ever won a beauty contest. I'd see them or their shells all the time, and my usual reaction was to walk away saying "Ew!"

Horseshoe crabs are an ancient species, older than dinosaurs. The Delaware Bay is the world's largest spawning grounds for them, which explains why the Jersey Shore has so many. The Delaware Estuary is also the largest staging area of shorebirds that travel the Atlantic Flyway, largely due to its location and horseshoe crabs—they eat horseshoe crab eggs. Horseshoe crabs can also save your life, indirectly. According to the Ecological Research and Development Group, extracts of blood from horseshoe crabs are used to make sure that items like intravenous drugs, vaccines, and medical devices are bacteria-free.

You can get up close and personal with horseshoe crabs at the Nature Center of Cape May (609-898-8848, www.njaudubon.org/centers/nccm, 1600 Delaware Avenue, Cape May). Gretchen Ferrante, program director, will pick one up and run her finger along its body, claws and all. My heart clenched when she did it, but it was the easiest way to see that horseshoe crabs aren't dangerous at all. A pinch is more like a love tap—that's how weak their claws are.

If you see one on the beach, it's usually just a shell. But if there happens to be a live one inside, leave the old guy or gal alone. They couldn't harm a fly, but they help a lot of people and critters, so you're doing yourself a favor but letting the horseshoe crab live on.

Alpacas

At first, I didn't believe what she said.

"You're going to see the alpaca farm, right?" asked Mary Ann Gorrick over breakfast. I was staying at the Inn at the Park, which she runs with her husband, Jay.

"Excuse me?" I asked, almost choking on my pancake.

"Oh, yes, the alpacas. We'll call them and say you're coming over," she said.

Believe it or not, there is an alpaca farm located in Cape May, which is better known for its Victorian buildings than its livestock populations. But as I pulled up to Bay Springs Farm, there they were, these mini llamas, curious about who the newcomer was.

Fernando, a young, black alpaca, bounded right up to the gate to meet me. Warren Nuessle had waved me over and said it was okay to pet Fernando, but only on his back. The other animals gave me the quizzical eye, and I wouldn't dare pet them, but as Barbara Nuessle led me through the farm, they didn't lunge or try to attack (no such luck at an ostrich farm I visited later in North Jersey for a magazine article I was writing).

Barbara Nuessle had always been a knitter, and she loved working with the yarn that was spun from alpaca fleece. So when she and Warren were trying to decide what to do when they retired, alpacas came to the top of the list.

They moved from Bryn Mawr, Pennsylvania to Cape May and now live with the alpacas. Nuessle still makes things from the alpaca fleece, and she spins the yarn herself. The goods are sold in the farmhouse store. They also breed and sell alpacas, and tried to convince me that they make good pets. It's not that I don't believe them, but I can barely find enough space for a 12-pound dog, though I wouldn't mind having my dog go to the bathroom in the same spot all the time, which is what alpacas do.

Alpacas at Bay Springs Farm

Bay Springs Farm

609-884-0563

www.bayspringsalpacas.com

542 New England Rd., Cape May 08204

Barbara Nuessle liked to knit, especially with yarn made from the fleece of alpacas. So when she and her husband, Warren, decided to retire, they opted for Cape May and a brood of their own alpacas. Now, the couple raises and breeds alpacas, which look like small llamas, on this 10-acre farm. It's open to the public on weekends. Check out the animals, and how Barbara spins their fleece into yarn, which she uses to make sweaters, scarves, blankets, and a host of other alpaca gear, all sold in the farm store. Open 10 AM–4 PM Saturdays and Sundays, and by appointment. $

Canyon Clipper Sport Fishing

609-374-4660

www.canyonclipper.com

1218 Wilson Dr., Cape May 08204

You can charter the Canyon Clipper for your small party—up to six people—to fish for drum, flounder, sea bass, shark, stripers, bluefish, and tuna. They'll bring all the bait, gear, ice, and tackle. You bring your fishing know-how. If you're after big game, the boat also has a fighting chair. $$$$.

Cape May Day Spa & Holistic Center

609-898-1003 and 609-898-2425

www.capemaydayspa.com

607 Jefferson St., Cape May 08204 and Congress Hall, 215 Beach Ave., Cape May 08204

Take a break at the Cape May Day Spa, which specializes in spa packages that will relax, scrub, and primp you from head to toe. They also offer treatments for couples, if you're eyeing romance as the reason for your Cape May trip. Open 10 AM–6 PM at the Jefferson Street location and 10 AM–5 PM at the Congress Hall location. $$–$$$$.

Cape May Bird Observatory: The Northwood Center

609-884-2736

www.njaudubon.org/centers/cmbo

701 East Lake Dr., Cape May Point 08204

Two main tourism draws for Cape May are romance and birds—though not necessarily together. Cape May's location at the southern tip of the state and along the Atlantic Flyway makes it an ideal resting spot for birds. You can join in on a daily walk or hire a guide for a private tour. Don't worry if you forgot your binoculars—you can rent them here as well. If the hours seem wonky to you, consider where you're at—the peak time for birding is in the spring and fall. Open 9:30 AM–4:30 PM April through May and September through November; closed Tuesdays June through August and December through March.

Birding

Cape May is known as a romantic place, but it's also one of the most popular spots in the world for birders.

Cape May is a common stopping area for birds migrating to and from the Caribbean and South America. In the fall and spring, birds rest in Cape May, and birders come to watch them. It's such a popular spot that the World Series of Birding ends here. The competition to identify the most types of birds starts in northern New Jersey and ends in Cape May, 24 hours later.

Where to go? Cape May Point State Park is one hot spot—it's the southernmost tip of the state. The Cape May Bird Observatory: The Northwood Center, is another. Higbee Beach, which was once a nude beach, is another popular birding spot. If you're looking for more expert guidance with your bird viewing, head up to the Wetlands Institute in Stone Harbor. There, you can watch from the inside, too, in inclement weather, and they have exhibits and instruction for kids.

The most popular times for birds (and tourists) are spring and fall, though you can see birds here throughout the year.

The red knot is one of the many birds that stops in Cape May Robert Lego

Cape May Miniature Golf

609-884-2222
www.capemayminigolf.com
315 Jackson St., Cape May 08204

The only mini thing about this course is its lack of fairway. This miniature golf course has the same types of water hazards and fine-tuned landscaping as the real deal, but at mini golf proportions. Open 10:30 AM–10:30 PM in season.

Whale Watcher, Career Changer

My spring 2007 trip on the *Cape May Whale Watcher* wasn't my first. That had been 10 years before, when I was a high school junior with a penchant for anything science-y and an unfortunate short hair-cut, more fluffball than Meg Ryan in *You've Got Mail* cute (thanks, mom, for saving the pictures). I went as part of a high school club trip, though I can't remember what club I was with. I know it had something to do with science because that's where I thought my career was headed—I swore that I was going to dedicate myself to the science of marine biology. I even went to college for it. But the first indication that it might not be the career for me was on the deck of the *Cape May Whale Watcher*.

The trip was in the fall—the best time to see whales—and I made it through most of the trip unscathed. I even saw a whale breach, which is when it comes up out of the water and flops back in. I drank in the commentary about the Cape May coastline, giggled about the nude beach (Higbee Beach, which is no longer a nude beach) and felt my face freeze in the wind before I walked down to the first deck to use the restroom.

That's when it hit me—a jumble in my stomach. I tried to push the sensation down, but the more I concentrated on *not* feeling sick, the more queasy I felt. I stepped out onto the back deck and let it go. It was more embarrassing than the unfortunate haircut.

"It's okay, dear," a kind older gentleman said as I chucked up my lunch over the side of the boat. He suggested I get a ginger ale and sit outside. After a few deep breaths, and that ginger ale, I was fine and walked steadily back onto the dock.

I switched my major from marine biology to English literature my first semester of college. I like to say that it's because I liked reading and researching rather playing with fish. But I know that one sea-sick experience had something to do with it.

I didn't get sick the second time around on the *Cape May Whale Watcher*. The tour was largely the same (except for that nude beach), and I went in the summer as opposed to fall. I got a tan instead of a windy chill. The entire time I sat on the top deck of the ship, took in the sights, and snapped pictures of the dolphins following our ship, I kept waiting for the seasickness to hit me. It never came. Maybe it really is all about timing.

Cape May Point State Park

609-884-2159
www.state.nj.us/dep/parksandforests/parks/capemay.html
299 Light House Ave., Cape May Point 08204

The Cape May Lighthouse isn't the only thing at Cape May's point. It's also home to nature trails, bird watching areas, and this museum, which showcases New Jersey wildlife and the history of Cape May, including a map that shows what areas have been lost to beach erosion. Some of the birding trails are handicapped accessible, too. If you'd like a guide to show you what's what, just ask—the tours are free, but you must schedule them in advance. Open dawn–dusk. Free.

Cape May Whale Watcher
1-800-786-5445
Second Ave. and Wilson Dr., Cape May 08204
www.capemaywhalewatcher.com

More than 500 dolphins live in Cape May's waters from spring through fall, and a great way to see them while being taught about Cape May's nautical past is by taking a ride with the *Cape May Whale Watcher*. The best time to see whales is in the fall. A sighting of whales or dolphins is guaranteed, or you'll get a coupon for a free ride. *Cape May Whale Watcher* runs dinner cruises, too. Cruises at 10 AM, 1 PM, and 6:30 PM. Open March through December. $$–$$$

East Coast Parasail
609-886-6887
www.eastcoastparasail.com
1121 RT 109, Cape May 08204

Take a ride 500 feet above the water at this parasailing outfit, which includes two boats and the choice of flying tandem or solo. Stay dry or request a "dip" into the water during your sail. Check Web site for coupon. Open 8 AM–sunset in season. $$.

Haunted Cape May Tour
609-884-4202
www.hauntedcapemay.com

Is Cape May really haunted? That's for you to decide, and the best way to reach a conclusion is through the Haunted Cape May Tour, which is a lantern-lit walking tour that highlights the best (or worst?) of Cape May's haunted past. The 90-minute tour (which involves less than a mile of walking) is popular in season, so reservations are highly recommended. $$.

Nature Center of Cape May
609-898-8848
www.njaudubon.org/centers/nccm
1600 Delaware Ave., Cape May 08204

Now located in what was a summer home, the Nature Center of Cape May is the place to go to learn about the habitat surrounding your vacation spot. Kids will enjoy the hands-on activities, including a touch tank, and the daylong camp activities, and everyone in your group can enjoy family programs, like bike tours and harbor safaris. Open 10 AM–3 PM Tuesday through Saturday, January through April; 10 AM–4 PM in season; and 10 AM–3PM Tuesday through Saturday October through December. Nature Center: free. Events $–$$.

Sinks Like a Concrete Ship

It might not be the lost city, but there is an *Atlantus* by the shores of Cape May. She's a concrete ship off Sunset Beach.

Yes, you're reading right: a concrete ship. Steel shortages during World War I led the U.S. government to experiment with different shipbuilding materials, and while concrete might not seem like a viable option, whoever floated the idea was onto something. The government built 38 concrete ships, 12 of which were put into service.

At the time of her construction, *Atlantus* weighed 3,000 tons and was 250 feet long. She served as a coal steamer for a year, and was decommissioned at the end of World War I.

In 1926, *Atlantus* was towed to Cape May. She'd already been stripped and bought by a salvage company, so there wasn't much of her left. She was going to be put into service as the base for a drawbridge, but while she awaited her fate, a storm knocked her off her moorings, and she found her way onto the beach. She was so heavy that no one could move her, so there she stayed. You can still see her today, but she's not exactly on shore anymore—erosion has eaten away the coastline, so she's out in the water, close enough to be viewed from the shore.

The concrete ship Atlantus

William J. Moore Tennis Club

609-884-8986
www.capemaytennisclub.com
1020 Washington St., Cape May 08204

This tennis club, which is set amid what was once a garden owned by Dr. Emlen Physick of the nearby Victorian Emlen Physick estate, features 16 courts—14 are clay and two are hard surfaces. Yearly, monthly, and weekly rates are available, as well as fees for hour-and-a-half blocks. Lessons and rentals available as well. Open 8 AM–dusk. $

NORTH CAPE MAY

Turdo Vineyards & Winery

609-884-5591
www.turdovineyards.com
3911 Bayshore Rd., North Cape May 08204

Turdo Vineyards makes 12 different kinds of wine, many of which have won state awards, and they invite you inside to take a look at how it's done. Tastings are conducted Thursday through Sunday, but call ahead to set up a time. $.

Higbee Beach

If you're a birder, you know Higbee Beach. Located on the western side of Cape May—on the Delaware Bay—it's one of the most popular birding sites in the state.

But until 1999, it was also famous for another type of sighting. Higbee Beach was a nude beach. For decades, people came to the beach to sunbathe au naturel. But complaints of so-called "lewd" behavior led to the state banning the practice. After a lot of protests and appeals to whether Upper Townships could enforce a ban (Higbee is on state property), the ruling still stands today, and you must wear your bathing suit at Higbee.

Classic Theater

Victorian architecture isn't the only game in town. Cape May is home to the Beach Theatre, a prime example of the work of W. H. Lee, a Philadelphia architect who was known for designing cinemas. He designed 40 in all, and only nine are still operating today. The Beach Theatre in Cape May is one of them, though it's always teetering on the edge of meeting the wrecking ball.

The Beach Theatre opened on June 29, 1950. It was one of Lee's last projects and the only one still around in Cape May County. But it wasn't just the architecture that made it work—the Beach Theatre was owned by William Hunt, who helped Lee with the design. Hunt was in the movie business, but not the Hollywood version—he owned and operated movie theaters all over New Jersey. By the 1930s, he had 22 theaters in all. In 1947, he started to winnow his empire, focusing exclusively on the South Jersey Shore area. He had such clout in the industry that he got first-run movies even before Philadelphia theaters did.

Many of Lee's—and Hunt's—theaters are now closed and/or destroyed. The Beach Theatre now has four screening rooms instead of one big room, and the Harbor Theatre in Stone Harbor has been cut up into five.

The Beach Theatre is always on the brink of closing and being torn down in favor of condominium construction, but the Beach Theatre Foundation, a nonprofit group, is working toward saving and restoring it. As of publication, it was still operating. For more information, or to see how you can help, go to www.beachtheatre.org.

ERMA

Cape May National Golf Club
609-884-1563
www.cmngc.com
RT 9 & Florence Ave., Erma 08204

Cape May National Golf Club isn't nicknamed "The Natural" because it's a power hitter or has a relation to Roy Hobbs. It earned this nickname because of how it's designed, and how it works with instead of against its native environment. It's surrounded by a 50-acre bird sanctuary. Just because it's bird-friendly doesn't mean it's golf-friendly—this par 7, 6,900-yard course is a challenging one to play, and you won't be playing into anyone's backyard. $$$–$$$$.

SHOPPING

NORTH CAPE MAY

The Book Shoppe
609-884-7878
3845 Bayshore Road, North Cape May 08204

Tired of big-box bookstores? Then pick up your summer reading at The Book Shoppe, which stocks the latest and greatest books atop the best-seller lists along with more classical fare. They have an impressive stock of just-for-kids items, too. Open 9:30 AM–9 PM Monday through Saturday and 10 AM–6 PM Sunday.

CAPE MAY

39 Degrees
609-884-6677
Congress Hall
251 Beach Avenue, Cape May 08204

39 Degrees has everything that the preppy, fashion-conscious gal could ever want, from Lilly Pulitzer items to designer denim. The Congress Hall shop also stocks kids' clothes and equally preppy guy designs. Open 10 AM–10 PM.

Antiques Emporia
609-898-3332
405 West Perry Street, Cape May 08204

Over 40 vendors display their wares in this packed shop. And because there are so many different dealers, you'll see a lot of different items for sale. I like the booth that sells vintage T-shirts, most themed around New Jersey, Philadelphia, and New York interests. Where else could I get T-shirts dedicated to the 1983 Philadelphia Phillies, 1988 Broad Street Run, and Lucy the Elephant? Open 10 AM–10 PM in season. Call for off-season hours.

A Place on Earth

866-400-SOAP
www.aplaceonearth.com
526 Washington Street Mall, Cape May
08204

All the soaps sold in this basement shop are made from organic plant life, and they're hand cut and packaged in Cape May, so you know nothing funny's mixed in. And with over 40 scents, A Place on Earth is sure to have something that pleases your nose. Check out the Sugar Scrub bar, where you can pick up fresh scrubs in however much you need—the perfect way to exfoliate and revive your skin. Open 10 AM–10 PM in season. Call for off-season hours.

Bath Time

800-424-BATH
www.bathtimecapemay.com
223 Jackson St., Cape May 08204

They stock over 250 varieties of soap, plus bubble bath, body lotions, and anything you'll need to keep your skin glowing and your hair healthy and shining at this shop. They have kid-friendly items, too, like over 45 types of rubber duckies. Open 10 AM–10 PM in season, 10 AM–5 PM off season.

Caroline Boutique

609-884-5055
400 Carpenter's Ln., Cape May 08204

You'll find everything you need to dress cool and casual at this shop, which looks right at home in its distressed wood setting. The brands hit the designer scale while staying casual—you'll find Michael Stars and Eileen Fisher pieces snuggled on the racks. Keep an eye open for accessories. The woven baskets sold here will work on the beach or at home. Open 10 AM–9 PM in season. Call for off-season hours.

Cheeks

866-5-CHEEKS
www.cheekscapemay.com
101 Ocean St., Cape May 08204

This 20-plus-year-old store specializes in cool, comfy, breezy flax linen clothing, though they also offer shoes, gifts, soaps, and cards in the attached gift store. If you're looking for a deal, check out their warehouse store at 600 Park Boulevard in West Cape May, where prices are knocked down 20 to 40 percent. Open 9 AM–7 PM.

A Note About Shop Hours

In season, most Shore shops have a set schedule. Off season is a completely different story. If I had tried to track every nuance of every off-season schedule, you'd be reading an encyclopedia—almost every shop is of the mom-and-pop variety, which means they can pick and choose when they'd like to stay open in the off season. Good for them. But it would have made for a messy guidebook.

In these cases, I've listed the in-season hours and a note if you should call for when the stores are open in the off season. Some are open weekends, some have weekday hours. Some open whenever the owner feels like it, so call ahead. Also, some shop owners told me that they'll close early in season if the weather's bad or if they're not seeing much foot traffic. So it's worth calling ahead any time of year.

Sugar Scrub Bar at A Place on Earth

Shopping and strolling on Washington Street

Dellas 5 & 10
609-884-4568
503 Washington St., Cape May 08204

Dellas is the place to stop for all those little things you forgot to bring, or souvenirs to take home as a reminder of your Jersey Shore trip. Browsing is fun, too, since Dellas keeps a retro '40s and '50s feel. Open 7 AM–11 PM Sunday through Friday and 7 AM–midnight Saturday in season. Call for off-season hours.

Exit Zero Store
609-884-1125
www.exitzero.us
Congress Hall
251 Beach Ave., Cape May 08204

What is exit zero? That's Cape May, at exit zero off the Garden State Parkway. Pick up hats, T-shirts fleeces, beach towels, and much more emblazoned with this city nickname, plus Cape May–related artwork. Open 10 AM–10 PM.

Washington Street Mall

For the most shopping packed into one area, check out Washington Street Mall. It's not a mall in the department store sense, but a strip of shops, restaurants, art galleries, and ice cream parlors. The streets are walking-friendly, too—no cars allowed.

Lace Silhouettes Lingerie

609-898-7448

www.lacesilhouetteslingerie.com

429 Washington Street Mall, Cape May 08204

Looking for a little something special for your romantic Cape May stay? And we do mean little, at Lace Silhouettes Lingerie, which sells romantic and sexy pieces. They also sell comfort staples, like fuzzy socks and robes. Open 10 AM–10 PM in season. Call for off-season hours.

Love the Cook

609-884-9292

www.lovethecook.com

404 Washington Street Mall, Cape May 08204

Did you ever know you needed an elephant teapot so badly? What about sea-themed BBQ tongs, or a cow-esque oven mitt? You'll find what you never knew you were looking for at this kitchen specialty shop, along with spices, rubs, and gourmet coffees and teas. Open 10 AM–10:30 PM in season. Call for off-season hours.

Mary Ann's Jewelry

609-898-8786

511 Washington Street Mall, Cape May 08204

Don't overlook this galley-sized store. It stocks both estate and new jewelry, including engagement rings and wedding bands. They buy jewelry, too, and sell antiques. On one trip to Mary Ann's, I found a stunning red and glass antique mirror. Perfect for trying on jewelry—better in your home. Open 10 AM–10 PM in season. Call for off-season hours.

No. 5 Trading Co.

609-898-6013

www.no5trading.com

31 Perry Street, Cape May 08204

You'll find lots of items inspired by other countries in this Carpenter Square Mall store, like jade jewelry, African art, and clothes with Asian dragon or character patterns. They also sell the basics, like easy breezy jersey dresses, silk scarves, and hand-embroidered purses. Open 9:30 AM–10:30 PM in season. Call for off-season hours.

Oma's Doll Shop

609-884-8882

www.omasdollshop.com

315 Ocean St., Washington Commons, Cape May 08204

These dolls look so real you'd think you were stepping into a nursery. But everything's just an imitation here at Oma's, which sells doll babies that are almost like the real thing—in terms of weight, movement, and clothing. They also sell paper dolls and other non-lifelike dolls, like Raggedy Ann and Precious Moments pieces. Open 10 AM–10 PM in season. Call for off-season hours.

Swede Things

Original Fudge Kitchen

1-800-23-FUDGE

www.fudgekitchens.com

728 Beach Ave. and 513 Washington Street Mall, Cape May 08204

What a way to entice you inside—someone is always standing outside these Fudge Kitchen locations to offer you a free sample. Pick from fresh-whipped, thick, delectable fudge, or other candies like licorice, truffles, and almond clusters. They sell sugar-free varieties, too, and ice cream. Open 10 AM–10 PM in season. Call for off-season hours. $.

Stitch by Stitch

866-563-5399

www.stitchbystitchnj.com

315 Ocean St., Unit 9, Cape May 08204

Needlepointers, delight! You can find just about any pattern you could ever want to cross-stitch in this airy store. They sell kits, patterns, and yarn for cross stitching, and also kits to make beaded jewelry. If they don't have what you're looking for—ask. They'll know where to get it. Open 10 AM–10 PM in season, 10 AM–5 PM in the off season.

Swede Things in America

609-884-5811

www.swedethings.com

307 Washington Street Mall, Cape May 08204

You'll find the best of Sweden in this quaint shop, including china, crystal, and lamps. The lace goods are a big draw, and they last—all the pretty lace runners and curtains in my mother's house are from Swede Things, and still going strong after 20 years. Open 10 AM–10 PM in season. Call for off-season hours.

Victorious

609-898-1777

www.victoriousantiques.com

Congress Hall

251 Beach Ave., Cape May 08204

Browse through new and estate jewelry and décor, nestled among bags and Victorian-era décor. The Congress Hall location has more estate jewelry than the Stone Harbor outpost, which is mostly re-creations. Victorious also has a location at 315 Ocean St. in Cape May. Open 10 AM–10 PM.

Wave One Sports

609-884-6674

www.waveonesports.com

324 Washington Street Mall, Cape May 08204

They don't sell just any old Cape May gear at Wave One. Their items, which range from embroidered sweatshirts to hats to T-shirts to sweat pants, are high quality and last for years (I have three sweatshirts that are older than my college diploma, if that says anything). Look out for the sale bin, which is where odds and ends are piled together, unfolded and ready for sifting. Open 9 AM–11 PM in season. Call for off-season hours.

Whale's Tale
609-884-4808
www.whalestalecapemay.com
312 Washington Street Mall, Cape May 08204

Whale's Tale is the kind of place that has something for everyone, but not in that cheap, dollar store sort of way. It's a hut full of possibilities, from the jewelry counter that sits in the middle of the front room to the puppet tower in the kids' section to the cards and Christmas ornaments. They stock a heavy supply of locally themed books, too. Open 10 AM–11 PM in season. Call for off-season hours. Closed January and February.

Winterwood Gift and Christmas Gallery
609-884-8949
www.winterwoodgift.com
526 Washington Street Mall, Cape May 08204

It's all Christmas all the time in this two-story shop dedicated to the holiday season. You'll find any kind of ornament you ever dreamed of wanting for your tree, plus beach-themed décor, jewelry, and even Halloween decorations. Winterwood also has shops in Rio Grande and Wildwood. Open 9:30 AM–10 PM in season. Call for off-season hours.

The Zoo Company
609-884-8181
www.capemaypuppets.com
421 Washington Street Mall, Cape May 08204

These plushes are the real deal—Zoo Company sells plushes and puppets of licensed characters, meaning that the Elmo or Dora or Cookie Monster you get is the real deal, not a knock-off. Zoo Company also stocks marionettes, people puppets, and Hello Kitty items. Open 10 AM–11 PM in season. Call for off-season hours.

NORTH CAPE MAY

Southend Surf Shop
609-898-0988
311 Beach Dr., North Cape May 08204

Southend stocks everything you'll need to surf—or at least look like a surfer. They have an impressive stock of Reef sandals, as well as Quicksilver and Roxy clothing. They rent surfboards, too, and their location across the street is convenient to go from store to surf. Open 9 AM–10 PM in season. Call for off-season hours.

Winterwood Gift and Christmas Gallery

WEST CAPE MAY

The Bird House of Cape May
609-898-8871
www.birdhouseofcapemay.com
109 Sunset Blvd., West Cape May 08204

Cape May is a bird watching hot spot, and this shop caters to those who come to town to see what's flying through. Most of the stock is items designed to draw the little birdies to your back yard. Open 10 AM–5 PM. Closed January through March.

Cape May Linen Outlet
1-866-884-3630
www.capemaylinen.com
110 Park Blvd., West Cape May 08204

Dress your house for less at this outlet shop. They stock goods for your bed, bath, and kitchen at knockout prices. Open 10 AM–6 PM.

Flying Fish Studio
1-800-639-2085
www.theflyingfishstudio.com
130 Park Blvd., West Cape May 08204

Who needs another boring "Here's where I went on vacation" T-shirt? You won't find that at Flying Fish—they make catchy beach-themed gear, like sweatshirts with a big lobster on the front, or retro-designed shirts dedicated to Cape May's smaller beaches, such as Poverty Beach. They also provide gear for the annual Lima Bean Festival, plus all those fashion extras you might have forgotten, like flip-flops, wedges, plaid hats, and organic cotton tees, at affordable prices. Open 10 AM–6 PM.

Simply Unique
609-884-3233
www.simplyuniqueofcapemay.com
479 West Perry St., West Cape May 08204

This looks like a general store but is dedicated to out-there home wear, like purple fish stools, flip-flop wine glass coasters, and hand-painted jelly cabinets. Simply Unique also has a coffee bar that sells brews and light sandwiches, and a candy store. You can take home beans, teas, or one of 12 different flavors of candy sticks, if it's too much for in-store. Make sure to check out Simply Unique Garden next door—it'll add some fantasy to your shrubbery. Open 9 AM–5 PM.

Weddings by the Sea Shoppe
866-459-7900
www.weddings-bythesea.com
139 N. Broadway, West Cape May 08204

Catherine J. Walton set up shop as a wedding planner in Cape May before the town became one of the most popular destination wedding spots in the country. She was on to a good thing, because now she has three wedding-related business, and the shop is one of them. Browse among the finer things a bride needs for the big day, like fans, gloves, and a little something special. Most of the items are Victorian-themed, though there are options for the hip bride. Walton runs her wedding planning business out of the store, so don't be surprised if you run into a bride or two while you're there. Open 10 AM–5 PM. Closed Sunday.

Cape May Area Trolley Tours

No need to hurt your feet in the course of exploring all Cape May has to offer. Take one of the town's many trolley tours, all operated by the Mid-Atlantic Center for the Arts. There's the classic Historic District Trolley, the Welcome to Cape May Trolley Tour, and the ever-romantic Evening Trolley Tour. But you can get much more specific with the following tour types:

Children's Trolley Tour

Ghosts of Cape May Trolley Tour

Holiday Season Evening Trolley Tour

Natural Habitats Trolley Tour

Spirit of the Light Trolley Tours

U.S. Coast Guard Base Trolley Tour

World War II Trolley Tour

   Check in with the Mid-Atlantic Center for the Arts about tours, times, and spots where the tours pick up riders—and keep in mind that some of these tours are seasonal. They can be reached at 609-884-5404 or at www.capemaymac.org.

EVENTS

March

Ocean Drive Marathon
609-523-0880
www.odmarathon.com

Take in the Shore sites through this spring marathon, which starts in Cape May and ends in Sea Isle City. The course is all on paved roads or on boardwalk and is a qualifying course. If you're not quite up to 26.2 miles, you can also run a 10-miler, 5k (or 3.1 miles), or 1.5-mile fun run and walk.

Sherlock Holmes Weekend
1-800-275-4278
www.capemaymac.org

This mysterious event, which is held in both the spring and fall, honors Holmes and Watson. The weekend mystery kicks off on Friday night, and you have the weekend to figure out who done it, with live actors working by your side. Sleuthing is free, though tours and events require tickets.

May

Cape May Music Festival
1-800-275-4278
www.capemaymac.org

For four weeks every spring, Cape May plays host to music performance from orchestras, and jazz and brass bands. Concerts are held at the Cape May Convention Hall, Beach Drive at Stockton Place or at the Episcopal Church of the Advent. $

Cape May's Spring Festival
1-800-275-4278
www.capemaymac.org

This townwide events welcomes in the warmer temperatures and its Victorian heritage in this combination outdoor and historical celebration at this 10-day event. Free.

Spring Arts & Crafts Festival
609-884-9565
Cape May Convention Hall

Check out arts and crafts from over 30 vendors from all over the Northeast.

World Series of Birding
609-884-2736
www.worldseriesofbirding.org

This 24-hour bird watching competition (how many can you identify in one day?) starts in North Jersey and ends up in Cape May. Yes, you can participate, even if you didn't know that "seagull" isn't an appropriate term to describe any bird.

June

NJ State Film Festival
609-884-6700
www.njstatefilmfestival.com

Take in short films, documentaries, and independent flicks from all over New Jersey at this state festival. Film students can sign up for workshops and classes, or in the five-day summer institute, which runs parallel to the film festival. Tickets can be purchased per film or in packages. $$–$$$$.

West Cape May Strawberry Festival
609-884-8382
www.westcapemaytoday.com

They don't call it the Garden State for nothing. Eat strawberries straight up, built into strawberry shortcake, or any of the other dozens of ways local farmers and chefs have figured out how to use this berry for your benefit.

World War II Weekend
1-800-275-4278

Celebrate the history and music of the World War II era. Events include concerts, lectures, and a boat cruise. Saturday also features a Veterans Memorial Ceremony at Sunset Beach during the daily casket flag lowering. Many events are free, though you can buy a weekend package for ticketed events.

July

Union Encampment
609-898-2300
www.hcsv.org
Historic Cold Spring Village

Take a peek at what Civil War life was like at this reenactment, where you can see how Civil War soldiers lived, slept, ate, and trained. $.

August

Baby Parade
Beach Avenue, Cape May

Think your kid's the cutest? Then enter him or her into this long-running baby parade. Or just watch the cute kids go by. Free.

Hotel and Guest Night
1-800-275-4278
Center for Community Arts

Got a talent? Show it off at this annual event, which dates back to the 1940s and brings all kinds of performances from Cape May visitors and hotel employees to the stage. Free.

Peach Festival
609-886-4554
Our Lady Star of the Sea Auditorium

How many ways can you eat a peach? Depends on what you put it in—the best of the best will be ready for tasting at this annual event, including cobblers, cakes, pies, and barbecue. There'll be fresh peaches, of course, as well as books, plants, and jewelry.

Railroad Days
609-898-2300
www.hcsv.org
Historic Cold Spring Village

If the choo-choos get you going, then check out this two-day event, which includes demonstrations by garden railroad groups and working scale model railroads, as well as displays of train memorabilia. $.

September

Revolutionary War Encampment
609-898-2300
www.hcsv.org
Historic Cold Spring Village

Take a peek at what Revolutionary War life was like at this reenactment, where you can see how soldiers in 1775 lived, slept, ate, and trained. $.

Cape May Food and Wine Festival
1-800-275-4278
www.capemaymac.org

If you love to cook, or just eat, come to town in September for his event. You can take classes and seminars, tour the kitchens of Cape May restaurants, and vote for your favorite clam chowder. Don't miss the Restaurant Relay Race, where teams from local restaurants compete to be known as the fastest at what they do in the Cape. The most popular race has servers pitted against each other to deliver a cocktail through an obstacle course without spilling a drop.

October

West Cape May Lima Bean Festival
609-884-8382
www.westcapemaytoday.com

Don't grimace. They really don't taste bad, so give the mighty lima bean another chance (or taste again) at this annual festival. Don't forget to stick around for the crowning of the Bean Queen and King. Free.

Pumpkin Festival
609-898-2300
www.hcsv.org
Historic Cold Spring Village

Pick your favorite and make that pumpkin unique at this annual festival. Aside from the pumpkins, there are also crafts, music, games, and a Halloween Parade. $.

Rest in Peace, Victorian Style Combination Tour
1-800-275-4278
www.capemaymac.org
Emlen Physick Estate

Ever wonder how the Victorians buried their dead? Check out a living history presentation as the Physicks mourn the death of a family member at this show, which is held on select Saturdays in October. $$.

Victorian Week
1-800-275-4278
www.capemaymac.org

This week is actually 10 days long and features tours and events, like Victorian feasts, murder mystery dinners, Victorian fashion shows, and glass blowing demonstrations.

November

Cape May Jazz Festival
609-884-7277
www.capemayjazz.org

Jazz takes over the town for a weekend in November, with shows all over Cape May's halls and hotels. If you want to do more than just listen, sign up for one of the workshops that set up during the week or, if you've got at least one year of playing time under your belt, the jazz improv session.

Sherlock Holmes Weekend
1-800-275-4278
www.capemaymac.org

Victorian Week Mid-Atlantic Center for the Arts (MAC)

This mysterious event, which is held in both the spring and fall, honors Holmes and Watson. The weekend mystery kicks off on Friday night, and you have the weekend to figure out who done it, with live actors working by your side. Sleuthing is free, though tours and events require tickets.

December

Annual Holiday Show
609-884-1341
www.capemaystage.com
Cape May Stage

Every holiday season, the Cape May Stage puts on a Christmas-themed show or two, from the classic Scrooge tale *A Christmas Carol* to *Every Christmas Story Ever Told,* which zips through holiday traditions in one sitting. $$.

NEWSPAPERS

Cape May County Herald
609-886-8600
www.capemaycountyherald.com

Cape May Gazette
609-624-8900
www.thecapemaygazette.com

Exit Zero
609-886-0079
www.exitzeropublishing.net

TRANSPORTATION

Aart's Cape May Taxi
609-898-7433
www.capemaytaxi.com

High Roller Transportation
609-425-5819

REALTORS

Coastline Realty
1-800-377-7843
www.CoastlineRealty.com
1400 Texas Avenue, Cape May 08204

Jersey Cape Realty
1-800-643-0043
www.jerseycaperealty.com
739 Washington Street, Cape May 08204

Wilsey Realty
609-884-1007
www.wilseyrealty.com
501 Lafayette Street, Cape May 08204

EMERGENCY NUMBERS

In an emergency, dial 911.
Poison information: 1-800-222-1222
Non-emergency: 609-463-6570

HOSPITALS

Cape Regional Medical Center
609-463-2000
www.caperegional.com
2 Stone Harbor Blvd., Cape May Courthouse 08210

TOURISM CONTACTS

Greater Cape May Chamber of Commerce
609-884-5598
www.capemaychamber.com

Mid-Atlantic Center for the Arts
1-800-275-4278
www.capemaymac.org

New Jersey Travel and Tourism
www.state.nj.us/travel
1-800-VISITNJ

General Index

Lodging by Price

Dining by Price

Inexpensive: up to $10
Moderate: $11–$25
Expensive: $26–$40
Very Expensive: more than $40

ATLANTIC CITY

**See also Brigantine; Galloway Township;
   Margate; Ventnor City**

Inexpensive
Adam Good Deli, 22
Irish Pub, 26–27
White House Sub Shop, 31

Inexpensive to Moderate
Atlantic City Bar and Grill, 22–23
Beach Bar at Trump Plaza, 23
Noodle Village, 28–29

Moderate
Angelo's Fairmount Tavern, 22
Back Bay Ale House, 23
Chef Vola's, 25
Flying Cloud Cafe, 26
Harrah's Waterfront Buffet, 26
Los Amigos, 27–28
Mia, 28
Phillips Seafood, 29

Moderate to Expensive
Chef Vola's, 25
Cuba Libre Restaurant & Rum Bar, 25
EVO, 25–26
OPA Bar and Grille, 29
The Trinity, 29, 31

Moderate to Very Expensive
Capriccio, 24–25

Expensive
Buddaken, 24
Cafe 2825, 24
Caruso's, 25
Dock's Oyster House, 25
Knife and Fork Inn, 27
Sonsie, 29

Very Expensive
Bobby Flay Steak, 23–24
Old Homestead, 29

AVALON

Inexpensive
Avalon 29th Street Deli & Grill, 126

Avalon Anchorage Marina, 126
Avalon Freeze, 126
Brady's Hoagie Dock, 127
Brian's Waffle House, 127
Circle Pizza, 127
Circle Tavern at the Princeton, 127–128
Concord Cafe, 128
Cooper's Original Snowballs New Orleans
   Style, 128
Mallon's, 128
The Mouse Trap, 128–129
Nancy Lynn Candies, 130
Tonio's Pizza, 130–131
Uncle Bill's Pancake House, 131

Inexpensive to Moderate
Maggie's, 128
Oceanside Seafood, 130

Moderate
Avalon Seafood and Produce Market,
   127
Cheese by Isabel, 128
Sylvester's, 130
Tortilla Flats, 131
Whitebriar Restaurant, 132

Moderate to Very Expensive
Bobby Dee's Rock 'n Chair, 130

Expensive
Cafe Loren, 127
Dining Room at the Golden Inn, 128
The Sea Grill, 130
Via Mare, 131–132

BRIGANTINE

Expensive
Laguna Grill and Martini Bar, 31

CAPE MAY

Inexpensive
Hot Dog Tommy's, 207
MagicBrain CyberCafe, 208–209
Mario's Pizza, 209
Martini Beach, 209
McGlade's on the Pier, 209
Ugly Mug, 211
Uncle Bill's Pancake House, 211–212

Inexpensive to Moderate
Dock Mike's Pancake House, 205–206